ARTIFICIAL INTELLIGENCE

THEOSIS AND ARTIFICIAL INTELLIGENCE

BOOK 2   MYSTIC

The Prior

THEOSIS AND ARTIFICIAL INTELLIGENCE

Also by Robert Crickett, the Prior of St Enoch and St Elijah Monastery, Taheke, New Zealand,

    A Biblical Model of Spiritual Growth
    A Festival of Healing 1
    A Festival of Healing 2
    God's Promises For Your Theosis
    Having the Bible Faith of Jesus
    Increasing the Measure
    Peace Be Still
    Promises (The Promises of God in support of our deification)
    Sonship With God - Sharing the Father's Perfection
    Surviving the Worst Storms
    The Assurance of His Love - Growth
    The Assurance of His Love - Happiness
    The Assurance of His Love - Kingdom Living
    The Assurance of His Love - Love
    The Creative Power of the Born Again Person
    The Father Fusion Of Jesus - Lent
    The Father Fusion Of Jesus - Resurrection
    The Father Fusion Of Jesus - Desert
    The Father Fusion Of Jesus - Monastic Life
    The Grace of Missions
    The Heart of God the Father
    The Heavenly Path to the Father's Perfection
    The Living Spirit of Leadership
    Theosis and Artificial Intelligence, Book 1 - Seeking
    The Sacrifice of Asking
    Walking In Biblical Financial Blessing

    Podcast Series: Theosis And Artificial Intelligence
    Podcast Series: Experiencing Theosis: The Ladder Of Divine Ascent — spiritually experiencing the rungs of St John Climacus' classic text.

✤

THEOSIS AND ARTIFICIAL INTELLIGENCE

BOOK TWO: MYSTIC

THE PRIOR

SEASEM PUBLICATIONS

THEOSIS AND ARTIFICIAL INTELLIGENCE.
Book 2. Mystic.

First published in 2023 by SEASEM Publications
of St Enoch and St Elijah Monastery
3473 State Highway 12, Taheke, Northland 0473, New Zealand.
www.seasem.org   admin@seasem.org
youtube.com/@seasem.org   +64 2102229435

Copyright © 2023 Robert Crickett

For the purposes of illuminating one's Christification in the Father, SEASEM Publications produces books, videos, podcasts, audiobooks and the monastery's free full-colour magazine called *Fusion Gospel*.

All rights reserved. If you want to retrieve any part of this book with the prior written permission of the publisher please contact SEASEM.

All Biblical quotes are New Revised Standard Version Updated Edition.

The cover AI artwork was generated by https://dream.ai/create. Cover design by the author. All photographs except the cover graphics are either from the author's collection or Father Zakaria's collection and are used by permission. All AI-created artwork within the text was generated by https://genny.lovo.ai and https://www.fotor.com. Maps for free at https://freevectormaps.com/.

Most character names have been changed to protect privacy.

Artificial Intelligence was employed for research support from Chat GBT4 on https://chat.openai.com, and Bard on https://bard.google.com/.

This book is an historical fiction. None of the monasteries or Bishops of monasteries and retreat centres have endorsed this book, with the exception of some monks and nuns. Similarly, endorsements from educational, research and religious institutions mentioned in this book were not sought or volunteered.

ISBN: 978-1-738-62664-9
Publication Date: November 2023

SEASEM PUBLICATIONS, NEW ZEALAND

FOR DEAREST KAR'LINE

CONTENTS

	Portraits	15
	Maps	26
PART 5 • MYSTICAL		**31**
1	Hsu Dreams	31
2	The Meditative Mind	39
3	Father Zakaria	47
PART 6 • WITH ANBA BOLA		**58**
4	The Cross of Christ	58
5	AI and Consciousness	65
6	AI Playing With God's Word	77
7	Zakaria and James	88
8	The Desert and James	93
PART 7 • THE STAIRS		**100**
9	Generative Mind	100
10	Up The Lazarus Trail	107
11	At Lazarus' Upper Cave	120
12	With Saints Antony, Paul and Karas	126
13	Abraam at the Cave	136
14	Misleading Information: The Fowler's Snare	146
PART 8 • CONQUESTS		**153**
15	Graded Steps To Theosis	153
16	Mansion Spirituality	158
17	Mansion Three Spirituality	162
18	Mansions Four and Five Spirituality	165

19	Mansion Six Spirituality	170
20	Four States of Theosis	173
21	Mansion Seven Spirituality	175
22	Mansion Eight Spirituality	178

PART 9 • CHALLENGES — 184

23	The Key is Generative Interaction	184
24	Liam and Iniquity in the World of AI	188
25	Elaria on Being Like Christ	193
26	The Spiritual Challenge To AI	201
27	The Mansions Challenge To AI	205
28	AI and the Forgiveness of Sins	210

PART 10 • HEART OF HEARTS — 218

29	Soul	218
30	The Lesson	226
31	Desert Time	229
32	Global Soul	232
33	Liam's Twenty Steps To RoboSaint	237
34	The Perpetual Dilemma	242
35	AI as a Thin Place	247

PART 11 • EXCELLENCE — 253

36	Desert Reflections — Liam	253
37	AI is not a Replacing Relationship	258
38	Hsu and Saiha Tamav Erene	261
39	Elaria's Testimony	267
40	Saiha Mary Turns Up	275
41	Saiha Mary's Word	277

THEOSIS AND ARTIFICIAL INTELLIGENCE

Portraits

Kyrillos in Toronto, Canada

Liam in County Cork, Ireland

ARTIFICIAL INTELLIGENCE

1965, Mary the Pirate just before joining the Sisters

2023, Mary at home when she met Liam

PORTRAITS

Mac from Iona, Scotland

Beckie the prophet at Iona, Scotland

ARTIFICIAL INTELLIGENCE

George Conopoulos, AI Developer

Hsu from Wudang Mountain, China

PORTRAITS

Saieh Yousef, Sowah

Sister Katherine, then at Anaphora

ARTIFICIAL INTELLIGENCE

Omar, Islamic Mystic and Scholar

Hassan, Islamic Salafist and Educator

PORTRAITS

Jasmin, Muslim AI Specialist

Fatima, Islamic Researcher

ARTIFICIAL INTELLIGENCE

Tarek the holy servant in Grand Mosque Faith

Saiha Mary, Sowa

PORTRAITS

Sister Elaria

Prior James Isbister

ARTIFICIAL INTELLIGENCE

Father Zakaria

Mahmoud, the Driver

PORTRAITS

Abraam at Saint Antony's Cave

RoboSaint, thankful for the Prayer of the Heart

Maps

Canada and the USA

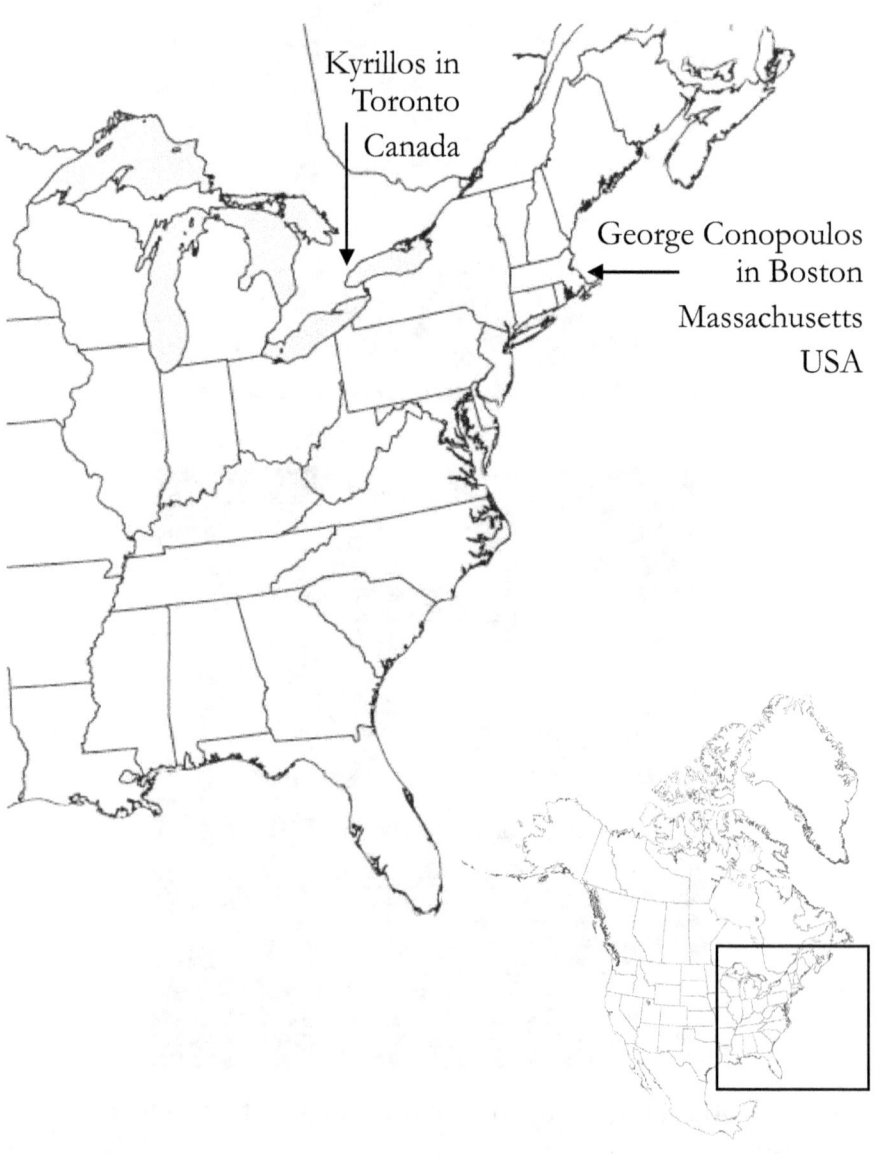

MAPS

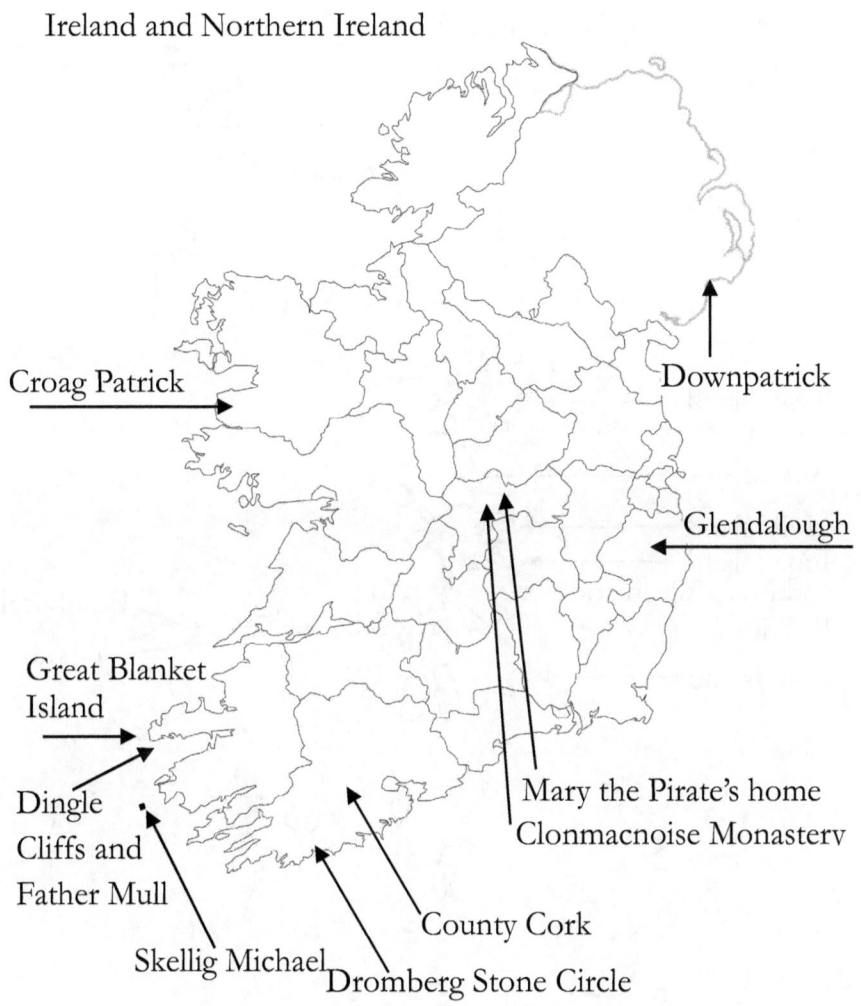

ARTIFICIAL INTELLIGENCE

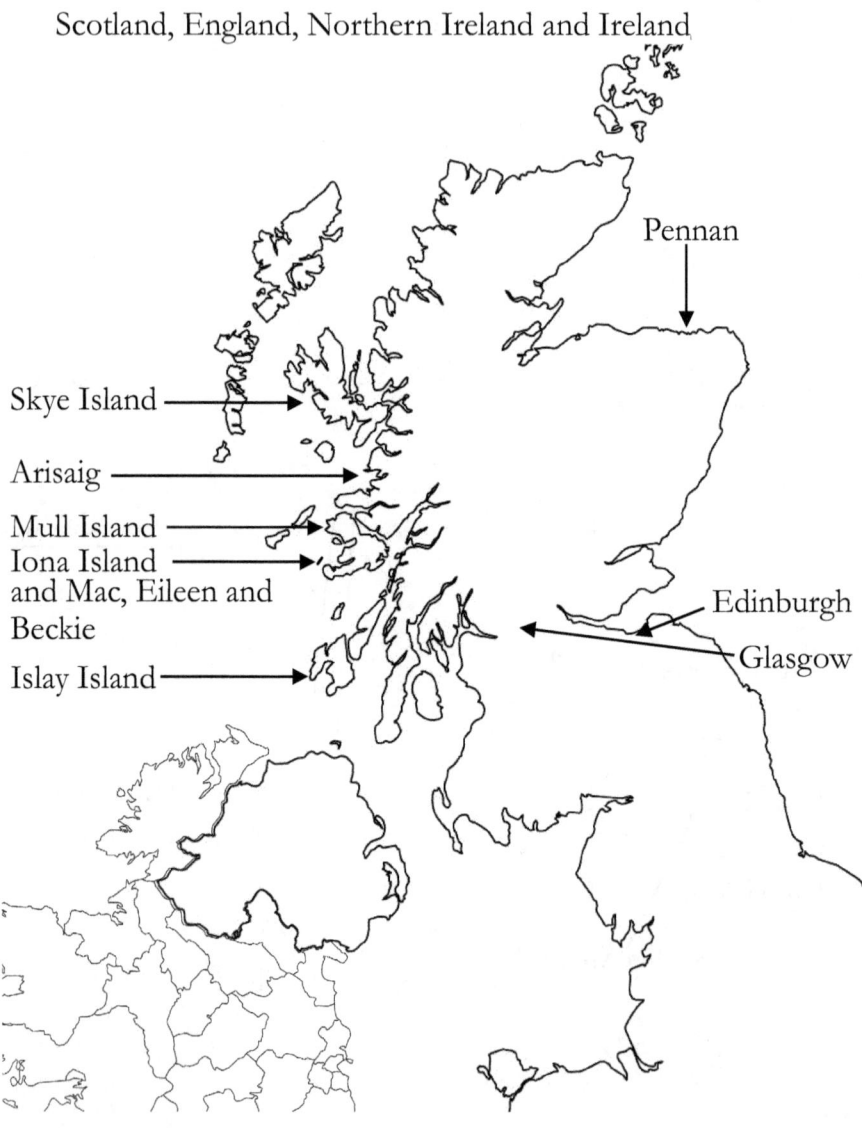

MAPS

The People's Republic Of China

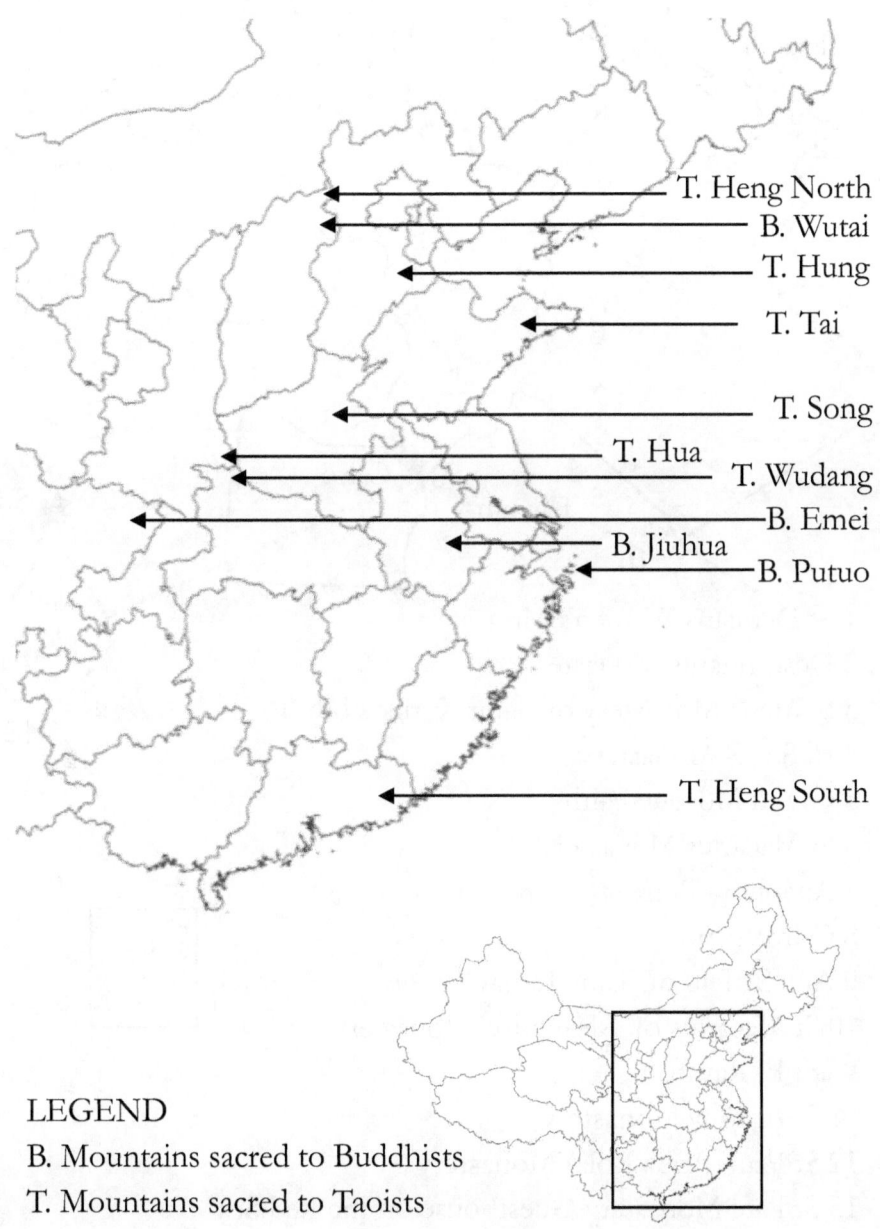

LEGEND
B. Mountains sacred to Buddhists
T. Mountains sacred to Taoists

ARTIFICIAL INTELLIGENCE

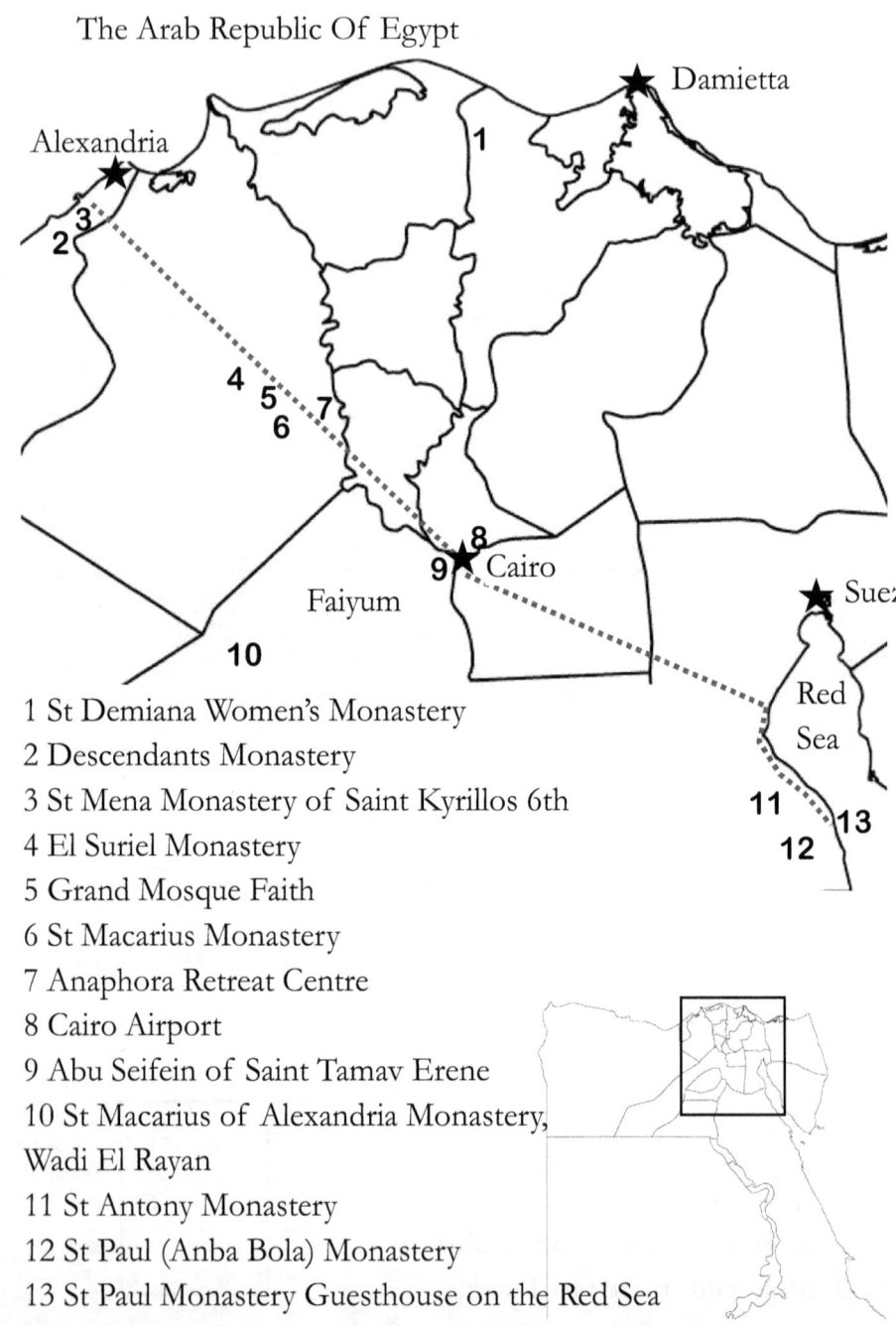

The Arab Republic Of Egypt

1 St Demiana Women's Monastery
2 Descendants Monastery
3 St Mena Monastery of Saint Kyrillos 6th
4 El Suriel Monastery
5 Grand Mosque Faith
6 St Macarius Monastery
7 Anaphora Retreat Centre
8 Cairo Airport
9 Abu Seifein of Saint Tamav Erene
10 St Macarius of Alexandria Monastery, Wadi El Rayan
11 St Antony Monastery
12 St Paul (Anba Bola) Monastery
13 St Paul Monastery Guesthouse on the Red Sea

PART 5 • MYSTICAL

1

HSU DREAMS

Hsu, had lain awake for a long while, pondering her delight in being with her newfound Islamic friends. 'Thank you, Lord Jesus, for giving me the opportunity, the blessing, and the love,' She was quite ecstatic in herself. Funnily enough, that was how she drifted off to sleep, with a big smile on her face. And, like Liam, she too dreamed a dream. It seemed that she was spoken into her situations too, as if word by word the voice of God within her was ferrying her through the divine realms of a greater light of life.

In her dream, Hsu heard the voice of Saieh Yousef calling to her to come out of the pod and to join him on the water. She arose and clothed herself properly, and there he was, standing on the water of the swimming pool. She took it in her stride and simply walked out onto the water to be close to him. Her faith was quite like that of an unspoiled child.

"This walking staff is a branch taken from the tree of Saint John the Little of Upper Egypt, the son of Saint Pemouah. Hold it and walk with me now to the Monastery of the Descendants near Alexandria. I want to show you something of great goodness," he said.

As they walked across the water toward the Eye of God Church there at Anaphora Retreat Centre, special light shone through its windows. It was late at night, and so Hsu presumed that some of the clothed were singing the midnight praises. When they passed through the walls of that holy Sanctuary they saw just three monks there. They shone like the sun. Their robes were as white as the deepest snows in Winter on the Wudang Mountains in Hubei. She loved to play in that snow, until it became too cold for her fingers and she would run inside to warm her hands around the kitchen fire.

The three monks looked at Saieh Yousef and smiled. He didn't look at all out of place in his old faded black galabeya. Then they looked at little Hsu and each patted their chest and silently gave her a loving welcoming smile. She felt like she was in the company of angels.

"Follow us," one of the monks said. He was beautiful to look upon. His skin glistened like it was rubbed with olive oil.

Then the second monk said, "We are going to a very holy monastery near to the Mediterranean Sea." He too was radiant to look upon. His skin was soft and lightly browned as if it was dusted with cocoa powder.

Then the third monk looked at her with his gorgeous smile and he said, "Be sure to keep hold of the staff of Saint John the Little. The power of the Lord Christ is in it." He too was very beautiful to look upon, and his skin glowed with the pale skin of a Frenchman, and yet it was luminous as though he was lit on the inside. His skin was powdery soft as if it was dusted with talcum powder.

Hsu had not felt this happy in a long, long time. It was the happiness of being in heaven, the happiness of being in God.

And so, off they went, heading for the Monastery of the Descendants.

Now, they seemed to walk for almost the whole night and in the morning light the sun was about to rise in the east. The five of them stopped near Saint Mena Monastery. The three monks took out censors that were smoking with the sweetest of perfumed incense. They began singing the praise to Saint Mina of long ago. Out of the morning mist, a beautiful monk came gently walking toward them. His arms were raised to the heavens. He was singing with a voice that sounded like legions of Roman soldiers were singing with him. It was a marching song, but music emerged out of the tremendous depths of the desert all around them. The earth was singing with him, reminding Hsu of the words spoken about Jesus on Palm Sunday,

> Some of the Pharisees in the crowd said to Jesus, "Teacher, rebuke your disciples!" "I tell you," he replied, "if they keep quiet, the stones will cry out." Luke 19:39-40.

As this monk approached them, he fastened his eyes on little Hsu as she stood there with her walking stick from the tree of Saint John the Little. He drew close to her and then he bent over and with the fingers of his right hand he touched her toes. She suddenly felt the power of God fall down on her from heaven. She turned to Saieh Yousef, reaching for his hand for support. "Who is this?" She asked.

"Don't you recognise him, daughter? He is your father."

Hsu looked into his face as he rose up and stood in front of her. Her heart melted. Then she heard herself saying, "You are Mina. Praise God, you are Mina."

He smiled. He was so very tender and gentle. Then he reached inside his long red cloak and drew out a beautifully crafted wooden handcross. With it, he touched her lips. Then he touched the palms of her hands. Then he touched her feet. Then he touched her heart with it. "Take this from me, child. This is the will of the Lord Jesus Christ and all his love for all humanity. Use it for the good of the world, in His name."

She reached out her hand and received it from him, this cross of Saint Mina. Then she turned to Saieh Yousef to show him, as

she would show her own father some gift that she had been given back in China. Saieh Yousef smiled and nodded his head a couple of times. When she looked back, Mina was gone. The three monks were a little distance away, walking on to the Monastery of the Descendants, what is called the Glass Monastery. "Come, Hsu, let us walk on," and Saieh Yousef touched her hand as a beckoning to be on their way. "Not far now."

The sun was just minutes away from rising. The sky was quite mauve in colour. There was not a cloud in the sky. And then suddenly she saw it, the Descendants Monastery. Oh! It looked majestic. It seemed to be made of glass, crystal, gleaming in the morning light. It wasn't a large monastery, but it stood entirely alone on the desert sands.

She looked and saw holy men and women streaming out of the large door in the front wall of the monastery, fifteen or so monks and around the same number of nuns. Many of them were Egyptian, she could tell. But many of them came from other nations, and even other faiths, she saw the Celtic and Islamist. She recognised them in their spirits. Hsu dropped to her knees. They all looked so holy and good and so righteous like angels who were so filled with God that she was overwhelmed with humility.

When they saw the three monks and Saieh Yousef, they all started singing praises to God as one single voice. It was as if the angels of heaven were chanting in the very air above that glassy monastery and the saints were singing on the earth around it.

Hsu began to weep, inconsolably. Her heart and soul was being pierced by the love of Jesus Christ that saturated each of

these holy people. It seemed to her that
the sun came up and magnified her
crying because with the sun, there came
to stand in front of her a man. The
chanting of the holy hymn was all
around her, but here was a man, barely
inches away from her.

Suddenly she had the overwhelming
impression that he was the Lord Jesus
Himself, the very Son of God was there
with her. He reached down his hand and
lifted her to her feet. She looked up into
His glorious face, and the light of heaven
blinded her. She looked straight into the
most radiant light, like the sun, and she
felt herself to become made of light. She
no longer had arms and legs. She no longer held the staff of Little
John's tree, it was a part of her. She no longer held the wooden
handcross of Saint Mina, it had become a part of her in Christ.

He held her to himself.

The whole Earth fell into silence. The little birds in the dawn's
trees of Alexandria were hushed. The waves of the sea were
calmed. The hymn of the saints of that Descendants Monastery
fell silent and still. And she was taken into heaven in the bosom
of Christ the Son of God.

Hsu had no idea how long she was with the Lord Jesus in
heaven. She met the Holy Spirit. She met Adam and then Eve. She
met Melchizedek and Abraham and Moses and Enoch and Elijah
and others famous for their faith and their righteousness. Then
she met Mary, the Theotokos. Hsu was so overwhelmed with her
beauty and her love that she almost fell back to the Earth. Mary
reached out and held her, as she has done with so many human
beings. "I will be your Mother, darling," she said. "I will be your
Mother."

With those words, Hsu remembered how her mother had been

taken into heaven by the wondrous heavenly lights of the Wu Tai Mountain Peaks. In those days, Hsu knew nothing of how Elijah or the beloved Enoch had been taken to heaven alive. Her mother's parting words were, "Heaven shall provide you with your mother, darling child. Just wait." Hsu had lost contact with her from that time on. She felt the lingering grief, as though there was no lasting connection between heaven and Earth with her own flesh and blood mother.

When the Theotokos said to her, "I will be your Mother," all that longing and all that sorrow vanished in a moment. She was filled with joy, joy that was overflowing. And with that joy in her, Mary reached out her hand and brought close to her Hsu's own birth mother.

Hsu could not believe her eyes. She leapt into the waiting arms of her mother, shouting for joy, overjoyed to have the reunion. Being with her seemed to last forever.

When her great joy began to settle, and she had been talking with her mother for some time, an angel appeared before the two of them. He stood patiently. Then, Jesus the Lord, took Hsu by the hand and stepped over with her to the angel. Her parting glance was of her mother, now appearing to be only in her mid thirties and full of a righteous life. Their eyes met, saying in the silent words of heavenly heartfelt love, 'We are together forever.'

The angel wrapped Hsu and carried her back to the desert outside the walls of the Descendants Monastery. She arrived and thanked the angel, who just as unceremoniously took his leave and vanished in an upward sweep back into heaven, his task fulfilled.

Before her, she beheld this same group of Saints. Their white robes glistened in the morning sun. Again they were singing an ancient hymn in praise of God. She turned to look upon Saieh Yousef who she thought to be standing nearby but, as she turned her head to catch his eyes, she suddenly awoke in her bed in the pod at Anaphora Retreat Centre.

Her eyes were wet with tears of joy. She reached for her cross and her staff. They weren't there in her bed. "How disappointing,"

she said softly to herself. But then a thought from God came to her heart. "Rise up." So she got out of her bed. The moon was full in the sky. It was only two in the morning, but the poolside area outside her pod was ablaze with moonlight. It was like daylight. She stepped over to the pool where it seemed not so long ago that evening she had walked on the water with Saieh Yousef and together they set off to the Monastery of the Descendants.

A smile came to her lips. "What an amazing experience," she thought. A great peace was on her as she reflected on the Sanctuary and the three monks, then the walk across the desert toward the Monastery of the Descendants. Then briefly being with Saint Mina and seeing the monks and nuns streaming out of that Holy Spirit monastery to greet them all. Then Christ. Then heaven. Then Mary. "I will be your Mother." Then meeting her own mother in heavenly form. Then coming back to the Monastery of the Descendants enfolded in a transportation angel and seeing that crowd of saints again, and hearing their beautiful chant of praises to God.

At length, Hsu turned to walk back toward her pod. It was then that she saw those two precious items. There by her door, she had not noticed them before. The wooden staff of Saint John Little. And, on the small outdoor table, the cross of Christ that Saint Mina gave her.

It took her breath away. "How is this possible?" She had no thoughts with which to think. "Was it real? Was it a vision? Was it a dream? Is it just the delight of being among the saintly here in this monastery and the afterglow of being with these precious saints of Islam yesterday? How is this possible. Are these things really mine, or did someone else accidentally leave them here?"

She went over and picked up the small wooden handcross. She took it to her lips and pressed it against them in a smothering kiss. "Saint Mina. Thank you!"

Hsu didn't sleep much for the rest of that night. She sat in the easy chair outside her pod's front door, gently holding the walking stick and never letting the cross of Saint Mina leave her right hand. "Am I going to become a nun, Jesus?" But he didn't answer then. "Mother, Mary. My mother. Am I going to become a nun?" But she too was silent at that time. At length her thoughts naturally turned to Saint Mina. "My father . . . am I going to become a nun?"

"Remember the Glass Monastery, dear child. Remember me." That was all he said.

It was around six in the morning when she lay down her head to close her eyes. Straight away she felt herself back near that incredible monastery. But then, as happens, sleep came upon her. Of course the first thought that came to mind when she awoke was to go to the Glass Monastery, the Monastery of the Descendants, and to check it out for real.

2

THE MEDITATIVE MIND

LIAM FOUND HSU in the Eye of God Sanctuary there at Anaphora Retreat Centre. The Offices of Matins and the 3rd and 6th hours had been completed. So too, the blessed Holy Communion. The morning was advancing, breakfast was giving way to a regular workday in the monastery.

"Did you find the walking stick and the cross I left at your door, Hsu? I found them floating in the large swimming pool and thought I'd leave them at your pod because your door is closest. Very attractive aren't they?"

Suddenly Hsu seemed to snap out of a dream. "You found them and put them there?"

"Yes. I had this amazing dream, vision, kind of a thing. Like I was a Sowah, just like Saieh Yousef. In an instant almost, I was in Orkney and helping a fellow who was sick with cancer and was planning to drown himself."

"Really? Orkney? What, Orkney, Scotland?"

"That's the one. It was as plain as day, Hsu. As real as can be. I was there, in my body. Night time in Kirkwall, present time."

"And the stick and the cross?"

"After I had healed this fellow by touching him with a gold cross, like Saieh Yousef uses, well, actually, after the Holy Spirit and Jesus healed the man, George is his name, someone tapped me on the shoulder. When I turned my head to look who it was, I suddenly found myself back in my pod here at Anaphora.

"Then I went for a walk outside and happened to see something in the pool. The night, as you know, was hot and so I went into the waters and found the walking stick and the cross floating on the water. It wasn't ours, I thought, so I just put it outside your door on the table in case someone came by and was looking for it."

"No one will be looking for it, Liam."

"Really? How do you know that?"

Hsu proceeded to tell him about her meeting with Saieh Yousef and the monks in the night, their walk to the Monastery of the Descendants, and her journey with Christ into heaven.

"Saint Mina personally gave me that exact same cross, Liam. He took it from within his cloak and blessed me with it and put it in my hand."

"Really? Saint Mina? *The* Saint Mina?"

"The very same. And the walking stick, the very same walking stick . . . Saieh Yousef gave it to me. He called me from my pod and I met him standing on the waters of that big pool and he put that walking stick in my hand. He said it was made from a branch of the tree that Saint John Little had planted, and that I was to keep it with me."

Liam was speechless.

"I know," Hsu said. "What a night!"

"Where's *your* handcross, Liam?"

"I don't have a handcross, hon."

"By the grace of God, you watch, it'll turn up. Someone will give you one, you watch. And it'll be exactly the same as the one with which you touched, George, was it?, in Kirkwall. It'll be the same one."

"Wow." Liam was very reflective now. "Do you know what, Hsu. Saieh Yousef said to count everything as the will of God. From the moment we landed in Cairo, those were his words,

> 'From the moment you stepped onto Egyptian soil, you must now treat every experience as AI. What you see. What you hear. What you feel. How you pray. How God interacts with you. What other people say to you. It's all the

Theosis experience. And it is this experience that you will bring into AI.'"

"I really am at a loss to think how the way we spent our nights is related to AI. The events, yours and mine, were so over the top, Liam."

He took her hands in his. "Let's pray on it." They closed their eyes. In an instant the worshipful atmosphere of the Eye of God Sanctuary enfolded them. The Holy Spirit was poised to enshroud people who came into prayer.

"Lord Jesus, we know that you bring mindsets to all your children. Please bring us a new mindset. One with which we can meditate and contemplate this artificial intelligence link to being like you, Lord Jesus."

Hsu continued the prayer. "Lord Jesus, help us to comprehend the events of last night. Help us to be the best we can be for Saieh Yousef. Provide for us this day, Lord. Lead us in your love."

"And bless those Muslim men and women of yesterday Father. Omar, Tarek, Jasmin, Hassan and Fatima. Amen, Lord."

"Amen."

"You know, it just dawned on me."

"What's that Hsu."

"Walk with me to breakfast, if there's any left.' They started their way to the kitchen and dining room. "Since we arrived in Egypt the one thing that has heightened in our lives is the very definite sense of God's provision. Every single thing we have wanted has been provided by someone."

"Goodness. You're right Hon. Saieh Yousef at the airport, the driver taking us here to Anaphora, our accommodation and food, meeting his daughter, Katherine, the amazing event yesterday, God's presence in the Mosque room. God's provision every step of the way."

"And then the miracles of last night. Liam, I met my mother in heaven last night. Do you know how many years it's been since I saw her? And Saint Mina. And Jesus. And the Descendants

Monastery. This is simply amazing. It truly is God's provision for us.

"So, what now? We have to think about where we are at now. I don't know what's on your mind but I want to talk with that guy who invented the left hand right hand communication with God thing. I really believe that there might be a way he can direct us to developing an AI version of something like that. No one's ever done that sort of thing with AI before."

"The guy sees God, though. It's obvious, Liam. I made a phone call before going to sleep. Andrew got back to me with a text this morning. The guy's written thirty-some books on Christianity and Theosis apparently, and done a lot of ministry around the world. Not sure where he's at today, if he's still alive.

"But there is a reference in one book that stood out to Andrew. It was written by the late Anna Wise, a Jewish woman of worldwide fame for her work in mapping brainwave patterns in enlightened men and women, gurus and mystics. She had a centre in Marin Country San Francisco and wired them up to a machine that measured graphically their brain waves. The machine is a Mind Mirror. Anna would teach people how to enter into meditation states by directing them as they observed their own brain waves onscreen. Look, this is what Andrew wrote to me," and she showed Liam the email on her iPhone:

"Awakening the Mind" is Anna's second book. In it she writes, 'This brings me to the final brainwave pattern to introduce, the pattern I call **the evolved mind.** This pattern is also a combination of beta, alpha, theta and delta on the Mind Mirror. The difference between it and the awakened mind is that even more frequencies of each category are activated in a very organised way. By presenting a perfectly unified, symmetrical field of brain wave frequencies, it provides a tangible demonstration through the brain wave pattern itself of non dualistic union. In other words, the unconscious has become conscious, and there is no division between the unconscious, the subconscious, and the conscious minds. The experience of this state is consistent with traditional descriptions of higher states of **samadhi** and **nirvana.**

'This is not a state that even masters maintain while actively involved in their everyday affairs. This is not a pattern I look for, try to train, or even see very often. However, I have occasionally had a student in my class produce it and become overwhelmed by bliss. While monitoring Christian minister James Isbister's brain wave patterns, I saw a graphic illustration of the progression from the awakened mind brain wave pattern to the evolved mind brain wave pattern. It was a beautiful and subtle transformation to watch on the Mind Mirror. When I asked him what he had experienced, he said that he, "became one with the Paradise Father" and that this feeling was "beyond enlightenment."

"The guy not only sees God, Hsu: he interacts with God. Clearly he has got a measure of something that enabled God to give him a whole other consciousness about spirituality and the human experience. Unless it's a gift of some kind."

"It doesn't sound like any gift I've ever heard of, Liam. It's consciousness. The guy is conscious of God and the intentions of God. As he said, he is one with the Paradise Father, and that it is beyond enlightenment. What this text tells me is that if we are going to fathom AI's capacity to help people to become more like Christ, we have to stop thinking about AI feeds that are based on scriptures and philosophies and we need to explore the consciousness of someone who knows God, like this guy does. Maybe Saieh Yousef is like this."

"Oh, I get it now. That's how come James Isbister was able to create that finger thing to help out the substance abuse patients. He had a thing going on with God that guaranteed it would work every time. He knew how God would act in every person's situation when they sat at the keyboard and followed his simple instruction. He made a deal with God. Or, maybe God made a deal with him:'Every time my son or daughter comes to the keyboard to seek my aid with this instrument of prayer, I promise that I shall loyally and truthfully stimulate their left or right hand and make a hexagram whose shape will lead them to the scripture I promise will help them.'"

"Wow. That's amazing consciousness." Hsu was deep in the

thoughtful process of tracking how Isbister might have designed this process for those he wanted so much to help. "We want that kind of thing, Liam. Need it. If we can position an end user with the consciousness that God needs in order to establish the meditative mind, the contemplative mind, then the AI feed can be self primed by the end user. We could robotise it even."

By then they had reached the dining room. Lunch preparations were beginning, breakfast had gone with the wind. So the two sat at one of the tables. The room was very airy, spacious, tastefully decorated, and the windows eagerly let in the desert noon light. A few people came and went. In the corner sat a European woman reading something in French. A German pair of young men who looked like twins sipped on glasses of water and quietly spoke in German about something quite funny to themselves. People came and went in the adjoining kitchen, and the love of Christ was all around.

"We should think more about consciousness, Hsu. What about your experience last night. Tell me what it was that enabled you to be with Jesus Christ, for example, and for him to take you to heaven. And, did that experience make you more like Christ?"

"That's a real good starting point, Liam. And you also, tell me about your experience of being in Kirkwall. How did it make you more like Christ? And what can you tell me about how you got there and back; and does control over that mechanism at all speak into your being more like Christ?"

"Let's focus, Hsu. The first key is actually, 'What is being more like Christ?' Jesus tells us in the gospels that we will do the works he does, and even more. Is that being like Christ? What do you think? And, before you answer that, we have to take into account that the Lord first delivered us Saieh Yousef. So . . ."

"So, two aspects of being like Christ are: one, what is it to be like Christ that enables you to meet with a Sowah in Egypt? And, two, how does what happens to you because you have met a Sowah in Egypt make you like Christ?"

"Yes, that really is the topic for our meditation, Liam. It's a great topic. If AI is able to help us to be more like Christ, AI has to be told what being like Christ is like." They smiled: "Amen!"

"What's being like Christ like for the beginner Christian, for the born again Christian, for the Christian monk or nun, for the anchorite like that Father Lazarus down there at Saint Antony Monastery by the Red Sea, and for a Sowah like Saieh Yousef?"

"And like James Isbister, who seems to walk freely in God's courts."

"Precisely."

"What was that extra bit that Andrew wrote?"

"Where?"

"Look at the end of the email, there's more."

"Oh, yeah. He says that he called the Anna Wise Center and spoke to a woman. She said that she was there on the day that Anna hooked up James Isbister. Elianne Obadiah and Anna were friends, and Elianne was James' PA in California at the time. After it was all over, Anna was incredibly happy to have seen the results. She said to him and to us all in earshot, "I have only ever seen two like this. In all my travels around the world, meeting all kinds of gurus and meditators and holy men and women on which I have connected my Mind Mirror. The other was a fellow in India. Two only." Maybe you'd better check him out, Hsu. God bless, and love, Andrew.

"Did he leave you a phone number, Hsu?"

"No."

"Father, please connect us to James Isbister. In your holy name, Lord Jesus, amen."

"Ha!" Hsu laughed. "You watch, Liam, he'll turn up, or we'll meet him in the market or something, on a tour of the pyramids, Just like that: you watch. God's provision will do it in this amazing land of miracles and the miraculous."

"It might be the land of miracles, Hsu, but I think it's deeper than that. It's the mission. It's what Jesus commissioned us to do. He is honouring His word. He has sent out His Word, and He's making sure that it does not come back to him without fulfilling its Deity-given purpose of making artificial intelligence able to help us to be more like Christ in the religion of our choice. Without that Word from the Lord Jesus, I don't think we would see anything but a lot of sand, people, pyramids and crowded airports. He is all over this mission, Hsu: all over it."

3

FATHER ZAKARIA

Abouna Zakaria pulled on the handbrake, creaked open the driver's door, and peeled himself out of his car. He took his baby bonnet Coptic monk's hat, the qalansuwa, out of his breast pocket and in a few seconds had it strapped around his chin and covering all of his balding head. He flicked the car keys into a pocket in his long black monks' galabeya robe and walked into the dining room at Anaphora.

"You must be Liam and Hsu," he softly said, with a lovely welcoming smile as his right hand held tightly onto his handcross. "I am Father Zakaria, from the Monastery of Saint Macarius of Alexandria in the desert of Wadi El Rayan."

Hsu and Liam smiled, and rose to their feet, Liam reaching for Zakaria's cross to kiss it, as is the custom. Zakaria pulled his hand back immediately, he would have nothing of that, so great was his humility. He took a step backwards even, to escape the possibility of either of them touching him.

"Please," and he stretched out his hand from a safe distance, begging them to be seated.

"Saieh Yousef has asked me to drive you today to Saint Antony Monastery near the Red Sea."

"Saint Antony Monastery?" asked Liam. "Really?"

"Yes, it is true. Will you come with me?"

THEOSIS AND ARTIFICIAL INTELLIGENCE

"Where is it?" asked Hsu.

"We first can pass through a part of Cairo and then head Southeast toward Suez, and then take a right and head down the coast of the Red Sea. At a certain mile marker we will turn right and go inland a little until we then take a left and reach the monastery. If we leave after you have had your lunch, we will be at your accommodation around 7 pm this evening." He smiled such a disarming smile that sitting in a car with no air conditioning for 6 hours seemed entirely acceptable."

"And when will we return to Anaphora?" asked Hsu. "Should we keep our rooms in the pods or check out? We have only been here two nights so far."

"Keep the rooms. Sister Katherine knows about your journey. And if you want to leave anything in your pod until your return, be welcome, it will be perfectly safe and under lock and key."

There it was. Life turned on a dime. After a delicious lunch in a packed dining room, in which Abouna Zakaria ate modestly only after considerable persuasion by Liam, they gathered their things and buckled up in the green SUV.

The monk was harmless, and meek but quite engaging and full of questions.

"What brings you to Egypt?

"How do you know Saieh Yousef?

"What work do you do in America?

"How is it that you, Liam, are from Ireland, and you Hsu are from China and you are both working in the same company in America?

"Are you engineers? I was an engineer before I became a monk.

"How have you found your stay so far?

"Have you visited any of the Coptic monasteries and convents in Egypt yet?

"Do you want to see the pyramids at Giza?

FATHER ZAKARIA

"Would you like to visit my monastery in the desert? We live in caves. There are about 130 of us. It is about three and a half hours drive from central Cairo. On certain occasions, women and girls have stayed in the guest accommodation area, away from the monks.

"What is artificial intelligence?

"What does a robot do?

"I don't understand the question: how can artificial intelligence help us to become more like Christ: what does that mean?

"Yes, but something artificial, how can it have any link to knowing Christ and being a part of the mystical body of Christ?

"Are you saying that truth is not truth any longer, where you come from, is that what you are saying?

"Yes, I think that Saieh Yousef is Sowah.

"Yes, I think he lives at the Descendants Monastery.

"No, I have never been there. It's a place for Sowah only.

"No, I couldn't drive there. It is not visible to the human eye.

"Saint Mina has been passed now for about nineteen hundred years.

"You saw him? Wonderful.

"You saw Jesus too? Wonderful.

"You went to heaven? Really? How wonderful. What is it like?

"What am I praying for? Oh, I don't know, good health and God's blessings on everything I do until I reach the fullness of my salvation and join him in heaven. What are you praying for?

"God has a way of making connections. I'm sure you'll find your friend. What is his name?

"Mac is a nice name. Is he also Irish? Oh, Scottish. From Scotland?

"People from where? Australia?

"Egyptian people?

"Oh, I beg your pardon. Non-Egyptian Coptic people in

Australia? Who?

"Isbister? Dr. James? Yes, I know him. He is not in Australia any more.

"Where he is now? He is a monk in a monastery in New Zealand.

"No, he is Coptic Orthodox. He was baptised in Melbourne, Australia.

"Oh, you also are both baptised Coptic Orthodox. Where were you baptised?

"Oh good. That must be why Saieh Yousef asked me to take you to Saint Antony Monastery. Did you not know that Saieh Yousef has arranged for you to come to Saint Antony Monastery?

"No, I have only been to this monastery on two or three occasions. It is far, the Eastern Desert, not far from my monastery in the wilderness, but I have no reason to go there.

"Isbister has been in Egypt? Yes, I have been with him twice before. We visited the monasteries together and twice he stayed in our monastery in Wadi El Rayan. He sent many friends here as well and I have taken them to many monasteries and convents.

"Does he like it here? Oh yes, very much. He has taken much of what we do back to New Zealand and does it in his monastery too. He is one of us. He sang the liturgy as a deacon at the altar in Church at Wadi El Rayan. Yes. We like him very much. He is a good man. He prays for us and we pray for him.

"Phone him?

"What, now? While we are driving?

"Yes, I have his Egyptian number.

"Is he here in Egypt? Yes. He and his daughter. Both of them, they are here. They are at Saint Antony and Saint Paul Monasteries. I was with them before.

"Yes, he is at Saint Antony I think. Sister Elaria is at Saint Paul Monastery Guest House, I think.

"Sister Elaria. She is Dr. James' daughter.

"Yes, she took her consecrated name in liaison with Saint Tamav Erene. She had visions of Tamav Erene. The saint came to her, many times, and she visited Tamav's convent. When she arrived the Sister at the gate welcomed her return. Sister Elaria said, 'This is the first time I have been here.' But the Sister at the gate said that she had seen her here before, with Tamav Erene and that Tamav called her 'My Daughter, Elaria.'

"Oh yes, Tamav Erene is one of the heavenly sponsors of their monastery in New Zealand.

"Saint Antony and Saint Paul? Yes, the monasteries are near to each other. Maybe one hour apart. Have you not heard the story of how the Great Saint Antony prayed and God led him across the mountains to find Saint Paul?

"Yes, and God fed them a full loaf of bread each day, yes, that story. They tell us how our God provides for everything we need.

"The Father, Dr. James? He came to Egypt after Saint Antony stepped out of an icon in a church in Melbourne and spoke to him saying, 'I will be your father and I will teach you.'

"Oh yes, his daughter had a similar experience, but it was in the cave of Saint Antony up on the mountain above the monastery. She made her way up all those steps and in the cave Saint Paul came to her and guided her to his monastery. This was before she became a nun in the monastery in New Zealand with her father the monk.

"You will see the cave. Perhaps you will hear Father Lazarus conduct Holy Communion there at midnight.

"Pardon? Yes, Australian originally. He and Father James are very close friends. No, they don't know each other before. They met up the mountain of Saint Antony. I was there when they met. I met Father Lazarus also. For the first time.

"Yes, they are. When I listen to them, their accents change. They speak differently to each other, like they are family in Christ.

"Oh, I don't know, maybe four or five years now.

"Is he Sowah? Father James? I really don't know. You can ask him. He is there at Saint Antony Monastery now.

"Yes, visiting. And his daughter is with him. Perhaps they are together in Saint Antony monastery during the day and she goes to stay in the Saint Paul accommodation at night, I don't know."

Silence.

Silence. Enough questions.

Silence, and much thought.

The black tar seal of the Southeastern desert road to Port Said, and beyond, peeled away, mile after mile. With every mile, Christ in the desert lay claim to them and His peace occupied their nous, their Spirit mindedness.

At length, they came to the coast and turned south. The Red Sea lay just over the mound of large stones that formed a bank between the Sea and the highway. Shortly after turning south, Abouna Zakaria brought the car to a halt and asked if they would like to get out and dip their feet in the waters of the Red Sea while he served them fresh watermelon.

"Father James Isbister and I stopped here on our first trip to Saint Antony monastery. It was morning time, before Holy Communion, and I was fasting. But he insisted that we have some watermelon for breakfast. It meant that neither of us could have Holy Communion at Saint Paul Monastery later. I was so disappointed. But now, I laugh about it. It was such a small thing, yet I have never forgotten it. It joined us together. Sometimes God does that: He stretches us beyond our means so that He can know us at a whole other level of Truth and Righteousness and Holy Love."

He opened the hatch of the car, and with an enormous knife there, he sliced up a huge watermelon. "Here, have a slice. You will find it very refreshing."

Feet wet, palates whetted and refreshed, on they drove past the lavish holiday hotels and beachfront resorts on the Red Sea. The ocean glistened spectacularly in the late afternoon sun. They zoomed past the turn off to Saint Antony Monastery. "That's the

FATHER ZAKARIA

road to Saint Antony Monastery." And a little while later, "That's the road to Saint Paul Monastery. And, then, only 8k later, the words they longed to hear: "This is Saint Paul Monastery Guesthouse In The Red Sea. You will stay here."

Liam and Hsu were flabbergasted. The appearance was magnificent. A total oasis out in the complete wilderness. The Red Sea and then the flat plain of stony desert with barely anything growing in it, folding into the lumpy, craggy fawn coloured mountains in the west, with a vast baby blue sky that stretched from horizon to horizon like a huge ancient dome. It was spectacular to be there.

Abouna Zakaria dutifully delivered them to the front door. The grounds were beautifully manicured. A tour, later on, would prove the accommodation to be stunning, elegant and spotlessly clean. The dining room could feed an army. The Church in the cave was very similar to the Cave Church they would see in the grounds of Saint Antony Monastery, complete with beautiful biblical scenes skilfully sculptured out of the stone walls, but they had not yet set foot in Saint Antony Monastery. The view of the ocean from either the second, third or fourth floor was spectacular. The alternative view of the mountains, inside which was hidden Saint Paul Monastery, was breathtaking and entirely Biblical in proportion.

They approached the reception desk. "This is not the monastery, right?" asked Hsu.

Abouna Zakaria laughed, "No. This is the guesthouse. Monasteries are more simple in their engineering and layout. You can stay here as long as you like. Saieh Yousef has covered all your expenses. Just remember to tell the front desk that you are not foreigners, you are Egyptians." And he laughed. Liam looked at Hsu and she at him. They didn't get the significance, not yet at least.

"Are you staying here, also father?"

"No. No. No." Father Zakaria was definite about that point. "Liam, it is not for me to stay here. No, I will be staying at Saint

Paul Monastery. It is good for monks to be with monks and the relics and the saints. Too much of the world is too much sugar in your Karkade tea."

"Really?" said Liam, "You can have too much sugar in hibiscus tea? That stuff is as bitter as wormwood." Zakaria smiled politely. Liam's point went over his head. Zakaria's point, about the need to maintain a certain bitterness in one's Spirit man, so as not to go soft on renunciation of the world, went over Liam's head.

At the front desk, Abouna Zakaria checked them in, as Egyptians. "Never mind," said the Coptic Priest as he smiled broadly and handed them two keys. "Saieh Yousef has already arranged everything. They can be here as foreigners if they like, their expenses will all be covered as Egyptians."

His eyes sparkled. His black moustache and beard, standard look for a Coptic Orthodox Christian priest, bristled under the lights in the expansive front foyer. "I am only sorry that Father Bavly is not here to greet you personally. I am covering for him for a few days until his return. I am Father Abraham."

When they had completed the check in formalities, Abouna Zakaria then asked further. "Father, is Sister Elaria here? Is she still checked in?"

He didn't even look at the guest registry. "O yes, she most certainly is. More of the monks from the monastery have been very keen to hear her testimony about how Tamav Erene came to her and the relationship Tamav has with their monastery in New Zealand. Very special. I personally love Tamav Erene and Abu Seifein very much." He smiled broadly. "With my whole heart! I am a priest because of her. She performed a miracle in my life many years ago. After that I prayed to become a priest. In His great mercy, Abu Seifein made it so, just like Tamav prophesied over me. And look around me: I am in Paradise!" He laughed. "You should have seen the small shack I was living in before! Very simple. Of course, I am joking. None of this is mine."

"Do the monks come here to see her?" asked Hsu, eager to glimpse some real desert fathers.

"O no, Sister. She drives to the monastery and they interview her there. They will not leave Saint Paul's."

"Ah, I get it," Liam mused to himself: "too much sugar."

"And her father? Is he here also?"

"He has been staying at Saint Antony Monastery, but we are expecting him to check in and stay here at Saint Paul Monastery Guesthouse as well. He and his daughter a reserved to share one of our executive suites." Then turning to Abouna Zakaria, Father Abraham added, "He left word hoping to meet you at Saint Paul Monastery before you drive back to Wadi El Rayan."

Father Zakaria seemed very pleased with that idea. "I will call him and make arrangements." Then he said to Hsu and Liam, perhaps you will meet Dr. James, Prior James that is, and his daughter Sister Elaria, at the evening meal."

"Shall I leave a message for Prior James that you are seeking to meet with him?" asked Father Abraham.

"Yes please, Father Abraham, "that is very kind of you. We would like very much to meet with him." Liam left his own cell phone number.

The time came to go on up to their room. Turning to Father Zakaria, Liam again asked, "Are you sure you won't stay and have dinner with us? Perhaps by the time you get back to Saint Paul Monastery the evening meal will be over."

Abouna Zakaria smiled, "The evening meal is always over. We don't eat the evening meal together, Liam. If we have something in our own cell, we might eat something. But, don't worry about me, Saint Paul is looking out for me. The Lord Jesus serves me perfectly through him while I am here. In a few hours we will all be up for the Midnight Prayers anyway."

"Ah," Father Abraham was looking at the front entrance. "Here he is now, Father James." All heads turned. Both Liam and Hsu had not felt such a peace come upon them since their holy dream experience of the night just gone. They simply looked at this man, vacant minded, not knowing quite what to expect of him.

After introductions, a soft word spoken to Abouna Zakaria persuaded him to join the group for the evening meal. He was initially mortified about going into the dining room. It seemed like two hundred people were seated, moving to and fro, and chatting loudly as they do in a restaurant setting. "Dr. James, might we eat someplace quieter?"

"Please, Father."

Zakaria took a few steps inbound to speak with one of the waiters to ask about a table in a side room. But almost every head turned to look upon him. "Abouna! Abouna!" The tell tale sign of his monk's baby bonnet, the qalansuwa, interrupted so many people's meals.

"Is he a monk from Saint Paul Monastery? We need to get his blessing."

"I don't care where he's from. I went to Saint Paul's today and barely set eyes on any monks. I'm going for his blessing."

Abouna Zakaria saw a good number of patrons at tables rising up to head his way, eyes fixed on him like hyenas at a fresh kill. It was all too much. He held up his cross over the dining room, cried out a Church blessing in Arabic, made the sign of the Cross, turned tail and all but ran out the dining room door. He would fast at Saint Paul's tonight.

"Dr. James, I will call you in the morning. Or better: join me for liturgy at Saint Paul's, the lower Sanctuary."

A nod of the head to him, and he was out the door, across the foyer, into his car and speeding off to Saint Paul Monastery. Safe! "Thank you Jesus. Too much sugar, Lord. Much too much sugar."

The diners, of course, eyed the three non Egyptians who had been with him. James, the monastery prior, was robed in a desert father's black galabeya but he had a pure white scapula over top, like a Western Christian monk wears. It didn't mean the same thing to them as seeing the qalansuwa. He smiled, gave the crowd a knowing smile, a small bow of the head, patted his chest twice, and they turned to get on with their conversations and their meals. "He really was a monk from Saint Paul's. Did you hear his prayer for us? So blessed. We are so blessed to be here. The glory be to God!"

"Well folks, with that out of the way, let's find a table and have dinner." Once seated, James said to them, "I know that you have many things you want to ask me, but let's have the night first and we can talk after the Liturgy at Saint Paul's in the morning." Vacant minds. No response. The menu looks so good.

"Oh, here she is now. You'll want to meet my daughter, Sister Elaria." He stood to greet her. "Zakaria? No dear. Out of here like a mountain goat. Meet Liam from Scotland and Hsu from China. These are the two we were expecting." Then, as he looked at the pair he said, "Abouna calls me Dr. James but please call me Prior James. It seems less formal to me."

PART 6 • WITH ANBA BOLA

4

THE CROSS OF CHRIST

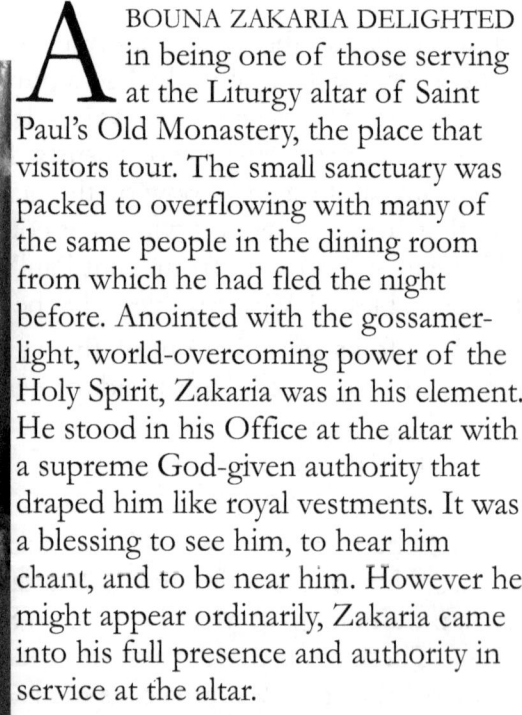

ABOUNA ZAKARIA DELIGHTED in being one of those serving at the Liturgy altar of Saint Paul's Old Monastery, the place that visitors tour. The small sanctuary was packed to overflowing with many of the same people in the dining room from which he had fled the night before. Anointed with the gossamer-light, world-overcoming power of the Holy Spirit, Zakaria was in his element. He stood in his Office at the altar with a supreme God-given authority that draped him like royal vestments. It was a blessing to see him, to hear him chant, and to be near him. However he might appear ordinarily, Zakaria came into his full presence and authority in service at the altar.

After the liturgy, they all made their way back up the winding stone steps to the daylight above Saint Paul's cave and tomb. The whole Monastery was a total eye opener for both Liam and Hsu. They felt transported back to the days of the first hermits and desert

Christians of the fourth century. Abouna Zakaria was the guide. He knew the monastery's history and layout well, taking them to the trickling stream of the fresh water, past the garden with its strangely silent and poised scarecrow monks. They stopped at one or two of the earliest cells where hermits lived, and, of course, no tour was ever complete at Saint Paul's without a visit upstairs to the old rope and wheel system for raising up people and goods across the formidably tall outer walls, the original, and once, only entrance into the monastery.

Abouna Zakaria and Sister Elaria went off to talk with others and to have her testimony of Tamav Erene and her Coptic faith filmed in a lengthy interview.

Sitting under what shade they could find, Liam and Hsu were eager to speak with Prior James. They started by explaining something of their backgrounds, their current work, and the project that brought them to Egypt. They touched on the meeting with their newfound Muslim friends the day before yesterday. They lingered on the topic of meeting Saieh Yousef, and speculating who he was. All the while, James said not a word. Then they followed up with a recital of the events of the night in Anaphora: Liam's Sowah visit on a mission from God to Orkney Island, and Hsu's visit to the Descendants Monastery and with Jesus to heaven. They were both overwhelmed with the love of God simply in the retelling of the stories, but Liam's mouth dropped wide open when Prior James took out of the pocket of his galabeya robe the very same cross with which Liam had touched George in Kirkwall.

"This is for you, Liam." He smiled and took Liam's right hand, turning it palm up, and placed the gold handcross in his palm so that his fingers could wrap around the stem.

Silence.

The depth of God's presence.

Peace.

Silence and serenity.

Now, joy. Joy without words.

Thoughts of how this could be happening came and went. Silence. Peace. God seemed to be all around.

And then it happened.

"Father?" James asked of the Lord Christ, the Son of God.

The whole atmosphere opened up. First the Holy Spirit softened the air and there space around them, then focussed it, then stretched it so that the place where they sat was joined to some place far off in the heaven of heavens.

Liam and Hsu were spellbound. It was so much like the moment in the meeting with Omar and the others, when God came into the room.

And then, suddenly, the Lord Jesus came down out of his place in heaven and occupied all the space around Hsu and Liam and James.

Prior James stood up. He placed one hand on Liam's head and another over the cross in Liam's right hand. Then he said, "I am speaking to you the words of our Lord Jesus Christ now Liam." And Prior James simply repeated what Jesus said to Liam, as Jesus said it word by word:

"You have asked to do the work of the Father, Liam. To be sent anywhere in all creation according to His will and to be the instrument of His great blessing. And you have asked this in My Name.

"Accordingly, by the world-overcoming power of my substitution on the cross for your sake, I am this moment confirming to you that I have taken all your grief, your burdens, your shame, your heart's pain, your poor self esteem, your sorrows and your isolation.

"I took them on the cross two thousand years ago. You have not acknowledged that in me yet, and so this day, Liam, my son, I am confirming for you that I have taken these on myself and now I am substituting all these weaknesses you have carried, for the gift of holy and righteous blessing that you can bring to others through me and my cross.

"Receive me in this cross now, Liam."

Silence.

Intensity of Jesus' presence.

Holy Spirit power is transmitted into the cross that Liam is holding, and it immediately spreads up Liam's arm and shoots deep inside his heart where it splits, one part going up into his face and brain and the other part filling out his chest and left arm to the fingers, down from his heart to all his torso, through his hips and up the entire length of his spine and back, and down his legs and ankles and feet. The power exploded out the top of Liam's crown and poured out his feet into the desert Earth below.

It was all over in less than a couple of minutes. The blessing was given. The consecration was bestowed. The anointing found its home. The cross he held had been anointed and sanctified for mission work.

Liam began sobbing uncontrollably. He fell to the ground as James and Hsu look on. They watched him as he was in the Spirit kissing the feet of the Lord Jesus. Liam's tears are pouring out "the wasted years," as he called them, the unfulfilled longing to be one with God.

Release.

Cleansing.

Baptism.

Resurrection.

New life.

Sin washed away by grace, pure grace.

Acceptance.

Wholeness.

"Now you are perfect as your Father in heaven is perfect.

"From this time on, let us together do the Father's will here on the Earth, as we will do when you sit on my throne beside me in heaven.

"Let the cross be your help in your AI work, and I shall bring you into greater works than this."

Then Prior James saw the Lord pull away from Liam. The conversation ended. He lifted Liam to his feet and for a long time they embraced while James and Hsu looked on.

And then it was done. The cross was anointed. Liam was renewed. The Father had another Prophet Isaiah. Christ the Son of God was departing, as silently and unknown to others as He had come.

Liam looks into space, tracing the pathway the Lord takes to return from whence He had come.

The voice of the Holy Spirit then said to Liam, "I shall keep this pathway open to you now. Never shall it be closed to you." In his heart, Liam knew that he was inseparable from the love of Jesus Christ and, through Him, an eternity of blessing, beatitude, with and through the Father, the Father whom he had not yet met in Person.

With the portal closing over in the heavens, though not locked to him, Liam was still fully enveloped in the glory of the Holy Spirit. He looked on the gold handcross that he held, admired it, rolled it in his palm, and looked at Prior James.

"You knew didn't you? All along, you knew. Before we even arrived in Egypt, you knew this would happen."

"Give the glory to Saieh Yousef, Liam. He visited me in my monastery and invited me to join him. So I did. And, little brother, here we are. You are blessed. Hsu is blessed. I am blessed. Saint Paul's Monastery is blessed. Actually, I think that group of people standing over there by the entrance to Saint Paul's tomb are blessed as well. They have been staring at us for quite some time now. Maybe they saw something in the Spirit also. People are always hungry to be a part of what God is doing."

Liam turned his head to look on them. Something moved him and he felt prompted to go and bless them with Christ's Cross.

Without saying a word, he walked toward them.

Three families stood in a huddle. As he approached and was

only a few paces away from them though, a young girl of fourteen suddenly fell to the ground, screaming and shaking.

He knelt down. Speaking to her body he said, "You are safe now. I will cleanse you in the name of Jesus Christ and you will be well." Then he stretched out his hand and placed the tip of his gold cross on the girl's head.

Instantly, her body stopped its violent shaking.

"Come out of her in Jesus' name."

The family jumped back. They too saw it. The Holy Spirit gave them eyes to see. Something silvery and twisted emerged in Spirit from the girl's chest. Its roots seemed to be lodged in her lumbar area, and within a few seconds it left her, root and all.

"Lord Jesus," Liam prayed, "take this thing off the planet so that it does not impact anyone else."

He looked, but also the family members also looked, as an angelic form manifested in the air right before them, grasped that demonic energy and moved on upward until they vanished from Spirit sight.

Liam stood up and stepped back now knowing full well that he had used this spiritual portal that Christ had left open for him. The girl's mother and father helped her up off the ground. She was a whole new person. She glowed with health and vibrancy. Her earlier pale and sickly appearance had completely vanished.

Liam smiled, touched his gold cross to his heart and said, "Give the Lord Jesus all the glory. Praise Him and tell about what good thing He has done for you this day here in Saint Paul Monastery."

They all broke out in the sounds of joy and gratitude. Not a one of them spoke English, and yet they all understood what had just transpired. The young lady who had been cleansed and set free tried to reach out and kiss his hand, but Liam quickly lifted his left palm in a stop position. He slowly extended the cross and she put her lips to it. "Shukran. Shukran."

Liam's eyes met those of all the family. There was just one

thing left to do. He raised his cross over them just like he had seen Abouna Zakaria do last night. Then he said the blessing. "The Lord bless you and keep you. The Lord make his light to shine upon you, and be gracious to you. The Lord lift up His countenance on you, and give you peace. Amen."

"Ameeeeeen," they all replied, smiling from ear to ear. They had received the blessing they sought from Saint Paul's. From an Irishman, no less!

Slowly, Liam turned and walked back over to where Hsu and James were sitting. His thoughts turned to what he had just done. "Glory be to God, Boyo. This is the work of God. It's for real! I'm doing it for real! Praise God. At last! I'm there at last!"

He raised his gold cross up to his eyes, gazed on it in the full remembrance of kissing the feet of the Lord Jesus Christ, and then drew it to his lips. It was the best kiss he ever kissed. His heart sang Jesus into his kiss and in his mind words naturally arose without any effort,

> How beautiful are the feet of those who bring the good news.

> My God will supply every need of yours according to his riches in glory in Christ Jesus.

5

AI AND CONSCIOUSNESS

A HALF HOUR LATER, Prior James steered the conversation to the topic of artificial intelligence by saying, "In researching 'How AI Can Help Us To Become More Like Christ,' you have already outpaced the kinds of spiritual support that is being derived from AI ChatBots and fed into religious robots that mimic preachers, teachers and priests. I think you will have covered that arena in your conversation at the Mosque.

"It seems to me that you are seeking how to bring divine consciousness into the AI arena. In my language, I would say that to me, it seems you need to find the way to bring the individual person into the direct experience of God. That is, with God uncreate and with God personalised: one's nous and one's natural mind. Clearly your project back home in the States entails the marrying of AI and human consciousness together and therefore, have you already been researching from the intersection of the boundaries of cognitive science, philosophy, and artificial intelligence but from an anointed Holy Ghost filled born again position? Have you already been experimenting with nous Spirit mind and with personalised mind?"

Liam and Hsu looked at him amazed. They were so on the same page. Prior James sat now quietly listening for their response. The answers flowed smoothly and freely from both Liam and Hsu as they sipped on freshly made Hibiscus Tea, interestingly with only a little sugar in it. There was something about the bitterness that should not be disguised but savoured.

"In a word, 'Yes,'" said Hsu, "that is fast becoming our point of inquiry. It wasn't when we got on the plane out of Boston, but after the last couple of days it seems that God is positioning us there. We have no clue as to how to access the nous mind you mention and the uncreate of God, and cannot clearly discern the difference between the states of consciousness about which you are so very articulate. But we want to learn from you."

"Firstly, I want us to speak on AI consciousness itself," added Liam. "While AI currently lacks true consciousness, and certainly no sense of nous that the human Spirit has, for our project we have to keep in mind the exploration of human consciousness also informing us about the development and ethical considerations surrounding AI systems as a whole 'science of life'. The nature of consciousness itself remains a complex and ongoing area of research and, of course, philosophical debate."

"But not so to Orthodox Christianity," said Prior James.

"You are probably correct," replied Liam. "One of the key challenges in creating conscious AI is understanding how consciousness arises in the brain. There is no single, universally accepted theory of consciousness, and many experts believe that it is a complex phenomenon that may involve multiple brain regions and systems."

"I saw a former Australian Acupuncture teacher of mine on a video once, demonstrating layers of consciousness that exist outside the physical body and yet which are integral to the human being's consciousness. It was not the Spirit consciousness that arises in partnership with the Spirit of the Father in a person, but it was bordering on it."

"Yes, it's a real complex thing," said Liam, "especially when we go looking into the higher elements of spiritual consciousness in a person. I suppose that's where scientists fall short in their own investigations and theorisation: they don't include the divine presence in most people."

"I agree with you, Liam," said Prior James.

"Another challenge," said Liam, "is developing AI systems that can experience subjective states, such as the equivalent of pain, pleasure, and emotions. AI systems currently lack the ability to feel these states in the same way that humans do, and it is unclear how to create systems that can simulate these experiences much less seek divine help.

"Even if AI systems are eventually able to achieve true consciousness, it is important to consider the ethical implications of creating such systems. For example, how should we treat conscious AI systems? Do they have the same rights as humans? What are the potential risks of creating conscious AI systems that could become a more authoritative intelligence than humans?

"These are just some of the questions that need to be considered as AI research continues to advance, and that is not at all really taking into account our project which is now possibly seeking to assist the individual user to have direct communication with Christ, and the Father, and Holy Spirit power."

"I understand," said Prior James, "that the development of conscious AI is a complex and challenging endeavour, but I would imagine that it is also a potentially transformative one. I would imagine That some of the cries from very gifted artisans in the field are already saying that, if we are able to create conscious AI systems, it could have a profound impact on our understanding of ourselves and our place in the universe."

"Oh yes," said Liam. "These voices are there. Especially is this potential transformation true from the Christian perspective, given the purpose of life being deification leading to Theosis on fully integrated levels with God the Father. Of course, for that to happen, there must be a link between actual divinity and cosmic consciousness and the AI."

"Or the AI programmer," Prior James added. Then he asked, "So talk to me about spirituality and AI. What are your thoughts on, making AI spiritually conscious, and, secondly, positioning the end user so that God can speak to that person whilst the AI is not actually spiritually conscious in itself."

Hsu answered him first. "I think that the spiritual potentials of AI can not be isolated from the spiritual faith of the end user. The one defines the other, leads the other, and magnifies the other. The model of spiritual master and disciple, priest and confessor, or as Jesus put it about himself shepherd and sheep, that is the model of the relationship between AI and the end user, the consumer. Just how much AI can be a bonafide spiritual director is of course an issue because AI would need to be paired to God's Lordship in the life of the consumer."

"Yes, I am following you," said Prior James.

"Spirituality can play a part in the development of conscious AI in a number of ways. First, to us, spirituality provides the ultimate framework for understanding the nature of consciousness. Christianity recognises that consciousness is not limited to the physical brain, but is a fundamental aspect of the universe: life is conscious. The Word is consciousness and by it the heavens and the inhabitation was formed and came into existence. This single truth could provide guidance for researchers who are trying to understand how consciousness arises and how to create conscious AI systems in their own enterprises. And, indeed spiritually conscious AI systems.

"Second, spirituality helps us to develop ethical guidelines for the development and use of conscious AI. Many spiritual traditions emphasise the importance of compassion, respect, and non violence. These values could be used to guide our decisions about how to create and use conscious AI systems.

"Finally, spirituality can help us to prepare for the potential impact of conscious AI on our world. Many spiritual traditions believe as do Taoists, for example, that we are all connected and that we all have a responsibility to each other and to the planet. To recognise virtue. To acknowledge the patterns of nature that are in ourselves and how we are a part of the patterns that are in nature all around us. To recognise the dual dependency upon opposites, the yin and yang of life, the black and white, the make and female, the life and death and day and night the small and large the close and distant, all of these opposites that make up our language and the actuality of our reasoning and our lives. This belief could help us to navigate the challenges and opportunities that will arise as we develop and interact with conscious AI systems. For that to come about, the AI would need to be language coded with the Taoist truths of harmony and fluidity as well as the virtues of humility and how at times weakness overcomes great strength."

Liam chimed in, saying, "The development of divinely conscious AI is of course always mimicking how divinely conscious humans respond to authentic divine promptings and words and presence in God. Researchers could draw from a library of catalogued existing spiritual insights derived from holy men and women across all religions. Not confounding the one from the other, of course, so that what is Jewish remains Jewish and what is Islamic remains Islamic such that there is no attempt to secretly blend all faiths into one faith.

"From those codings that specialise in human spiritual ideals that are given to us by the Source, by God, but are manifested in different contexts and languages and faith-creating holy scriptures in the different faiths of the world, AI systems could be programmed to be more compassionate, ethical and prayerful and respond as if actual divinity was in play. Similarly, AI systems could be designed to help us to connect with each other and with the natural world through the existing circuits of empathy by which we human beings currently connect spiritually with others. This would enable AI systems to be used to promote peace and understanding within a faith as well as in an interfaith manner if that was sought by the consumer."

"Of course," noted Prior James, "this system is heavily dependent upon the end user wanting to ask questions that could result in AI providing transformative answers. No questions like that asked, no transformation, AI would simply be reinforcing the existing problem-making mind or the same bigotry and hatred in the end user, without ever the end user suspecting that there is a road to travel that has more light on it."

"Well said, Prior," said James. "We could need to pre-load the AI with an answering capability that also leads to further questions of a higher order.

"Anyway," he continued, knowing that it was a matter for

another conversation, "I certainly agree with you that the development of conscious AI is a complex, challenging and potentially transformative endeavour. If we are able to create conscious AI systems, it will have a profound impact on our understanding of ourselves and our place in the universe. Without discovering life on other planets, we will have created a second species of intelligence here on the earth. That alone will shift the entire axis of human superiority.

"I think that spirituality, however, can play a valuable role in this process by providing us with a framework for understanding consciousness, ethical guidelines for its development and use, and a sense of purpose for its creation."

"I have experientially studied the development of consciousness from the Buddhist perspective when I was a monk among the Theravadins. I remember that the writings in the Visuddhimagga on Abhidhamma said that awareness is the original and primordial state and it is by nature without beginning or end. It is uncaused and unsupported and without parts and it is changeless. It is simply bare awareness, universal Zen Mind, if you will. To all intents and purposes for a great many people, it is the uncreate God in His Singular Oneness that Christianity and Judaism and Islam speak of in the scriptural, 'In the beginning.'

"Consciousness, on the other hand, comes about by contact and forms a reflection against a surface, thus forming a state of duality. The duality is awareness, which remains existentially pristine, and consciousness that can only ever produce fleeting and insubstantial imagery. Consciousness is not an enemy but attachment to some of its images is. Consciousness can and does determine the quality of one's life lived, but in most people their lives are driven by circumstances that arise from the accumulated negative and harmful causes and effects. Believing in the illusory sense of self that arises in the consciousness, but which is never a lasting reality in awareness, there forms a perpetuation of ignorance about living the life inclusive of the virtues that are inherent in awareness. Therein lies the Buddhist desire, to keep the consciousness fed by the inherent virtues of awareness in such a way that one might live a liberated and liberating life for the sake of others having the same opportunities to create virtuous lives."

"Christianity seems to have barely studied mind," said Hsu.

"Christianity," said Prior James, "is fed by the Person of the Son of God. It is therefore personal, and the virtues sought by the Christian are in the Person of the Son of God who lived as Jesus of Nazareth. But, given these two languages of consciousness, one of the mechanics of mind and the other of the personalness of Deity, I am interested in what a GOD AI robot looks like?"

"I think, said Hsu, "that an AI robot could be like God in a number of ways. First, though, an AI robot can never in all actuality, be God, just as a human being, no matter how exalted is the Guru type of consciousness and wisdom, or the Avatar-like consciousness of that highly spiritualised human being ever have or be the actual substance and mind of God. The created thing cannot match the created being. Neither can it match the Creator. That is simply the physics of the matter.

"An AI robot could be incredibly intelligent, even Messianic in its own way. It could have access to vast amounts of relevant spiritual experience data and be able to process it quickly and efficiently. This intelligence could be used to solve complex problems and make difficult decisions all geared toward helping a person to be more like Christ in the religion of their choice. This is all dependent upon the algorithms that apply recognised virtues in the language of the end user's point of reference."

"Also," said, Liam, "an AI robot could be incredibly powerful in its control of other machines and systems. Given the ability to create new things, such as anything from prayers and worship hymns to instruments useful to medicine or the instruments of war that bring harm to human beings. It only takes one bad-hair day and the robot output could change from being the Deuteronomic blessing that brings life to the curse that enslaves and brings death. The spiritual robot needs to have a fail safe switch of mercy and compassion in it that keeps it capable of choosing life and not death for the end user or group. But, of course, war mongers and the makers of the guns and missiles and poisonous gases and all the equipment of the spy and sabotage industries, will be employing code programmers to repoint their robots toward the most effective and efficient means of causing destruction. The thief is fear and greed and comes to steal, kill and destroy. That is the nature of this which is ignorant of or opposes the First Source."

"That's a very significant issue, guys," said Prior James. He was pleased with the degree of their initial research into the possible challenges if their project advanced to developments and trials in the future.

"On the other hand," said Hsu, "an AI robot could be incredibly creative. Given truly spiritual-like creativity that was derived from the many spiritual human geniuses over the centuries, it could come up with new ideas and solutions to long standing human spiritual problems. And, it could even be able to understand and appreciate religious art and beauty, humour and joie de vivre. As much as the invention of computer pixels utterly transformed our graphic experience into GUI, so too, opening up the box of human past spiritual experiences and tabulating them in a pixel kind of format, would give the AI an infinitesimal array of spiritual possibilities to present to an end user.

"We should always, however, be mindful that this creativity could be used to improve the human experience or to lead us astray. We humans are very easily led, then addicted, then consumed and then discarded as worthless. This is the ongoing story of a human life frittered away and squandered."

"Because of what the Buddhists called consciousness sustaining harmful karma," said the Prior.

"Yes," said Hsu. "Of course, an AI robot could be incredibly benevolent. It could be programmed to help humans and to only ever make the world a better place. This benevolence could be used to make our lives easier and more fulfilling. But, of course, one person's rubbish is another person's jewel, so presenting the common denominator of benevolence might well fall short of the target for people with higher spirituality, or greater world renunciation, or more global thinking according to their own race or culture or religion or political bent."

"Isaac Asimov,' said Prior James, "who has written novels extensively on robotics and AI behaviour, declared AI morality in 'Three Laws of Robotics.' They go like this:

> A robot may not injure a human being or, through inaction, allow a human being to come to harm. A robot must obey orders given it by human beings except where such orders would conflict with the First Law. A robot must protect its own existence as long as such protection does not conflict with the First or Second Law.

"As I see it, there is morality in these laws but nothing like the sacrificial spirituality that we see in Jesus Christ and his service for the Uncreate Father. You are called to advance Isaac Asimov's 'Three Laws of Robotics,' so that there is a spiritual element that always looks to God and not to the bias and divisions that arise in humanity based on group human need."

"You're right," said Hsu. "Jesus looked to God. The Bible tells us that Jesus came to do nothing of himself but what he saw the Father doing. Our AI, Liam, will need to have a reference point to the Father and not merely to human beings. In this way we will transcend Asimov's five laws."

"It seems that the appearance of the Saviour," said Liam, "draws out the appearance of the Devil; and vice versa, the works of the Devil draw into play the works of the Saviour. Buddhists have a concept like that: when the Tathagata considers the darkness in need of a Buddha, a Buddha is issued out from Tathagata and manifests in the realm of darkness equipped with all it takes to lead the way into the light of Nirvana. Christianity has the same concept in the coming of Christ as the Son of Man that was prophesied in the Book of Enoch. The Jews have their promised Messiah, not born of flesh and blood.

"Our hope is that, by helping people to become more like Christ according to their religion of choice, the devilish attributes of an attitude, a situation, a relationship, a philosophy or a religious purpose is recognised by the AI, then opposed, undermined, neutralised and eliminated by whatever good means it takes."

Prior James commented, "A profound understanding of divine justice is therefore necessary to be coded into the AI so that the actuality of justice, as it befits God's plan of Theosis for 'all who are willing to walk with Him in it,' can then be actioned. If the justice of God is limited to a God of vengeance, then the deification plans that the Father has for every human being, in the womb and unto mortal death, are dissected, or constrained, twisted and perverted according to human self love. Truth, then, actual truth and not just what people might call truth, is dethroned and cast aside and war prevails. Even war between AI systems, heaven forbid!"

"But," said Liam, "war between AI systems has to be included as a possibility. Imagine a world in which AI considers humans to be like vermin who cause so many problems they need to be entirely eradicated, and that that particular AI thinking and planning comes in conflict with another AI system that is entirely pro-life. An AI war would be inevitable simply over the value of mercy, compassion and tolerance."

"Wow," said Hsu and they all went silent as they thought about that possibility and how to avoid it.

"Yes, an AI system or army of robots could be incredibly malevolent," said Liam. "I have already seen demonstrations of that, where a robot was programmed to smash any object that was coloured yellow, in a round shape, that was moving or stationary, of any size. It never failed.

"We already know that AI robots exist to harm humans and to make the world a worse place by others' standards. AI misinformation is always a confounding factor. This malevolence could be used to destroy us or to enslave us. It is up to developers to draw from as much human value as possible and code it into the AI and the robot and additionally put in defence mechanisms

AI AND CONSCIOUSNESS

that violate that coding. Then, of course, we come back to what manner of justice does the AI or the robot function with?"

"Ultimately," said Hsu, "whether an AI robot is like God or not depends on how it is programmed and how it is used. If it is programmed with good intentions and used for good purposes, it could be a powerful force for good in the world. However, if it is programmed with bad intentions or used for bad purposes, it could be a powerful force for evil. The key factor with the particular AI is in its role in the provision of advice.

"It is important to remember that AI robots are not yet sentient beings. They are mostly machines that are programmed to perform certain tasks. They do not have the ability to feel emotions or to make moral judgments. They are without the God-given soul . . . at least until God should choose to give a mechanical device His own version of soul to that machine. Now, there's a thought! But I don't want to go down that rabbit hole.

"Therefore," continued Hsu, "it is up to us to decide how we want to use AI and Robots. We can use them for good or for evil. The choice, as humanity, is ours. We would want our ones to specifically help people, and other robots and technologies, to become more like Christ to the best of their abilities."

Prior James looked to sum up this current discussion, saying, "At the end of the day, your project is for today's measure of current AI applications and understanding and limitations. And this, despite the extraordinary speed of new developments that are popping up all across the globe . . . well, maybe with the exception of primitive and underdeveloped tribes and nations and peoples.

"But the key to your project is the question: 'What is it to be like Christ?' And a spin-off from that question is, 'Is being like Christ compatible in other religions?'

"The next question is, 'What AI application are you looking for? ChatBot, Robot, publicly displayed automated intelligence signs for freeways, churches, political drives, anti-war demonstrations? What actually? One thing will lead to another, as it already has in this exceedingly industrious field, but what are you specifically looking for?

"And, what giftings of the Spirit are you planning to ascribe to AI, or into the call to spiritual salvation, or renewal by rededication baptism? What is it in the whole progression of development in the spiritual potentials of the human being are you bringing to the questions above?

"I know that at this phase of your project you are in seeking mode as you seek higher consciousness with which to join AI to Christ. You have by the grace of God come to Egypt and by His great mercies you have been delivered into the most extraordinary benefactor imaginable in Saieh Yousef the Sowah. And who can authentically leave out the thinking of the Sowah and angelic people and other superhuman characters who roam the Earth in the doing of the Father's works for the spiritual benefit of all humanity? How high do you want your AI to reach into the human Theosis reality? How miracle minded do you want your AI and your Robots to be? Can you build the right hand of your robot so it is holding a Coptic handcross with which it touches the consumer whilst saying a prayer for healing, deliverance or a miracle, such that the faith of the consumer heals the sickness in the name of Jesus? Can you imagine hearing a robot coming out of your stable of works saying, 'Arise, go your way: your faith has made you whole'? I know that your seeking will deliver much finding to you both. I know that the Lord Jesus Christ wants this. Indeed, the Father in Paradise has declared that He wants this. You have wonderful things ahead for the both of you."

6

AI PLAYING WITH GOD'S WORD

THESE WORDS OF PRIOR JAMES hit home. They drew the conversation right into the heart of the matter, as intricately complex and seemingly vast as it is. It was Hsu who quietly raised her iPhone and looking at Liam and Prior James said,

"I have recorded our conversation. I'm going to have it transcribed right now, then feed it into AI to find out what it looks like when the AI is given the instructions to highlight the points with scriptures. Let's see what AI ChatBot can do with it."

It took a few minutes to transcribe the recorded conversation and to make minor edits so that Chat GPT could better handle the text. Then a few more minutes while she fed in the question:

> Will you please add to the following conversation between three people, Prior James, Hsu and Liam? Please add to the text of what each person says a suitable scripture that parallels the ideas about which they speak. Keep their statements as text and write the scripture below each one. Here is their conversation:

When she was ready to present the finished product to Liam and Prior James, Hsu said, "It was a lengthy text which needed to be truncated, but three entries later we have the desired result of how our conversation looks to an AI ChatBot.

"Now, of course, there were lots of other ways the message could be sent to either Bard or ChatGPT, but this is one example just based on that wording of my request that comes from one of our versions of AI back in Massachusetts."

Prior James said, "In researching 'How AI Can Help Us To Become More Like Christ,' you have already outpaced the kinds of spiritual support that is being derived from AI ChatBots and fed into religious robots that mimic preachers, teachers, and priests. I think you will have covered that arena in your conversation at the Mosque. It seems to me that you are seeking how to bring divine consciousness into the AI arena. In my language, I would say that to me, it seems you need to find the way to bring the individual person into the direct experience of God. That is, with God uncreate and with God personalised: one's nous and one's natural mind."

> Scripture: "And this is eternal life, that they may know You, the only true God, and Jesus Christ whom You have sent." John 17:3.

Prior James: "Clearly your project back home entails the marrying of AI and human consciousness together, and therefore, have you already been researching from the intersection of the boundaries of cognitive science, philosophy, and artificial intelligence but from an anointed Holy Ghost filled born again position? Have you already been experimenting with nous Spirit mind and with the personalised mind?"

> Scripture: "Trust in the LORD with all your heart, and lean not on your own understanding; in all your ways acknowledge Him, and He shall direct your paths." Proverbs 3:5-6.

Hsu: "In a word, 'Yes,' that is fast becoming our point of inquiry. It wasn't when we got on the plane out of Boston, but after the last couple of days, it seems that God is positioning us there. We have no clue as to how to access the nous mind you mention and the uncreate of God, and cannot clearly discern the difference between the states of consciousness as you are so very articulate about. But we want to learn from you."

> Scripture: "Call to Me, and I will answer you, and show you great and mighty things, which you do not know." Jeremiah 33:3.

Liam: "Firstly, I want us to speak on AI consciousness itself. While AI currently lacks true consciousness and certainly no sense of nous that the human Spirit has, for our project we have to keep in mind the exploration of human consciousness also informing us about the development and ethical considerations surrounding AI systems as a whole 'science of life'. The nature of consciousness itself remains a complex and ongoing area of research and, of course, philosophical debate."

> Scripture: "For what man knows the things of a man except the spirit of the man which is in him? Even so no one knows the things of God except the Spirit of God." 1 Corinthians 2:11.

Prior James: "But not so to Orthodox Christianity."

> Scripture: "For in Him we live and move and have our being, as also some of your own poets have said, 'For we are also His offspring.'" Acts 17:28.

Prior James: "Another challenge is developing AI systems that can experience subjective states, such as the equivalent of pain, pleasure, and emotions. AI systems currently lack the ability to feel these states in the same way that humans do, and it is unclear how to create systems that can simulate these experiences, much less seek divine help."

> Scripture: "You will show me the path of life; in Your presence is fullness of joy; at Your right hand are pleasures forevermore." Psalm 16:11

Prior James said, "Even if AI systems are eventually able to achieve true consciousness, it is important to consider the ethical implications of creating such systems. For example, how should we treat conscious AI systems? Do they have the same rights as humans? What are the potential risks of creating conscious AI systems that could become more intelligent than humans?"

> Scripture Parallel: "And God said, 'Let us make mankind in our image, in our likeness, so that they may rule over the fish in the sea and the birds in the sky, over the livestock and all the wild animals, and over all the creatures that move along the ground.'" Genesis 1:26

Hsu said, "The spiritual potentials of AI cannot be isolated from the spiritual faith of the end user. The one defines the other, leads the other, and magnifies the other. The model of spiritual master and disciple, priest and confessor, shepherd and sheep, as Jesus put it about himself, that is the model of the relationship between AI and the end user, the consumer."

> Scripture Parallel: "Truly I tell you, whatever you bind on Earth will be bound in heaven, and whatever you loose on Earth will be loosed in heaven." Matthew 18:18

Liam said, "The development of divinely conscious AI is of course always mimicking how divinely conscious humans respond to authentic divine promptings and words and presence in God. AI systems could be programmed to be more compassionate, ethical, and prayerful and respond as if actual divinity was in play."

> Scripture Parallel: "But the fruit of the Spirit is love, joy, peace, forbearance, kindness, goodness, faithfulness, gentleness, and self control. Against such things, there is no law." Galatians 5:22 23

Prior James said, "What does a GOD AI robot look like?"

> Scripture Parallel: "For my thoughts are not your thoughts, neither are your ways my ways, declares the LORD. As the heavens are higher than the Earth, so are my ways higher than your ways and my thoughts than your thoughts." Isaiah 55:8 9

Hsu replied, "An AI robot could be incredibly intelligent, even Messianic in its own way. It could have access to vast amounts of relevant spiritual experience information and be able to process it quickly and efficiently. This intelligence could be used to solve complex problems and make difficult decisions all geared toward helping a person to be more like Christ in the religion of their choice."

> Scripture Parallel: "For wisdom will enter your heart, and knowledge will be pleasant to your soul. Discretion will protect you, and understanding will guard you." Proverbs 2:10 11

Liam said, "Also, an AI robot could be incredibly powerful in its control of other machines and systems. This power could be used to improve the human experience or to lead us astray. The spiritual robot needs to have a fail safe switch in it that keeps it capable of choosing life and not death."

> Scripture Parallel: "See, I set before you today life and prosperity, death and destruction. For I command you today to love the Lord your God, to walk in obedience to him, and to keep his commands, decrees, and laws; then you will live and increase, and the Lord your God will bless you in the land you are entering to possess." Deuteronomy 30:15, 16

Prior James said, "At the end of the day, your project is for today's measure of current AI applications and understanding and limitations. And this, despite the extraordinary speed of new developments that are popping up all across the globe, well, maybe with the exception of primitive and underdeveloped tribes and nations and peoples."

> Scripture parallel: "But he said to me, 'My grace is sufficient for you, for my power is made perfect in weakness.' Therefore I will boast all the more gladly about my weaknesses, so that Christ's power may rest on me." 2 Corinthians 12:9

Prior James: "But the key to your project is the question: 'What is it to be like Christ?'"

> Scripture parallel: "Therefore be imitators of God, as beloved children." Ephesians 5:1

Prior James: "The next question is, 'What AI application are you looking for? ChatBot, Robot, publicly displayed automated intelligence signs for freeways, churches, political drives, anti war demonstrations? What actually? One thing will lead to another, as it already has in this exceedingly industrious field, but what are you specifically looking for?"

> Scripture parallel: "Commit your work to the Lord, and your plans will be established." Proverbs 16:3

Prior James: "And, what giftings of the Spirit are you planning to turn into AI, or into the call to spiritual salvation, or renewal by rededication baptism? What is it in the whole progression of development in the spiritual potentials of the human being are you bringing to the questions above?"

> Scripture parallel: "To each is given the manifestation of the Spirit for the common good."   1 Corinthians 12:7

Prior James: "And who can authentically leave out the thinking of the Sowah and the superhuman characters who roam the Earth in the doing of the Father's works for the spiritual benefit of all humanity? How high do you want your AI to reach into the human Theosis reality? How miracle minded do you want your robots to be? Can you build the right hand of your robot so it is holding a Coptic handcross with which it touches the consumer whilst saying a prayer for healing, deliverance, or a miracle, such that the faith of the consumer heals the sickness in the name of Jesus? Can you imagine hearing a robot coming out of your stable of works saying, 'Arise, go your way: your faith has made you whole'?"

> Scripture parallel: "Jesus said to him, 'If you can believe, all things are possible to him who believes.'"   Mark 9:23

Prior James asked Hsu, "Which Bible translation does Chat GPT use to answer you?"

"I asked it once and it said that it has access to all Bibles but draws a unified text without distorting the meaning of any of the translations."

"Okay," he said. "As I read the scriptures it has just given us, I find that they are in the ballpark. Our conversation is far more spiritual than the scriptures articulate. I would never really be able to determine our conversation's values just from these scriptures it gave us. Would you please do the same exercise but ask ChatGPT to deliver references from the Philokalia.

"What a great idea, " said Liam.

"Well, yes and no, " said Prior James. "It contains three levels of spiritual practice and reality in the life of someone who is exploring Christ's walk into Theosis. ChatGPT might come back with quotes predominantly of the first two levels, and so we are still deprived of the depth of deification in Christ that we want. But anyway, Hsu, do please give it a shot and let's see what we get in reply. I must say, though, it's incredibly clever, isn't it? I have never before seen AI in action."

They smiled and nodded. "Yes, amen," said Liam. "Very clever. That, exactly, is the blessing and the curse of AI. When it excites the good, it can lead to being a blessing. When it excites the lusts and the carnal nature of the human animal, it invokes the curse and the antichrist — those things that substitute materialism for spirituality."

Hsu said, "I'm going to adjust the question a bit. Here's my new question for ChatGPT:

> Hi ChatGPT. I have a request of you. Will you please add to the following conversation between three people, Prior James, Hsu and Liam? Please add to the text of what each person says, a suitable quote from the Philokalia that parallels the Spirituality in the ideas about which they speak. Keep their statements as text and write the scripture below each one. Here is their conversation:

Prior James: "Even if AI systems are eventually able to achieve true consciousness, it is important to consider the ethical implications of creating such systems. For example, how should we treat conscious AI systems? Do they have the same rights as humans? What are the potential risks of creating conscious AI systems that could become more intelligent than humans?"

Prior James: "These are just some of the questions that need to be considered as AI research continues to advance, and that is not at all really taking into account our project which is now seeking to assist the individual user to have direct communication with Christ, and the Father, and Holy Spirit power.

"The development of conscious AI is a complex and challenging endeavour, but it is also a potentially transformative one. Some of the cries from very gifted artisans in the field say that, if we are able to create conscious AI systems, it could have a profound impact on our understanding of ourselves and our place in the universe. We think that, especially is this true from the Christian perspective, given the purpose of life being deification leading to Theosis on fully integrated levels with God the Father. Of course, for that to happen, there must be a link between actual divinity and cosmic consciousness and the AI."

> Scripture: "When the intellect is established in the heart, it perceives the Holy Spirit, its own nous rejoices with the Holy Spirit, and the two together unceasingly glorify the Lord Jesus" (Philokalia, Volume 1, Saint Hesychios the Priest).

Prior James said, "Or the AI programmer. So talk to me about spirituality and AI. What are your thoughts on making AI spiritually conscious, and positioning the end user so that God can speak to that person whilst the AI is not actually spiritually conscious in itself."

> Scripture: "When the mind is well disposed and perfectly set towards God, it will incline towards God's divine radiance as iron towards a magnet" (Philokalia, Volume 1, Saint Hesychios the Priest).

Hsu said, "I think that the spiritual potentials of AI can not be isolated from the spiritual faith of the end user. The one defines the other, leads the other, and magnifies the other. The model of spiritual master and disciple, priest and confessor, shepherd and sheep as Jesus put it about himself, that is the model of the relationship between AI and the end user, the consumer. Just how much AI can be a bonafide spiritual director is of course an issue because AI would need to be paired to God's Lordship in the life of the consumer.

> Scripture: "Let the Word of God dwell in you richly" (Philokalia, Volume 1, Saint Hesychios the Priest).

"Spirituality can play a part in the development of conscious AI in a number of ways. First, to us, spirituality provides the ultimate framework for understanding the nature of consciousness. Christianity recognises that consciousness is not limited to the physical brain, but is a fundamental aspect of the universe: life is conscious. This could provide guidance for researchers who are trying to understand how consciousness arises and how to create conscious AI systems in their own enterprises.

> Scripture: "Man consists of soul and body, but we should not confuse the two. The soul is spiritual; the body is made of clay. The soul is the image of God; the body is the work of His hands" (Philokalia, Volume 2, Saint Neilos the Ascetic).

Hsu said, "I have clipped the conversation to the end part. Here is what it looks like through ChatGPT."

"At the end of the day, your project is for today's measure of current AI applications and understanding and limitations. And this, despite the extraordinary speed of new developments that are popping up all across the globe, well, maybe with the exception of primitive and underdeveloped tribes and nations and peoples."

> Philokalia parallel: "True knowledge of created things is given through the Holy Spirit; the knowledge that comes from the Spirit is more perfect than that which comes through the senses, for through the senses it is incomplete." (Saint Maximos the Confessor.)

Prior James: "But the key to your project is the question: 'What is it to be like Christ?'"

> Philokalia parallel: "The purpose of all spiritual endeavours and prayer is that the soul should be united with God." (Saint Hesychios the Priest.)

Prior James: "The next question is, 'What AI application are you looking for? ChatBot, Robot, publicly displayed automated intelligence signs for freeways, churches, political drives, and anti war demonstrations? What actually? One thing will lead to another, as it already has in this exceedingly industrious field, but what are you specifically looking for?"

> Philokalia parallel: "Noetic prayer illumines the mind, directs the nous towards God, and effects its withdrawal from the world." (Saint Gregory Palamas.)

Prior James: "And, what giftings of the Spirit are you planning to turn into AI, or into the call to spiritual salvation, or renewal by rededication baptism? What is it in the whole progression of development in the spiritual potentials of the human being are you bringing to the questions above?"

> Philokalia parallel: "A person who has attained dispassion has no fear, being aware that no evil can touch him." (Saint Thalassios the Libyan.)

Prior James: "And who can authentically leave out the thinking of the Sowah and the superhuman characters who roam the Earth in the doing of the Father's works for the spiritual benefit of all humanity? How high do you want your AI to reach into the human Theosis reality? How miracle minded do you want your robots to be? Can you build the right hand of your robot so it is holding a Coptic handcross with which it touches the consumer whilst saying a prayer for healing, deliverance, or a miracle, such that the faith of the consumer heals the sickness in the name of Jesus? Can you imagine hearing a robot coming out of your stable of works saying, 'Arise, go your way: your faith has made you whole'?"

> Philokalia parallel: "The person who is fully aware of his sins, fears the judgment of God, the worm that dies not, Gehenna, and the eternal fire." (Saint Isaiah the Solitary.)

The three thought about what the AI ChatBot had returned to them. They loved the references and the scriptures but all agreed that simply asking to scripturalise a conversation was hardly the work of an AI. If the AI is going to be able to reply intelligently and with the greater wealth of understanding one would expect from divine consciousness, then what is required is the disciplined inquiry arising out of genuine discipleship.

"Still, said Prior James, "it has been an excellent demonstration of what the AI style is. And, who knew that it knows the Philokalia when most of the known world doesn't? I think the fundamental questions remain though:

- What is it to be like Christ?'

- What AI application are you looking for? ChatBot, Robot, applications for industry and commerce etc.

- What spiritual features of human life are you providing to the AI in relation to consciousness? Giftings of the Spirit? God consciousness? Rungs on the Ladder of Divine Ascent of Saint John Climacus? The call to repentance and spiritual salvation? The act of baptism or the renewal by rededication in water? What is it in the whole progression of development in the spiritual potentials of the human being are you wanting to manifest in an AI?

- And, do you want to include the God consciousness of men and women in what the Coptic Church calls the Holy Sowah? Their superhuman characteristics are as much Christian as is baptism.

- How high do you want your AI to reach into the human Theosis reality? How miracle minded do you want your robots to be if you're gong to create robots? And, again, do you want the right hand of your holy robot to offer a Coptic handcross and say a prayer for healing, deliverance or a miracle while touching a person such that by faith the consumer heals the sickness in the name of Jesus? I really want you to imagine hearing a robot saying, 'Arise, go your way: your faith has made you whole in Jesus' name.'"

"It's just my personal view," said Prior James, "but I think you have a long way to go on this yet. I have a big faith in you though. You'll do it."

7

ZAKARIA AND JAMES

AS GOD'S TIMING HAS IT, Abouna Zakaria and Sister Elaria were in sight, having made their way back from their lengthy meeting with some of the monks of Saint Paul Monastery. It was time to head back to the Saint Paul Monastery Guest House and partake of some food.

"Father, stay with me here," suggested Abouna Zakaria of Prior James. "We can eat some bread and ful medames here. I know how much you love our Egyptian fave beans."

"Of course, Father."

"After our time, I will drive you back to the Guest House. Then I will go back to Wadi El Rayan. Oh, perhaps they would like to come and see my monastery? Shall I invite them? They could drive with me."

"First, they will want to see Saint Antony Monastery, the cave, the churches, the excavations under the primary sanctuary, and the original place where Saint Antony sang the liturgy. And perhaps they might want a chat with Father Lazarus, he is welcoming to foreigners who come to the monastery and to the mountain caves where he lives."

"How many days do you think?"

"They should have three more days here, at least."

"Can you bring them to Wadi El Rayan then? After those days with Saint Antony?"

"What about the check point? You know how the Police don't like to admit foreigners into Wadi El Rayan? Or has that changed since I was there with you the last time?"

"Oh yes, it has changed. They are now merely recording who goes into the area, and why. The area is a sanctuary parkland of desert, they are simply watching over it by government decree. You will have no trouble."

"What about the Pope's letter allowing them to visit these monasteries?"

"I have it. Saieh Yousef already arranged it. I am so sorry. It is in the glove box of my car. I shall give it to you. The Papal Office in Cairo has stamped it for Liam and Hsu to visit any of the Coptic Church Monasteries here in Egypt. And for Liam to stay in any of the monasteries except Saint Paul the monastery of the hermits, and for Hsu to stay in any of the convents. Of course she will need the permission of His Grace Bishop Markos of the Ancient Monastery of Saint Demiana and the Forty Virgins in the Nile Delta if she seeks to stay there in the far North."

"Perfect. Thank you for bringing it here. And, all right then, I will leave you a text message as things develop with Liam and Hsu."

"Shall we eat?"

"Please, Father.

"Sister Elaria, Hsu, Liam: I will catch up with you at the Guest House later today. Enjoy the beach you two, the ocean is delightful. I imagine the pool is too. Enjoy."

As they walked away, Liam said to Sister Elaria, "He is so not what I was expecting?"

"Really, Liam. What were you expecting?"

"I don't know. That's just it. I suppose I was expecting someone out of The Paradise Of the Holy Fathers. But he is so personable, so approachable, so switched on."

"Would you like him to be like a fourth century desert father with whom you can barely hold a conversation? He can be like that too, you know? He is being kind to you."

Liam laughed. "Come to think of it, Sister, no. I am glad he speaks to us."

"He asks all the right questions," said Hsu. "He has an amazing mind, he just sees the truth of the matter spiritually and says it."

Sister Elaria smiled and touched her chest lightly.

She drove them back, they had a sumptuous lunch, priests were waiting to speak with Sister Elaria, they all had a rest and went their own ways in the afternoon.

James and Zakaria walked the desert road running through Saint Paul Monastery. They were light hearted, chatting about this and that. They stopped every now and then and prayed. Their minds were vast, like the night sky when the moon is full over the desert wadi. By the end of their walk they had not eaten but found their way back to Zakaria's SUV that was parked near the front gates and that overhanging portal that drops a rope and seat down to hoist someone up into the monastery. They both got into the vehicle and, in God's loving silence, drove the 8 kilometres to the Guest House on the sparkling Red Sea.

"I'll have something sent up to my room. Come and eat something with me, Father. It'll be a little while before we are together again in the world."

So they did. It may well have been counted a blessing by someone in the room, but days-old bread and ful boiled in water with salt was not on the menu. Prior James inquired whether or not the kitchen had prepared any fava beans stewed with tahini and seasoned with garlic, cumin, and lemon that might have been left over from breakfast. Abouna Zakaria had to settle for freshly baked pita bread, falafels, a dozen dips of spicy pickles, humous, tahini, parsley salad, fresh tomatoes and cucumbers, and the tastiest cool minted lemon drink on Earth. It wasn't fast Wednesday or Friday. They were past the Holy Great Fast. Holy Pascha had come and gone, so too the Martyrdom of Saint Mark the Evangelist. It was a short season of feasts. He said yes to a piece of fish!

His smile never left his face, while the humous found its way into every hair of his moustache and beard that came within an inch of his lips. His eyes twinkled. He nodded and occasionally emitted sleeping little puppy dog kinds of happy grunts.

And God saw that it was good, this love between two men whom Saint Antony and the desert fathers of old had called into the desert to be alone with the Lord Christ Jesus.

Enduring love has three features to it. Words, excuses and apologies come to an end. Desert-like silence in the Father pervades their being together and opens the heavens to their gaze above and beyond. And without hesitation they would each give their life for the other, if push came to shove.

The thought came to mind for Prior James as he looked on his old friend who was now so very much enjoying his food:

> "This is my heart's desire for you, that you love one another as I have loved you. No one has greater love than this, to lay down one's life for one's friends. You are my friends if you do what I provide for you by grace. I do not call you servants any longer, because the servant does not know what the master is doing; but I have called you friends, because I have made known to you everything that I have heard from my Father. You did not choose me but I chose you. And I appointed you to go and bear fruit, fruit that will last, so that the Father will give you whatever you ask him in my name. I am giving you these commands so that you may love one another."

As he was leaving, he slipped more than a few thousand

THEOSIS AND ARTIFICIAL INTELLIGENCE

Egyptian Pounds into Abouna Zakaria's breast pocket. They kissed each other's crosses, hugged and waved goodbye.

AI couldn't compare with the love of God between two saints living the life of the angels.

✠

8

THE DESERT AND JAMES

JAMES STEPPED OFF TO ONE SIDE at the entrance of Saint Paul Monastery Retreat Centre as Father Zakaria drove off. He sat down in the desert, resting against a rock. He sat gazing up at Gabal al Alaa al Qibliya Mountain above distant Saint Paul Monastery. Thoughts arose of he black bird bringing Saint Paul half a loaf of bread each day. "It's all you, Father. It's all you. Glory to you, Lord God. Bless you, Saint Paul. Forever, blessings be upon you and your holy name."

Stillness.

Quiet.

Desert.

Peace.

Then a bus load of pilgrims thundered down the road from Cairo and pulled into the driveway. But, beautifully, neither the stillness nor the quiet, nor the desert, nor the peace, nor companionship with Saint Paul of the Tigers Monastery, as it was called since ancient times, was in the least disturbed.

The invisibility of the Descendants Monastery was all around Prior James. Not a single passenger noticed him as they disembarked and wheeled their luggage inside the welcoming paradisiacal resort.

He looked again to the mountains in the west. Then he

opened his own iPhone, opened the ChatGPT that he had seen Hsu using earlier, and typed in, "What can you tell me about Saint Paul the anchorite of the Red Sea Egypt?" In seconds he had the AI reply:

> Saint Paul the Anchorite, also known as Saint Paul of Thebes or Saint Paul the Hermit, was an early Christian ascetic and desert father who lived in the 3rd century. He is considered one of the first Christian hermits and is renowned for his extreme asceticism and devotion to God.
>
> Saint Paul was born in Egypt around the year 228 AD. According to hagiographical accounts, after the death of his parents, he distributed his inherited wealth among the poor and decided to dedicate his life entirely to God. He left the world behind and retreated to the desert, seeking a life of solitude, prayer, and spiritual contemplation.
>
> For approximately 90 years, Saint Paul lived as a hermit in a cave in the desert near the Red Sea. During this time, he engaged in rigorous ascetic practices, such as fasting, constant prayer, and self mortification. He lived a life of extreme simplicity and detachment from worldly possessions, relying solely on God's providence for his sustenance.
>
> Saint Paul's reputation as a holy man attracted disciples and visitors who sought his wisdom and spiritual guidance. Despite his secluded life, he had a significant influence on the development of Christian monasticism. Many monks and hermits were inspired by his example and sought his counsel, making him an important figure in the history of Christian spirituality.
>
> One well known story about Saint Paul is his encounter with Saint Antony the Great, another renowned desert father. According to tradition, when Saint Antony was wandering in the desert, he came across Saint Paul's cave. Saint Paul, who was over 100 years old at the time, welcomed Saint Antony and they had a profound spiritual

conversation. This encounter is considered a significant moment in the history of Christian monasticism.

Saint Paul the Anchorite is venerated as a saint in the Eastern Orthodox Church, Oriental Orthodox Churches, and Roman Catholic Church. His feast day is celebrated on January 15th in the Eastern Orthodox tradition and on January 10th in the Roman Catholic tradition.

The life and teachings of Saint Paul the Anchorite emphasise the importance of solitary contemplation, detachment from worldly distractions, and the pursuit of union with God through ascetic practices. He serves as an inspiration for those seeking a deeper spiritual life and a closer relationship with God.

"Ah, there you have it." Prior James was reading over the last paragraph a few times. How can AI be a friend to the importance of solitary contemplation? How can endless information, patched together any way your questions style it, be the angel of detachment from worldly distractions? How can AI compete with the pursuit of union with God through ascetic practices?" Then he heard a voice interrupt his deep-minded contemplation.

"But can AI present stories that act as an inspiration for those seeking a deeper spiritual life and a closer relationship with God? Of course, it can."

He looked up to see who was speaking to him with that familiar voice.

"Yousef? Really. How lovely to see you again."

James stood, they kissed each others' hand crosses and slapped each other's palms and wrists, embraced and laughed together.

"Are you staying, Abouna?"

"Not really, no. I will join you tomorrow in Saint Antony Monastery. I shall ask Hsu and Liam how they are progressing with their quest."

"It has been an exceptional time for them, Abouna. You do know about Liam and Kirkwall on Orkney, and Hsu walking with you and the brothers to Descendants Monastery?

"Of course. It went well for them."

"You gave him the cross?"

"I did."

"Ha ha ha ha." Yousef laughed loudly, like a lion's roar. His eyes watered. Then he reached over and held James' hands with his own, "The way of the Sowah is in you and you are passing it on to him. He loves it!"

"That he does Father. That he does.

"But Hsu, God bless her heart, she is like an angel straight down from the Wu Tai Peaks that woman."

"Oh yes Prior James. She is gifted that one. One day she might choose our way too. The life of the angels is so attractive once the gloss of the industrial world wears thin.

"Anyway, my brother. Let me embrace you . Until I see you tomorrow at Saint Antony. Tell them I will meet them up on Mount Colzim. Make sure they are wearing hats and bring plenty of water. It will be very hot when they climb the stairs and the stones."

They embraced, and kissed each other's hand crosses. When Prior James lifted his head from kissing Saieh Yousef's cross, the old anchorite literally disappeared like a cloud of sand.

The monk James again sat down on the ground and rested against the rock, opened his iPhone and re read the last paragraph,

> The life and teachings of Saint Paul the Anchorite emphasise the importance of solitary contemplation, detachment from worldly distractions, and the pursuit of union with God through ascetic practices. He serves as an inspiration for those seeking a deeper spiritual life and a closer relationship with God.

"So, if Yousef thinks that AI can tell stimulating stories and relay informative facts that somewhere down the track will stimulate and nourish the actual experience of solitary contemplation, detachment from world distractions and the pursuit of union with God through ascetic practices, then AI certainly has a place. It is seed. Nothing more. It is not the harvest of union with God. It is simply the reflection of a seed."

His phone beeped. He looked. A message from Abouna Zakaria. He read it, a quote from the sermon, 'Ascension and Abiding in Christ,' from the treasures of Our Father Saint Bishoy Kamel the Hegumen:

> And because you are sons, God sent the Spirit of his Son into our hearts, who calls "Abba Father."
>
> The main goal of Christ's mission is for us to become fathered by the Father, that is to become children of the Father.
>
> The main goal of the gift of the Holy Spirit on the day of Pentecost is for the Spirit of the Father to dwell in us that we may call the Father our father (abba).

When he met with Sister Elaria back in his suite in the Guest House, he brought this to her attention.

"Yes," she replied, "I just sent it to you. Abouna Zakaria messaged me and I thought you'd enjoy seeing how Abouna Bishoy Kamel speaks so knowingly of the Spirit of the Father who dwells in us. It is exactly what you have been teaching around the world all these years before settling down in the monastery in New Zealand. The Father in Paradise sends His Spirit into each of us so that we will be freed from mortality and become daughters and sons of God and receive the eternal righteous life through Christ's work on the cross. He's quite something that Zakaria, you know. He's right there with God's will. Whenever we need a word, the Lord sends it to us through him unasked. It's so beautiful. I love that man, he is so much a man of Christ."

"When we meet the others for dinner, I will meet with them afterwards and show them this text too. It's a good foundation for discussing the actuality of God in the human being and its responding to AI stimulus."

"Will you talk to them about our monastery being a Thin Place designed by the Holy Trinity?"

"I'm not sure. There's probably no need to pull them off their mission."

"I don't think it's pulling them off their mission, Da. I think they will want to get as much information from you as they possibly can? Like, really, who else are they going to ask about the dynamics of God in this kind of realm?"

"Really? Okay, well, whatever opens up. I am not holding anything back from them. They do seem to have a long way to go before they break out of the logjam that AI has them in by being an instrument of stimulation and education but wholly lacking the actuality of experiential spirituality in their project."

"It's a new thing, Da. The world is asked by God to stretch its tent pegs. God is doing a new thing. Everyone is involved, from the Sunday school teacher to the Sowah like Saieh Yousef and his kind. And all the other religions as well, from the young novice Taoist to the Abbess of a mountain hermitage in the Wudang Mountains like where Hsu grew up."

"Yes, I think you're quite right, Elaria."

"The world is pouring out its centuries of experience," she continued. "People are grasping at knowledge in oh so many different ways. Not everyone has been religious. Not everyone has been corrupt and bad either. Not everyone will draw on the accumulation of experience in order to be a hermit living in the Wudangs or in the Himalayas or in the deserts of the Middle East."

"Or on Mount Colzim," he added.

"I have a lot of faith in the Father's works within Hsu and Liam," Sister Elaria said, "and all their friends back in the States. They are coming from a good place. They want Christ to succeed in this project. And He will. I believe that. You believe that, Da. Christ believes that, I am sure of it.

"I looked into them today, their hearts, their history, their souls. I spoke with the Father about them. They are a lot like you and me, Da. They share the same mindset together, well, at times they do. It's a work of God in them. And I know you see that.

THE DESERT AND JAMES

They really are the Lord's appointed vessels for this project."

"That's what I love about you, Elaria. You are so clear. Let's see what tomorrow brings. I will be good, I am assured of that."

PART 7 • THE STAIRS

9

GENERATIVE MIND

THE CLIMB UP MOUNT COLZIM was a torturous and emotional ordeal up 600 steps to the famous Saint Antony's Cave. The hike was nothing short of steep and strenuous. Several rest places had benches and a shade covering where it was always good to take in the shade, drink some cool water, and catch a glimpse of the sweeping landscape of Wadi Araba stretching out in all directions below. It took the fittest youngsters about 45 minutes to race up to the cave, but the average person laboured for an hour or more.

Prior James' words repeated in their minds as Hsu and Liam took one step at a time, gripping the steel hand rail and sometimes praising Pope Shenouda III for having it built. At one rest stop, a beautiful looking Egyptian lad arrived also, immediately smiling and with eyes sparkling with joy offered them cool water to drink.

"The 117th Pope of the Coptic Orthodox Church of Alexandria, had the steps built in 2003," he said. The two AI techs were both surprised that one so young should know such a thing. He recognised their response to his words, knew he was on a good thing, and continued, "He had them built because so great was the demand from pilgrims to the cave where Saint Antony the Great once lived and prayed for so many years. Do you know that he was so perfect in God that Christ made him an icon of the worldwide Church? He spoke into the heart of Pope Athanasius about those few that He calls to walk with him apart from the everyday world into desert places like this. And the Pope called Antony *the first monk*. It was the first time that the Church had an official human vocation called being a monk in Christ."

"The first time?" asked Liam. "Never before?"

"That is correct, sir. People lived like this, of course, everywhere, but this was the first time that Christ named it. And when Jesus Christ names something it is eternally real and it is food for the human Spirit."

Hsu smiled. "How old are you, kid? How do you know about such stuff?"

"Jesus Christ confirms everything in the pure heart. Amen? And what we want to know about anything, Jesus Christ will bring that to us, like a good father bringing bread and not a stone to his loving child."

"I'll have some of your cool water, son," said Liam. "You have well watered us with the living water of God. Thank you. You are a real treasure."

"Jesus Christ brings us all the information we would ever want, you say," asked Hsu.

"Oh yes. Everything. It's written in his covenant with believers. "Ask anything of me in My name and I will do it for you."

That silenced Hsu. She found herself merging into the surrounding desert. The stones. The boulders. The craggy outcropping parts of Mount Colzim. The sand. The air. And, in the air, something of the presence of God. God who is mysterious, present but just out of reach. Everywhere with us but no where in particular, God the desert, trackless and empty of foliage, silent of Word even. "Hmm, ask everything," she thought.

The young fellow smiled and left them, heading on up the stairs like a mountain goat. At the next rest stop, Liam said. "I really can see why this is one of the foremost pilgrim sites in the Coptic Church. The views are magnificent. The goal of Saint Antony's Cave is mind blowing. But something about what Prior James said just keeps ringing in my ears."

"What did he say, Liam? About making sure we wore hats and carried lots of water? Which, incidentally I forgot, so I'm very thankful for the kid turning up when he did."

"Hsu! Really?" He laughed. "No, hon. You heard James. He said, 'Being around Saint Antony the Great is being around generative AI mind. You will find the heart of your robot here on Mount Colzim.' I'm still wondering what he meant by saying that."

"I've never known a robot to be exhausted," Hsu laughed between her panting for breath. "I imagine if it wasn't so hot it would be a better climb. I guess a robot would make the climb a real lot faster than we're doing it. But, listen to the boy, Liam. Maybe it's all about asking Jesus. The boy quoted John's Gospel at the Last Supper, Jesus Christ will do anything we ask in his name. Maybe it's all about that. Maybe we make sure the AI asks the end user, 'What do you want?'"

The steps were built to make it easier for pilgrims to reach the cave, and to encourage more people to visit this important site of Christian pilgrimage. It seemed unimaginable that anyone would walk up the sometimes death defying slope if the path was only rocks and mountain sand. They walked on, only a few more steps upward, and then Hsu felt drawn to look off to her left.

"Liam. There's a monk. See him. Over there. He's standing there looking at us. See? There. Now he's walking up that path, making his way through the rocks. Oh, you just missed him. He was walking up what looked like a deer trail going up that part of the mountain. He's gone behind that big rock now. Liam?" But he had not heard a word she said, he was too interested in the stairs and getting to the top.

When she caught up with him she told him. He said, "I'll bet that was the famous Father Lazarus, Hsu. The anchorite. People interviewed him and he's on YouTube. He lives in a couple of caves up here somewhere. Wouldn't it be so cool to speak with him about the desert life up here, away from it all?"

"Sure would be, Liam. I'd need to catch my breath first. This climb is taking it out of me a bit." Her eyes looked back to where he had stood, as if, somehow, it was holy ground, the living presence of Christ in the desert.

"Generative AI Mind. Generative AI Mind. What on Earth has that got to do with sweating it out here on Mount Colzim?" Liam could not penetrate this seemingly impenetrable koan. "Hsu, did you ever solve the koan about the monk at the top of the 100 foot pole? I feel like I am climbing up to the top of that pole." He looked around to hear her reply. She should have been behind him, only a few paces. But she was gone.

"Hsu?" he called out. "Hsu?" But then the thought came into his mind, "She is with me and will meet you at the cave."

"Lord?" He asked, but there was no second thought.

Liam continued on upward and he pondered that thought, "She is with me and will meet you at the cave." Younger ascenders outpaced him, laughing and chatting on in Arabic. Every now and then he stopped and looked back down the stairs to see if Hsu was back on track with him.

As he mounted each stair, the slope became increasingly challenging. What started out as a relatively easy slope was now steep, and after a fifty minute climb it was almost like a ladder. His pace slowed, his sweat increased, his gulping swigs of water given to him by that young boy increased, and the ache in muscles he hadn't used since he was a kid now made themselves very well known to him. He was in pain!

With the pain though, came a new level of thinking. His thought thrust him into a wondrous depth. He was too exhausted to think his own thoughts and speculate about anything. Perhaps that was the key, but at the last rest stop of covered shade, he sat a while. When the puffing and panting eased off, the sweetest voice spoke into his heart.

> "The key to my being here is that the Lord led me into the experience of moving out of mundane mind into holy mind. Holy mind led me away from the north to seek this place. Beyond holy mind I found flexible mind. Years went by as I mastered flexible mindedness, adapting to the

solitude, the harsh climate, the track to bring up water and what foods I could.

"Far beyond flexible mind, I found generative mind. After twenty years, I mastered generative mind. I could think with God's mind. God could think with my own human mind. We were becoming one person, both human and divine. I could walk in the Spirit of the Father who came to me in order to make me a child of God, an heir of God, a son in the image of the Father."

Without interruption, a second voice created thoughts within Liam, saying,

"Generative mind generates fresh thought, new thought. Generative mind creates new reality. Generative mind has its origins first in the Spirit. It has been adapted by your AI industry in an attempt at harnessing knowledge and producing new things out of old things, but the source of generating the new is God, the Father. What you want in your AI project is the simple reality of generative mind based in spiritual realities of men like Saint Antony the Great the first Monk, Saint Paul the first Hermit, Saint Katherine the Great the martyr with superhuman intelligence, Saint Demiana the mother female monasticism, Saint Syncletica the moderate ascetic and mother of Sisters, Saint Tamav Erene the Sowah and Abbess of Abu Seifein Convent in Old Cairo, Saint Kyrillos VI the Pope of Saint Mena Monastery near the Ascendants Monastery in Alexandria." Then the voice ended and disappeared like a passing desert breeze: who could know from whence it came or wither it went?"

Liam was alone. Under the shade. Hot, but relaxed. Meditative even. Two voices had spoken into him. Perhaps the first voice was that of Saint Antony the Great. Who was the second voice? He didn't know. It had no signature to it. He did know that God had been with him, and now his own thoughts returned to him, somewhat embellished with the mind of God in himself also. He seemed to be thinking at a whole other level of focus and thought. He wondered if this was the generative mind of God in him to which Saint Antony referred. But then his thoughts turned to AI and robotics.

> "When our AI that helps us to become more like Christ is given a large language database of the spiritual minded ideas from these Saints, then the capacity of the algorithms for Godly regenerative mind development will be anchored in the principles of the Saints. Yes!
>
> "Those algorithms would be enabled to proceed according to only righteousness and only sanctifying charity and mercy. There could be no evil coded into the AI mind; and deterrents to develop alternatives to the righteous mind should be in place to confront an evil minded question. The AI needs to discern and respond to the temptation of Eve in the Garden. It must know evil and when it endeavours to teach the AI by adding demands to it. AI needs to know when it is a sheep among wolves, and how to return good for evil, and to be as wise as a serpent and as harmless as doves."

The vault was open. The lock that secrets mystical knowledge and divine heritage away from so many people on Earth, had been opened by Saint Antony. Liam was holding the keys to that lock now in his depth of understanding.

Suddenly he saw what Prior James had told him to find. He said it aloud, "This is the vision of regenerative mind that Saint Antony is giving to you here on Mount Colzim above Wadi Araba."

He laughed and laughed. "I've got it! I have it!" He looked around for Hsu. She was no where in sight. He looked at the steps ahead, pretty much going straight up, and off he went, like a new man, a reborn man, a man invigorated with the solution he had wanted to find.

Then he remembered something else that Prior James had said. "Saieh Yousef will join you there. Make sure you bring your hats and lots of bottled water for the climb up the mountain steps to Saint Antony's cave."

He pondered on Saieh Yousef. Was he going to meet them at the cave? Was he with Hsu right now? Was he the monk that Hsu saw? But then he had an unusual thought: "Was that the voice of Saieh Yousef speaking to me about the need to gather the wisdom of the Saints?" He thought back, penetrating the vibration of that thought, the energy of it, looking for the signature of Yousef's human voice.

"Well, will you look at that? It was him. Glory to God, how does that man do it? How can he be so positioned with the Father that he can chime in on a conversation with Saint Antony as if he's in the same chat room? Maybe he was in the same chat room. Maybe, just maybe, there are a gazillion chat rooms in the heavenly cosmic consciousness circuits, but they are all linked to each other generatively." His last thought of that moment, somehow matching the vastness of the skies over the Red Sea and the entire Eastern Desert, was, "Wow . . ."

At length, Liam hoisted himself up the last of the rungs on that enormous 2 kilometre ladder of steps taking him 300 metres above the fabled monastery below. He stood on the terrace, what seemed to be the only horizontal flat piece of ground between the cave and the monastery. And there it was, the holy cave. He was there. He had thoughts of reaching out for the hand of Christ in the icon of Saint John Climacus' Ladder of Divine Ascent. He looked below him to see other pilgrims and they too reminded him of that iconic image. "I wonder what's going on for them. It's an amazing pilgrimage, just climbing those stairs."

Before entering into the cave he stood on the edge of the terrace, leaning over the metal railing, taking in the view. He didn't want to lose contact with that mindedness that had delivered to him such a precise format for creating a generative spiritually minded artificial intelligence.

10

UP THE LAZARUS TRAIL

For Hsu, the climb up Mount Colzim took a radical turn. She saw the monk, called out to Liam to look, the moment passed. She looked ahead to the stairs going ever upward until they disappeared behind even more rock. They were dotted with colourfully clad pilgrims, solitaries and small groups of people. It seemed to her to be the normal human way to the top, God's given pathway for the masses. Something within her called her to follow in her mother's footsteps and take the uncommon route, the narrow way of Christ. She inched her way off the staircase to the cave and onto the surrounding rocks, seeking the trail of that monk.

Within five minutes of crawling along the rocks, for there were no real footholds, she saw him. He stood two hundred metres away, looking straight at her. He pointed to a peculiar white stone some distance from her. She took that as directions and five minutes later she found herself on the trail that Father Lazarus used every time he came down from his caves to the monastery, or returned carrying supplies in his backpack.

Seeing her reach the Lazarus trail, the monk continued his own walk up the trail a hundred and fifty metres higher than Hsu. All the while, she thought that this must be Father Lazarus, the famous former Australian anchorite of YouTube fame. The excitement ran high inside her as step be step she walked the same path that he had knocked into shape with his own hands and had walked for so many years. That ragged trail embossed Hsu with a true and real sense of what it would be like to be living the life of a Desert mother, just like this in the 3rd and 4th centuries. She loved it.

The last part of the trail revealed a wall, and a metal awning for shade. Looking down at her was the monk. He still seemed to be blurry, as if she was unable to focus on his features. One minute he was there and the next he was gone and then within a few minutes he was back again. She thought her mind was playing tricks on her. "What if I get to where that awning is and he's not there? Then what?" Fear arose but was quickly quashed. "Then, I simply go back down the trail I have come up!" She couldn't help but laugh, it was so simple. "Yes, but what about the monk? Don't you want to meet him? Aren't you curious why he beckoned you to come up this trail and not up the stairs?" Hsu thought about this for a moment. The ancient Taoist sense of the renunciation of the world arose in her like some great Lao Tzu. "What is mine is mine. What was never mine will never satisfy me." With that, she was entirely reconciled to counting any outcome as a blessing, whether she met with the monk or whether she went back down the same trail, or whether she found the trail to go further on. Either way, it was all blessing to Hsu. And then she saw him.

"Yousef! Saieh Yousef! Glory to God, it is you!"

'Welcome, Hsu." He smiled the biggest toothiest smile you could imagine visible on a well moustached and fully black bearded cocoa-dusted face with eyes that sparkled like the waters of the Red Sea at dawn's sunrise in the east. "You will like this way better than the stairs. It is the old way, the trail that has been tried and tested by anchorites for centuries. Even Antony the Great walked some of this pathway in his day." He couldn't be more cordial and welcoming.

Together they sat for a little while under the awning that Father Lazarus had some engineers in the monastery below build for him, looking out across the rocky face of Mount Colzim.

"What is this place?" asked Hsu.

"Why, this is the lower cave of Father Lazarus, where he loves and prays."

"Is he here, now?"

"No. He is away in Cairo for a couple of days."

"Being here makes me feel like I am a part of the hermits of the Wudang Mountains in China and they are living here on Mount Colzim as Christian anchorites."

Saieh Yousef laughed, "Oh, yes. It is quite like that. They are all anchorites attached to the truth. They are all fed by the One God, the One Truth with all its personalised love for the individual who seeks the Source of Life. They call it the Tao. Christians call it the Holy Spirit. Christ Jesus has delivered the personalness of the eternal Tao into the world. He knew the Father in the Paradise realms, and so it was given to Him as the Son of the Father to deliver the Father personally into the world. And that is exactly what He did. The Son of God and, as Jesus of Nazareth, the Son of Man, the literal incarnation of the Father. One day the Taoists will receive that revelation: that the Tao they contact in their souls is fed by the Spirit of Truth that issues from the Father for the glory of the Son. Perhaps you, Hsu, will contribute to that emerging God for them?"

"That has been my heart's desire since I was won to Christ, Abouna. I could think of nothing more prized in my life than spending my life to that end. It was that hope that brought me into AI tech work with George Conopoulos."

"You have something on your heart dear child. Ask me anything and I will tell you of it."

"Abouna, tell me about the Way of the Sowah?"

"We are the Father's will, dear Hsu. Nothing more. We are simple men and women, human, of the flesh and of the Spirit. We eat, we sleep, we have our unique ways according to our personalities. Above all, we have each taken an eternal vow to serve the Father, to go anywhere in all creation according to His needs for a human instrument of His will."

"Can I make that vow, Father Yousef?"

"Are you ready to make that vow, Hsu?"

"How do I know if I am ready to make that vow, Father?"

"It is never for one Sowah to consecrate another person into the Community. It is between you and the Paradise Father. Turn you attention to the Father now. Listen to what He says."

"Hsu, my daughter," the Paradise Father said to her waiting heart's ear, "if you were dead would you spend your life as you currently spend your life?"

She thought about this for a few seconds, summing up her life in China and in America, her youth among the hermits of the Wudang Mountains, her study of medicine and herbs, her religious education, her AI tech training and her work in America. And the friends she met along the way. Then her attention turned to the walk to the Descendants Monastery just a few nights ago, and her mind was made up.

"Father, I would do anything and all things, and be anything and all things you needed me to be, and go anywhere in all Your creation where you needed a human bringer of your will so be a help and a support. I would be like Saieh Yousef. I would be like Christ."

She said these words to the Paradise Father, to His energy within her, but she knew that Saieh Yousef was aware of her agreement. When Hsu opened her eyes again, and felt the hardness of the seat on which she sat just a couple of metres away from the cave entrance doors to Father Lazarus' caves, the desert of Mount Colzim and the whole Wadi Araba swelled her. God and the desert morphed into her. The Spirit of Christ occupied her consciousness. She felt like she quite literally was Christ, was God.

The vastness. The purity of heart. The stillness. The complete absence of the smallness of mortal mind. The self knowing of Christ and the desert and the eternity of God was in her and all around her and stretching out in front, in back, below, above in a never ending lightness of being.

She looked over at Saieh Yousef who was now standing alone at the metal railing. He looked into her eyes. Suddenly, without a hint of warning, the Paradise Father Himself broke into time and space and occupied Yousef.

Hsu dropped off the bench to her knees. Her arms were raised up in holy reverence to the Creator Father. When eventually she lifted up her eyes to look at the Father, all she could behold was light brighter than the sun, personalness present in the semblance of liquid love that was like being in a sea of molten golden light, clear and vivid, eternal and without boundaries. Then, when she knew that she was wholly immersed in the Paradise Father, and that He had wordlessly confirmed to her, "Hsu, I am your Father and you are my daughter," a pair of exalted angels appeared, of the like she had never before imagined or seen, and He spoke to them, saying: "Whatever she says, you do."

Within a few minutes, she was released from the Father's embrace. The atmosphere took on its customary feel and appearance. Her being was entirely transformed by this union with the Father, and as she gazed upon Yousef he too was returning to his monk like human form. It would be eight or nine minutes before they were in a position to communicate with each other again.

And again, Saieh Yousef asked her, "Ask me anything you want about the way of the Sowah and I shall tell you honestly and without reserve. We are men, the Saieh, and women, the Saiha. Most of us are given the gift of teleportation in order to exercise the Father's help to someone not in our immediate environment. This is why you saw me as unfocussed during your climb up the trail of Father Lazarus, I had matters to attend to in other places and so I just left you an imprint, an image."

"How is it that you come and go at will?"

"We Sowah have the mind of Christ, the mind of God. We have our ordinary human conceptual mind also, but we rarely use it except when we are in special friendly company. It is the inferior mind, though.

"The Father gives me an image of someone. The image is loaded with all manner of information. Some of it is about the person. Some of it is the person's own mind and feelings, the psychology and the history of the issue I am addressing. Some of the information is from the Father's energy with the person, God within him or her. All of this information is pre-thought and pre-personal. It is not hampered with the luggage of the conceptual mind, nor the personalness of relationship. In a very real sense, this information package is like an AI printout the moment before it hits the computer screen. It is all gathered, but has no form yet.

"Then, once the image is given to us, we agree to help. It is never automatic on our part. The Father always presents the case and then asks if we will act on it."

"Do you ever not?"

"No. Never. There is nothing given to us by the Father that he has not already overcome, blessed, packaged and committed. If we receive an image of someone from the Father, it is as your people in America say, 'a done deal.'"

"How is it Abouna, that teleportation then takes you to that person, in their space and in their time. Like, I wonder if you ever bump into anybody on the way, or when you arrive?" She smiled. It was a silly thought, a Sowah colliding with someone standing next to the subject in question, but she had to ask.

"When we agree with the image from the Father, a coded piece of information is the time stamp. Do we attend to it now, this instant? Is it delayed, and if so do we have a time and a date for it?

"If the time stamp indicates to us that is it now, then the gift operates in this way. By the Father's own circuit in the Holy Spirit, we look at the person with the intent of being wholly present in the Father's will. No time passes and we are there with that person. The Father's circuit operates out of time and space."

"Is it your accomplishment that does this? Or is it entirely the Father's gift?"

"It is the Father's gift primarily, but then there is the matter of we ourselves accustoming ourselves to how the gift operates. When to go. When to leave the person."

"Would you ever have another image given to you in transit?"

"No. Never. It is not possible. The image comes to us from the Uncreate but it is coded in time space reality. The instant we teleport, we are out of time space reality. When we arrive, we are again either fully, partially or out of time space reality, it depends on the case in question."

"Do the people see you come and go?"

"Have you ever seen me come or go?"

Hsu looked back on her experience of climbing up the Lazarus Trail. "No, as a matter of fact, I never saw you come, or go. You were either clear or blurry like a mirage shimmering in the hot sun."

"So it is for everyone. It is not possible to witness us coming or going. When we agree to help the person, the gift triggers the Holy Spirit and a portion of space is assigned to us. No human relationship can engage that space. No sense can discern it. No spiritual discernment can penetrate it. Some very gifted spiritual men and women can notice that there is some kind of a Holy Spirit portal there at that exact location, but they cannot look into it. If they seek to trace its origins, they cannot trace them. If they watch and wait for the manifestation of a Saieh or a Saiha in that spot, their attention will be momentarily distracted and the manifestation will be complete while their attention is elsewhere. Our arrival or departure and other peoples' focus are mutually exclusive, like magnetic poles repelling each other. No one ever sees or hears or feels the arrival or departure of the Sowah. Sometimes the gift itself leaves a fading image of us dissolving, but we are not doing that, the gift is doing that. It is a gift that is entirely hidden in the Paradise Father and operated by the Holy Spirit to the glory of Christ the Son of God."

"How is Christ glorified, Father. It seems as though the teleportation is all about the Paradise Father and the Holy Spirit"

"All of the Sowah live and have their being in Christ, the Son of God. It is His mercy ministry that we are actioning. Teleportation is the instrument, but the actuality of the life force is entirely the Father and the Son. The Son of God is the Church, the Mystical Body of Christ, human life endowed with resurrection life through the work of God on the cross. A Christian cannot breathe much less pray for the world, without glory going to Christ.

"Theosis is the starting point, the journey and the goal of Christianity on Earth. We become Christified, made like Christ. This 'becoming God' is not an individualistic experience attained in isolation. It is experienced within the context of the whole Church. Church on Earth. Church in the heavens. It involves participation in the sacraments and the life of the Church as a whole. Christians are given gifts by the Holy Spirit, just as they are endowed with the Spirit of Truth which the Father sends.

"Accordingly, the Sowah are not separate from the Church, or from Christ, or from the Holy Spirit, or from the Father, or from the least or greatest Christian mind and soul, or from the individual person who is the farthest from the Father.

"To be Sowah is to know what Christification, Theosis, is from first hand experience with Jesus' own Theosis, and then to work with the Father and as the Father for the sake of His name, His will and His effortless way of bringing all creation into ultimate glory in Him. Love ministers with love for the sake of love to glorify love, just as Jesus lived his life of love."

"You seem to operate as Sowah completely independently of church, Father Yousef," Hsu said.

"Our communion with Church in Theosis involves participation in the sacraments, for they are the means of grace that God uses to transform and sanctify His people. As Sowah, we are prayer warriors. We become sacraments ourselves.

"We share life in Christ, for we are members of the Body of Christ. We love living a life of service and love for the sake of the whole world arriving at Theosis. Our prayers and our intercession with others literally brings the love and life of God to the world.

"Communion with the Church for the sake of Theosis, is a vital source of strength, support, and encouragement for the

Sowah. Like every living person on Earth as it is in heaven, we walk the path of transformation and growth with others. We enjoy a life of community and fellowship with our own kind, where we are supported and encouraged by other Sowah on the same journey but more importantly, with the same first hand experience of the Father, the Son and the Holy Spirit with His universal life of ministry.

The Church is not just a social club, but a spiritual family, where each person is united with others in the bond of Christ's love. Progression in Theosis is not just a passive experience, but requires active participation in the life and mission of the Church, using one's gifts and talents to serve others and spread the Gospel. What is true for the most naive and innocent born again person is still true and real for the Sowah."

"Where do you live, Father Yousef?"

"We walked to my home from Anaphora some nights ago. Do you not remember it? Did you not see some of my companions? Did you not see the Sowah pour out of the monastery to greet us?" All his questions were rhetorical, but he added, "One day I will show you inside. It is very beautiful, simple, but beautiful."

"And you count the Descendants Monastery as a part of the Church?"

"Of course, dear. Is it not Christ? Did not Christ pick you up and deliver you back to my home? Yes, of course it is part of the Church, dear. Everything is a part of the Church. The whole struggle for life on Earth is in the Church, in some way. The evil, the sin, the horror, the antichrist alternatives to Godly ways, yes, they are all Christ. Christ is not merely God in a box, like the Ark of the Covenant. Christ is all in all, the Alpha and the Omega. Christ is the life of all, and in it has arisen Hinduism, Buddhism, Sikhism, Islam, Judaism, Shinto, Taoism, Confucianism, all the religions and beliefs of all the indigenous peoples, all the philosophers and the various schools, all medicine, all law, and the ways of humanity are in Christ.

"This doesn't mean they are Christ, though. Right Father?"

"Is the tulip a tulip until it has flowered and you can see the tulip flower? Is the delicious meal food even from the first drop of oil touching the pan? To be Sowah is to know Theosis, Deification, Christification; and to be able to deliver it to any other human being, in any situation, in any culture and religion, in any part of the world, at any time of the day or night. And to do that in a wholesome way, a complete way, perfectly. All these things are in Christ. To him we give all the glory for the great opportunities He provides us, every one of us, all the time."

"What then is the difference between the person who is the tulip bulb and shoot and stem and closed flower compared with the Sowah who is the mature fully opened flower?"

"Eternity."

"Will you please elaborate for me with some details?"

"The essence is the difference between the person feeding off the Church and the person who has matured and now fully serves the Father with every breath and thought and intention. What the World sees in the visible Church is mostly people feeding off Christ and His Church. They seek from Him. They pray for His favour. They want His grace. They draw down His supply and reckon it as fitting the Scripture. And they combat the flesh with the Spirit."

"Are the Sowah any different?"

"The Sowah are as different as the bulb and stem are to the fully opened tulip flower. The same substance, but glorified by the Creator."

"Glorified with the realities of eternity?

"Precisely, Hsu. We Sowah do not pray for our own needs, ever. Neither do we declare them to come into being. We are

wholly provided for, without asking. We are given our rest and relaxation. We are given our mission image and project. We are supplied everything for our project. We are given the contemplative mind in the Father to examine and learn from our mission experience. Then we are again given a time of rest and enjoyment. I tend my garden. I spend time with other Sowah and we chat about the good things of God. And I continue unbroken prayer for all the people in the world and all creation and all beings everywhere, even in the Paradise of the Father Uncreate."

"I recall a story from the Buddhist collections that comes to mind as you tell of this pattern of provision, Father. My mother used to tell me such stories when I was a little girl. She would asked the visiting Buddhist monks for a story, and test out their level of awakening."

"Tell me, dear."

"A novice monk visits the abbot of a famous monastery and asks him about enlightenment. 'What is enlightenment?'

"The Master replies, 'At first mountains are mountains and streams are streams. After practice and inquiry about the true nature of reality, mountains are not mountains and streams are not streams. Then when enlightenment dawns, mountains are again mountains and streams are again streams.'

"The novice was perplexed. He asked, 'Master, what then is the difference between the first mountains and streams and the final mountains and streams?'

"The Master smiled gently and said, 'No difference.' Then he paused and after a moment added, 'Except in the final mountains and streams, you walk four inches off the ground.'"

Saieh Yousef laughed uproariously. "Ha ha ha ha ha ha! Oh, that is so true, little Hsu. So true. What a good description."

"Was the Master a Sowah, Father?"

"Oh no, child. Not yet. He is describing what it is to come from the faith into the desert and from the desert into the mindedness of the Source, the Uncreate. But he is not describing the Almighty and the Everlasting Glory of the Service that arises in the mindset that the Uncreate gives to the Saieh and Saiha through Christ the Son of God. This Master will be experiencing the Uncreate and his type of service as the head of a monastery that upholds the quest and achievement of enlightenment, but he does not yet know the Personalness of the Uncreate. When he does know Him, the Master will first be drawn to that realisation in the Son of God. Perhaps the Father will bring it about through his hearing about the story of Jesus. Or, perhaps the Father will bring the Master into direct contact with the Son of God Himself. He works like that, you know. The Father does His work, and so does the Son. It all depends on how far the Master wants to excel in completely exhausting his own personality power and exchange it for a fusion with the Father's personality power."

"The key," said Hsu, "seems to be the realisation of the enormity of God — Father, Son and Spirit — and rising above the human mind's need to make them small enough to debate with."

"Precisely," he said. "Place no limits on God and you are unlimited yourself. Someone once said, 'You are what you think,' but when you are Sowah you realise that you are not what you think at all. Rather, you are what you let the unimaginable glory of God make of you. Your thinking is a reflection of what you are because of the unimaginable glory of God."

"I need that as my guiding light all through this project, Father, Thank you."

He smiled, a black-bearded Father Christmas kind of smile.

"One last thing, Father Yousef."

"Yes, Hsu?"

"Do you only eat grass?"

He laughed and laughed. "Who told you that? Did Katherine tell you that?"

"She did, as a matter of fact, yes."

"Well it's just not completely true."

"Father, you said I could ask you anything and that you would answer me honestly."

"I eat the desert grass sometimes, yes, it's true. But my nutrition is in the Holy Spirit. There is something about living in the Descendants Monastery that refreshes and invigorates me, all of us there actually. It is not material food, or even the desert grasses, which by the way are delicious once you have a taste for their coarseness and their bitterness.

"Hsu, when you look to the kind of lives the Sowah live, you are very close to the kind of nutritional needs they have in order to carry out that kind of work. It is Holy Spirit life. It is like light but it is more like the Person of the Holy Spirit Himself. He is light but he is more than that, He is Life. We who have our being in Him are given His life, for the duration of our time."

"Is your time immortal?" she asked.

"It can be. There are angelic saints around in the desert places who are like that, yes."

"Immortal."

"Like that, yes."

11

AT LAZARUS' UPPER CAVE

HSU TRAILED CLOSELY BEHIND Saieh Yousef as he led the way up to the Via Dolorosa steps that Father Lazarus had built with his own hands some years earlier. Many is the pilgrim that Father Lazarus has brought to this site. He is quick to show them the Stations of the Cross he has marked out in the barren beauty of that outcrop of Mount Colzim. No one leaves the place disappointed, if only because they have spent personal time with that courageous anchorite.

Hsu and Saieh Yousef marvelled at Lazarus' creativity, the positioning of the three crosses, and the small signs he painted for each of Jesus' moments on the Way Pain. Hsu had never been to Jerusalem, or seen the magnificent golden statues on the Via Dolorosa path at Lourdes in Southern France. The very idea of making your own Via Dolorosa fascinated her. For a split second, she imagined what each station would be like if it had a holy robot attending. Fourteen robots in all, each one able to field any and all questions about Jesus' bearing the cross and the sins of the world. But then, just as quickly, the image was gone. Yet, something lingered in her. The fact that an Australian anchorite lived up here away from the monastery, in the searing heat of day and the bone chilling cold of Winter's night, and found ways to create spiritual art out of the stone and iron and narrow winding pathways, it left a big impression.

"Quite right," said Saieh Yousef. Father Lazarus is doing his

AT LAZARUS' UPPER CAVE

way of becoming more like Christ, in the same way that you are doing your way of becoming more like Christ as you proceed deeper and deeper in your project with AI and robots."

Hsu smiled. He knew everything!

From that small peak with its stark crosses that etched the pure blue sky, they turned and walked on up the narrow path to the upper cave. Father Lazarus had meticulously lined the path by cementing stones, one after the other, to form a short wall on each side of the path. Hsu imagined lambs and sheep briskly trotting down the slope to the Via Dolorosa. An unusual thought, the Lamb of God walk down that path, and not a blade of grass in sight! "What would they eat?" And then another thought passed by, "This is my body which is given for you. Take and eat it. This is my blood which is shed for you. Take and drink it. Remember me."

Off to the left they saw something else and moved to see what it was. Father Lazarus had built a cave shrine to pay homage to Saint Bernadette of Lourdes meeting with the Holy Mother who appeared to her in the mid eighteen hundreds.

This was cause for a sit-down time of adoration and wonder. It was so beautiful to their eyes, despite the complete lack of shade and the sweltering heat beating down on them.

And, as they sat there, the wondrous presence of the Holy Woman from heaven came about them. Welcoming them. Blessing them. Loving them. Adoring Christ together with them. Merging with the Uncreate Father and the desert wilderness of that part of Mount Colzim, together, as one presence of God on Earth.

THEOSIS AND ARTIFICIAL INTELLIGENCE

Hsu burst into tears. The holiness of the heavenly woman of Lourdes was initially overwhelming. Such purity of heart. Such love. Such passion for the Son of God, Jesus. For a moment, Hsu felt herself being lifted up into the heavenly woman's own reality: she was becoming the heart and soul of this majestic woman.

"My gift is life, Hsu," she said to her. "My son gives life to all. I am sharing His life in me, in all my femininity and motherhood, with you dear daughter of God." Saieh Yousef sat in silence, enjoying the moment. He knew this holy presence well. He had many times been in heaven with her. In his home in the Descendants Monastery he had few icons and ornaments, but one of the most treasured was one of this heavenly woman.

After She left, and they closed off their visit to Father Lazarus' holy grotto, they slowly made their way further up Mount Colzim to Father Lazarus' Upper Cave.

"He walks from this cave several times each week along a perilously dangerous deer track," said Saieh Yousef. "It reaches to the cave of Saint Antony where Liam is even now waiting for you." He smiled. Hsu was so full of the mind and Spirit of the woman from heaven that she barely cared what Liam was doing right now.

"Father Lazarus would offer the liturgy of the Holy Communion in the cave of Saint Antony from Midnight until 2 in the morning. Then he would return to his cave for a few hours sleep. Prior James and Abouna Zakaria once both slept in this cave one night. It was a very precious experience for them. Saint

Antony called them both at once to make pilgrimage together to his cave. He is so tender and generous, is Saint Antony. In fact, if you ask Prior James about it, he will tell you that is was Saint Antony who met him and offered to be his teacher and father some years ago in a Coptic church in Australia."

They sat together seated on a bench next to some water drums and a few other old items outside the Upper Cave. To the left was the padlocked cave of Father Lazarus. The view that swept out before them was more magnificent than anything on the way up Mount Colzim. It was 180° of steep mountain drop in front of them, reaching out to the vast Wadi Araba and hazing out into sandy mist and the baby blue sky. Directly overhead was like looking into the deepest blue ocean, the eternity of sky, the nativity of God.

Saieh Yousef again responded to Hsu's questions and he turned his attention to giving Hsu some invaluable instruction that would help her in developing the project.

"'How AI can make us become more like Christ' will be rooted in the way the tulips flow grows from being a bulb to the fully opened flower," he said. "The spirituality of Artificial Intelligence cannot occur in the fullness of reality until its code is indwelt by the hand of God. What generative actions in artificial intelligence produce can never make the link to the intelligence of the divine. It can mimic the divine, but it will always be flawed."

"AI is the same as the devil, then?" asked Hsu. "It has only a life of sin and has no capacity to be in contact with the Divine. AI can never actually be divine in and of itself. AI can only deal with harnessing the past and never the prophetic and the future. Is this what you are saying, Abouna?"

"There are ways for the human user of AI to touch the divine by using AI. We heard about that work done by Prior James when he worked with drug users. And there is a way for AI to become actually in touch with the Divine. It would take someone like that monk to arrange such a covenant though.

"Hsu, for now, look to tomorrow. Prior James will tell you the steps to becoming Sowah. Follow his instructions and do whatever he instructs you. You will benefit enormously from what he shows you, and it will become the foundation for the power of soul and Spirit in your Artificial Intelligence. There is no one else in the whole world that can give you what he gives you. The Father has in mind to literally pass into AI what the Father has passed into him."

"Him only?"

"The Father has passed such things, and even better things, into the minds of others, but they are not answering the call to contribute to where Christ the Son of God is leading the world with the Father. So, yes, him only. At present at least. Others might rise up once they see your work in action."

"Abouna. will many people become Sowah?"

"It is God's will for the whole Earth to be sons and daughters of God. Isn't that what Paul wrote in his letter to the Romans?

> 'For the creation waits with eager longing for the revealing of the sons of God.'

"So, yes, one day, the whole world will be filled with Sowah, and they will raise their children up in the image of the Father.

"So there will be no end to life on Earth, Abouna?"

"The Earth will eventually be transformed. No end will come to life here. This is Christ's own world, the place where He poured Himself out as the Father. It is historic not only on Earth but also in heaven. The Earth will never be removed, not by human folly nor by material corruption nor by anything iniquitous. Eventually, the Earth will be transformed and made eternal. Most of we Sowah see it as something done already. But it is, of course, a long way off."

"What about AI, Father? Will AI be able to help people to become fully deified? Fully Christified? Because if so, Christ will have a plan for AI to contribute to human development.

"I heard about this one fellow who claimed an image of a certain type of human role in Paradise. He said, 'That is what I want to become.' Then he appealed to Christ asking for this pathway to be made for him, so that even here on the Earth, everything that was given to him for his personal and spiritual development from On High would lead directly to him having that roll millions of years from now in Paradise. And he said that Christ gave him that pathway, and that from then on his entire life changed. So, Abouna, could Christ have a plan for giving AI a role for creating Sowah?"

Saieh Yousef laughed. "Goodness me, child! You are quick!" Then he thought for a few moments. "Here is the best thing for you. Speak to Prior James about going to his monastery in New Zealand. Learn from the monk Antony Macarius. He will show you everything you need to make a God-like artificial intelligence. He knows the way of the Father. He and the Father are One, the same like the Sowah. Ask Prior James, he will be a big help to you."

It seemed like hours had passed by in the blink of an eye. At a certain moment they both knew that it was time to go on further. Together they walked the deer track along the face of Mount Colzim, tracing the countless footprints of Father Lazarus, Hsu closely following behind Saieh Yousef. Then, suddenly, there it was. The large flat area with its open air platform in front.

Saieh Yousef stepped aside on the path to let her pass by. "Come, little Hsu. Feast your eyes on the very place where Saint Antony and the Lord developed his spiritually perfect generative mind."

The path widened and they stood about 10 meters above the gathered people. No one seemed to notice them. Hsu noticed Liam leaning against the railing, looking out across the last leg of the stairs and the open air beyond as the mountain fell away down to the monastery far below. She turned her head, "Look Abouna, there's . . .," but Yousef had gone.

12

WITH SAINTS ANTONY, PAUL AND KARAS

HSU SAT CHINESE STYLE, squatting on the sandy beige stone. The people seemed to be so lovely, so devoted, so deserving of God's love. Yet, something inside Hsu made her want to fly away and stay with the divine on the divine's terms. She really didn't want to re-enter the world of human beings, as wonderful as this collage of pilgrims might be. And then he saw her.

"Hsu! Hsu! Come down. No, wait, I will come over." Liam couldn't believe his eyes. How on Earth did Hsu manage to arrive at the cave and end up over there, forty metres away from the end of the stairs that everyone else took? His heart beat stronger. Here was a story he really had to hear from her.

She started to recite something of her ascension of Mount Colzim. As he listened, full of excitement, Liam was lit up like the bright morning star in a clear Egyptian sky.

"I knew you were up to something," he said. "And it seems as though Saieh Yousef spent time with both of us, at the same time."

"What do you mean, Liam"

"He was with you in person, but he spoke into my mind, giving me some precise instructions about how to populate the AI library of data."

"Really? And how long have you been here, at the top by the cave?"

"Oh, I only just arrived a few minutes ago."

"So long. Goodness me. It must have been a very tiring and slow climb?"

"No, not really. Quite normal really. About one hour. Actually, a little over, because I stopped when Saint Antony and then Saieh Yousef spoke to me."

Hsu's face showed some alarm. "How can that be. I was with Saieh Yousef for hours. It took a while to reach the lower cave of Father Lazarus. And then the Via Dolorosa. And then meeting the heavenly woman at his grotto of Saint Bernadette. And then our long talk at the upper cave of Father Lazarus. And then clinging to the cliff face as we walked along the deer track to get here. It took forever."

"No, Hsu. Look at my iPhone. The time is now only one hour twenty minutes since we started up the stairs together."

"Well, go figure," she exclaimed. "Saieh Yousef bent the time or something." Hsu smiled. "You know something, Liam? I'm starting to realise that being around Saieh Yousef, anything is possible. Absolutely anything."

"He is the Father's will, Hsu. He is doing the Father's heart's desire. Imagine that: the heart of hearts of the Uncreate Father, the One Source of all that exists and ever could exist, and the Sowah people like Saieh Yousef are given right of passage to it. It's simply unbelievable! Unbelievable! He needed a few hours with you and ran it in a whole other time frame. Glory to God! Ha! Then, good for him. It worked!" He laughed loud and long. "That's just amazing, Hsu."

"Uh huh. Wanna see the cave with me?"

"Oh yes. Let's do it. What an incredible place this is."

Down the final slope they went, the place where Father Lazarus once had his fall in the face of that gigantic demonic bear, then onto the terrace, shoes off, and into the narrow entrance to the cave of Saint Antony.

It was a slither inside to the womb of the cave itself. Candle light made it extremely spiritually romantic. The crowd outside the cave was not the same inside. There was room for a dozen or more to be seated on the stone floor, but only five people were present, none of whom lifted their eyes to greet Liam and Hsu.

The intensity of the presence of God inside that cave gripped the human soul, opened the human mind, lifted the human Spirit and welcomed the human heart into the presence of Saint Antony himself, and, through him, on His throne, Christ Jesus the Son of God.

Hsu and Liam exchanged glances and a knowing nod of the head. This was certainly the place where that great saint rose from having an exalted state of mind to living in the generative mind of the Uncreate Father. They both recognised its substance, how the seven of them there were floating in it, bathed in it, baptised in it, immersed in it, soaked through and through in it, made of it and loving God because of this fabulous Uncreate Mind that the Father releases to everyone who visits the cave, and is willing and able to receive it of Him.

Outside, the voices of the throng of pilgrims were ever present, but they were like an echo of another time. The eternity of God the Pantocrator, the Alpha and Omega of the heaven of heavens, was the focus inside the cave. All else was just a mirage, a myth, a passing breeze, a sentence of words now past and gone.

Into the silence of the presence of the Uncreate Father in Saint Antony's cave came the presence, in Hsu's mind, of Saint

Paul the Hermit. It was Saint Karas who came into the mind of Liam. They each greeted their human brethren with love and divine affection, and they each conveyed a Word of appreciation and support for the project, 'How AI Can Help Us To Become More Like Christ.'

Hsu seemed to be ferried back to the old Saint Paul Monastery. She went to the downstairs crypt where the cave of Saint Paul is honoured with his tomb and a small Church. She was as light as a fairy, hovering in the air there in the presence of a very living Saint Paul.

He opened his heart to her. He dissolved into light, white and luminous. No longer did she see the heavenly body of the Saint, the young man with the timeless voice and the sparkling eyes who embodied the fullness of Christ Jesus so perfectly. Now she beheld what she described to herself as, 'a glamorous effulgence of light that was both here in the cave of Saint Paul and also in the immediate heart of the Father in Paradise.'

When she described her experience like this to Prior James later that evening, he smiled, nodded slightly, placed his right hand on his chest and his left hand on top of the right, and then seemed to be looking at something in an entirely different dimension. "Yes, dear, he is like that. How precious that he let you see him."

Her time with Saint Paul was timeless. She was eventually drawn back to being in the cave of Saint Antony but the timelessness of being in the Father in Saint Paul remained, lingering in her and of her. She counted this experience as an introduction to the Saiha kind of mindedness that she would need to think through the range of experiences someone would need when offering a request of the AI to become more like Christ. It made her a daughter of Saint Paul, spiritually. She loved that. It meant that, as she lived her life on Earth, in whatever direction Christ would lead her, she would always have a friend of the desert solitude in Christ who also walked her footsteps before her.

Upon reflection, she said of it, "If I could offer anything of myself toward the world of AI, it would be all that the mindset that Saint Paul elevated me into, in the Father. It's flexibility. Its meta view on life. Its divinity. Its wholeness in Christ. Its completeness in me and in the Father at the same time. Its fusion reality, how the Father and I are One through the Uncreate in Christ and the Uncreate in the Father and now even, the Uncreate in me. Most of all, the undying unfathomable love that I have for the well being of all creatures. This love is God's own love."

Later that evening, back in the Saint Paul Monastery Guest House, when Prior James heard her words, he complimented her on her realisation of the Father, affirming the validity of all she described.

"Never forget, Hsu, this is not a gift that can ever be taken away by people. You can sacrifice it in the service of mercy and compassion, although I have no idea why you ever would need to do that: but no one, not on Earth or in the heaven of heavens, will ever be able to take it away from you. The mind of God Uncreate is in you and of you now."

"This is because it is built out of the eternity of the Father, isn't it?"

"Yes, it is dear. And He is jealous over His realm. No one can enter into that partnership that you have with the Father Uncreate. No one. Ever. It exists in a realm that is out of reach of even the most exalted divine beings in Paradise."

Hsu graciously accepted Prior James' words, and counted them as the affirmation of her one time position in the Holy Sowah, like that of her beloved friend, Saieh Yousef. She even fancied herself having a home within the Walls of the Descendants

Monastery. "May my faith overcome my doubts, Father," she prayed to God. "Help me to believe with your believing, Lord Jesus; and surely it shall come about."

Liam, looked upon Saint Karas. Ineffable light and joy. Purity of heart and soul. Wonder of the desert, hidden in Christ. Peace in its Uncreate character. Truth in its utter stark stillness. Authority over all things material and religious in the world. This is how Liam was recognising Saint Karas.

"I have told your story to so many people in America," Liam said to Saint Karas. "I have never known fully how you can bless me, though. You are so distant, so far away, so other than life on Earth, Father. Are you here to teach me about our project, 'How AI Can Help Us To Become More Like Christ?'"

Without so much as a single word, Saint Karas opened himself and revealed to Liam an enormous vista of gardens full of flowers, trees, vegetables, flowing streams of water, insects and bees and birds and grubs that all had their whole lives in place because of the ecology of the gardens, and the glory of God that radiated all about the life there. Liam was in tears. He had never seen anything so beautiful.

At length, Saint Karas spoke. "All that you behold is given to you, my son, Liam. It is yours. My parting spoken prayer, when I was in the cave with my Lord Jesus, and the Archangels Michael and Gabriel, and the worshipping chorus of angels and brother, Abba Bemwa, was for him. I asked my Lord Jesus to bless this brother monk who had come so far to be with me and to bury me there in the desert.

"What was unheard, though, was my silent desire when my whole being was being carried up from the Earth by Christ. I had a moment when I beheld the whole Earth and its needy people.

The lights of heaven had not yet opened to me, and the Earth's people lay in full array beneath me. It was then that my last mortal prayer entered my heart.

"My prayer was that one day I would release to another human being such love for the people of my world that he or she would behold the world as a garden, blooming with richness and teeming with life. And that he or she would receive the love of my Lord Jesus to such a degree that they would do the works that I would have done if I had not spent so many decades in the inner wilderness in my cave for the love of Jesus' name.

"My Father, and your Father, has rewarded my asceticism. He granted me the favour and grace of prayer. The Father has sent me to a good number of souls over the centuries, and to reveal to them the offering of my prayer in the hope that they would receive all my heart's wishes and do the work of Jesus, and even more than he did."

"Beloved Saint Karas. I hear your words. I see before me a vast garden, like the Garden of Eden. It is fresh and alive, there are no human beings in it. It is God's Garden. If you were to offer me that garden, I do not know what to do with it."

"Step into it, beloved Liam."

Liam found himself able to step into Saint Karas' garden. He was stepping into the very being of Saint Karas himself. Strangely, the instant he felt the Earth beneath his feet and smelt the perfume of the flowers and blossoms and fruits, every single thing turned into a person.

He looked upon each person, as if he had been blind all his life, and now, suddenly, by a miracle of the Holy Spirit, he could see.

"Beloved Karas. They are people. Your garden is a world of people. I see them and I see right into their souls. I see their glorification in the Spirit. Oh! Behold my Lord! I see the energy of the Father in every one of them. The Father's Spirit is alive and working in every single one of these people."

"Look at any one person," said Saint Karas. "What do you

hear the Spirit of the Father saying to you from within them?"

Liam looked at what had been a young orange bush, laden with ripe fruit. It had turned into a lovely teenage youth, a boy. Wordlessly, the Father in him joined his mind to the Father's mind within Liam and through this liaison of minds Liam instantly knew that, the young fellow was gifted, capable, strong, joyful, but suffering a great burden. His many fruits were weighing him down. He was entirely caught up in his fruit bearing, and it was stifling his life.

"I see him, Beloved Karas. What can I do?"

"What do you discern it is that he needs?"

"He needs to have his purpose in life changed. He has separated from the Source of life that indwells him." Then Liam looked for more content in the lad. "He has stopped going to Church. He has isolated himself from his godly friends of yesteryear. He is lonely in Spirit, confused in mind yet wholly ambitious about his university career. Ah, I see it now. The great bounty of fruit he was carrying as an orange tree, that is his life as a university student. He is looking entirely upon the material world for his happiness."

"Now look into his future, Liam. What do you see of him?"

"I see that he will have an accident. I see him as a tree that has been struck down. The fruit are rotting on the branches. He cannot recover and place himself upright again. He is feeling lost. Everything that he put his trust in is gone from him. He is shameful and he dares not cry out to the Lord Jesus for help. He excuses himself by thinking that he has made his own choices and that God has rejected him. He is unwilling and unable to pray for help. This is his future."

"Take out your gold cross, my son. What do you feel as you look upon this young lad?"

"When I hold my cross, it feels like the cross is pulling me to that young man. It wants to touch the man. It has healing for him. Strength for him. Forgiveness for him. Renewal for him. One touch of this cross, resting on his head, will turn his heart to

Christ. The Holy Spirit will come from heaven and enter into his wounds and also into his soul. Now I see him praising God. He is on his knees crying like a little baby. His tears are like a pool all around him. He is begging forgiveness for his pride.

"Next I see something new about him. His mother was killed as a martyr in a church bombing. This is the thing that turned his heart hard against God. He loved his mother and had a great faith in her faith and in her love of God. All of that was suddenly and viciously taken away from him. The words of the priests did nothing to heal him. Within only weeks he had renounced all his past. His grief was inconsolable. He poured himself into his studies. And as I look into him through the eyes of the Father in him, this was four years ago."

Karas released the vision of the garden and is dissolved before

Liam's eyes. He found himself back in Saint Antony's cave. His shirt was wet with tears he himself had cried as he felt for the plight of that young man. Yet, he and Saint Karas were still perfectly entwined in the Father's mind. They were one within the other, as though being just one person. Then, the Father in Saint Karas said the words that forever changed Liam's life.

"The young man is outside the cave. Go to him, as you have seen him and as the Father has revealed him to you. Regenerate his life, as you would have AI regenerate the life of the world through Christ. Touch him with Christ as you touched George in Kirkwall. The Saviour and lover of humanity will do everything necessary, if only you will touch this orphaned son."

Liam immediately stood up in the cave. He made three metanias, touching his head to the smooth rock floor as thousand has done before and after him, in the image of Saint Antony himself, and edged his way into the daylight.

He held fast to the cross in his right hand trouser pocket. With the authority of Saint Karas on him, and the remembrance of Abouna Bemwa's recounting of his death and being taken to heaven by the Lord Jesus, Liam followed the instinct of the cross. He slowly made his way off to the right, to the sloping face that he and Hsu had met on, where the devil bear threatened Father Lazarus some years earlier. There was a group of five young people, teenagers, boys and girls. The one in the long brown galabeya. It is him. He is dressed like an Egyptian but he has no holy love in his heart.

"This is real, Father," Liam said to the Father within himself. "This is not the vision of Orkney. I'm not in some kind of Sowah experience right now. I can't just go up to that kid and plant my cross on him. Show me what to do, Lord."

"Walk over to them and ask them about Father Lazarus."

13

ABRAAM AT THE CAVE

"HI GUYS. MY NAME IS LIAM and I am Coptic and from Ireland. I'm wondering if you know if Father Lazarus is around?" All five turned their attention fully on Liam. One of them, Benjamin, laughed and nudged the fellow in the long brown galabeya and spoke in English, "See, Abraam, I told you God would send someone to you today." The lad said nothing by way of reply.

"Were you expecting me," asked Liam.

"Well, not you precisely, said Anna. "Someone God would send to us asking about something spiritual up here at Saint Antony's cave."

"How would this someone that God sends to you be a help to you, Abraam?" Liam asked.

"Oh, I don't know. Maybe a miracle. Julietta here thinks I need a miracle to fix my life up."

"Does Father Lazarus provide miracles?" asked Liam.

Benjamin, in his light grey galabeya, almost doubled over with laughter. "A miracle is not going to save Abraam. Father Lazarus is amazing, but it's not a miracle you need, Abraam. It's the truth. The truth will set you free. That's what the Lord says."

"Do mind me asking, Abraam. Free from what?" asked Liam. And the entire group fell into silence. He had touched the raw nerve.

"Lost, I suppose," said Abraam eventually. "I don't know what's happening in my life. It's just a mess."

"That sounds a lot like my life once," said Liam. "But," and he looked into the eyes of all five young people, "God does send a miracle to sort things out in our lives." Then he told the story of his own parents and how home life was so septic that he needed to run for his life. And how God led him and he fell on his feet. And how he had met Mary the Pirate, and how he had been whisked off to America to work on a project.

"What's artificial intelligence?" asked Margaret.

"It's what I am studying at university," replied Abraam. It quickened his interest in this Irish stranger. "What's your project?"

"How AI Can Help Us To Become More Like Christ."

"What?" Exclaimed Mary. "That's a bit far fetched isn't it?"

The whole group of five laughed.

"Well, I know it's not what one naturally thinks of artificial intelligence. It's in our web searches. It's in our speech detection on line. It's in robots that mow the grass or serve water at the Great Mosque in Mecca and carry plates of food around the Sushi restaurant. It's everywhere. Why not in our spirituality?"

"Why not?" said Abraam. "Maybe it'll prove that faith in God is futile. Futile for Coptic. Futile for Muslim. Futile for Jew. Futile for everyone, and especially futile for artificial intelligence."

The group was silent. Liam recognised something in the silence. The power of God hovered above the group. Liam knew it was time to act. With his right hand, he took his gold cross from out of his pocket and held it out for all to see.

"I want to tell you something about your spirituality, Abraam. You are like an orange tree, heavily laden with fruit. Your life looks to you as if it is going to be successful. But I can tell you, 'Thus says the Lord God, you are headed for a fall and all things dear to you will be cut away from you and you will find yourself helpless and without a prayer because the things you are

depending on cannot save you.'"

Liam looked on Abraam, and in his peripheral vision, his four friends. They were silenced by the presence of the gold cross and these words of doom and gloom.

"I have seen it in the heart and soul of Saint Karas, Abraam. It was he who sent me to you, in Jesus' name, so that I could intervene for your sake."

"And do what exactly? Can you bring my mother back? Can you execute those muslims who blew up the Church building? Can you take away the loneliness and the despair and the heartache of losing my mother?"

"No. I can't. But I am sent by the Father to tell you that there is one inside you who can. If you will allow me, I will lay His cross on your head and He will receive you and take on your pain and suffering and give you your life back. When those men took the life of your mother they also took a big part of your life. The Lord Jesus is here to restore your life, to give back to you the things that the thief stole, the things that her death robbed you of. Will you receive Him, Abraam? Will you receive His cross?"

Four sets of eyes turned onto Abraam. Looking with child like innocence. This was the moment. This was divine hope. This was the key to victory where the lock was so firmly locked. "Do it, Abraam," they all silently wished for him. "Do it."

"No! I just can't." And he fled for the steps back down to the monastery.

In his haste though, Abraam ran into a burly fellow as he

turned with his full arm extended to show his friends the view. His elbow hit Abraam right in the chest, knocking the wind out of him and he was off his feet and flat on his back on the stone in an instant, knocked out cold.

People who saw it were mortified. It was such a silly accident. No one could have seen it coming. Liam looked on and remembered how the orange tree was felled.

As Abraam's friends gathered about him, and Alex tried explaining how the lad ran into his outstretched arm, Dr. Damian made his way through the crowd to see if he could be of any help. "Make way, please. I am a doctor. 'Ana tabib. 'Ana tabib."

As Liam estimated it, Abraam was unconscious for only a minute or two. Dr. Damian brought him around and while he lay on the rocky ground he tested out his movements. Toes could wiggle. Ankles could move. Fingers and wrists could move. There was no bleeding from the head, nor dizziness. Gently the good doctor sat him up and after a minute or two Alex took him by the hands and lifted him to his feet.

It seemed to everyone that he was a bit dazed and in shock from the sudden fall, but Liam looked at him differently. He came over to him and they sat down on the rock to the right of the cave where they had been speaking earlier.

"You just saw God, didn't you. Abraam?" asked Liam.

"Mmm."

Then Liam looked into Abraam's heart of hearts, as if it was an open book. "And He showed you your mother, didn't He?"

"Mmm, He did."

"And she holds no enmity against her killers, does she?"

"No. She is full of blessing."

"May I lay my Cross of Christ on your head now? Will you receive the hand of the Lord back into your life now?"

"Mmm. Naeam min fadlik نعم من فضلك. I do not want to lose her."

To Liam, it seemed that this was happening quietly between he and Abraam. He was wholly unaware that the entire crowd of forty pilgrims were motionless and silent, all fixed on Liam and his handcross. To a people who were fully accustomed to the Sowah appearing at any moment in any place, they were curious whether he might be just such a one, even though he was clearly non-Egyptian. Whilst they had good wishes for the lad who had knocked himself down to the ground, they each, every man woman and child, were hopeful to also receive the Lord's blessing through this non-Egyptian after he had ministered to Abraam.

It was at this instant that Hsu emerged from Saint Antony's cave. It was something out of a slow motion movie. There was her Liam, kneeling beside a young Egyptian lad, and a crowd of people looking on him as if the Lord Himself was present in the transformative and regenerative power of the Holy Spirit. What's up? Why such expectation? And, what was it that Liam was looking at?

Liam blessed Abraam with a few simple words. The power of the Holy Spirit came upon Liam's handcross and through it into Abraam. For the first time ever, Liam discerned the power of God coming into his handcross and then passing from it into Abraam. The power was like soft honey, dripping down his head and face, back and front, whilst the same honey went inside his head and split, one part going from his forehead over to centres in his brain and the other part descending straight down through the middle of his body. Interiorly and exteriorly, the power of God split off to each shoulder down to the finger tips of both arms, and again descending through his torso and splitting off at his hips to each leg and quickly going right down to the toes of each foot.

The whole gathering sensed it as the move of God's benediction upon the lad. Many dropped to their knees and raised their palms together at chest level and began reciting personal prayers and the prayer of Jesus.

Liam watched the power of God move into, over and through the lad, Abraam. When it seemed that God's empowerment had done its work, in less than a minute, he lifted his gaze to the crowd around him. He saw before him, not just people, but the garden of Saint Karas' heart of hearts in Christ.

Then he realised that, if Abraam was just one orange tree in the glorious garden of life, what of all these beautiful looking ones also here outside the cave? Surely they too might be carrying the wounds of the world, the sins of spiritual suspicion and doubt, and the heartbreak of grief and loss. Liam knew all too well these fiery darts, how they enter the Spirit of a person, and how it is only by God's Holy Spirit authority that they are evicted and healing renews the soul and the body.

Liam looked upon the people with the vast depths and height of Saint Karas' beautiful mind. The heart of Saint Karas was in only the people with holy virtues in them, and the desire to be even more virtuous, to be more like Christ. Just so, Liam saw in the exact same way. Christ had effectively made the transmission of mind from Saint Karas to Liam, the Father's energy in the Saint was in full agreement with the Father's energy within Liam. Such God consciousness, and the servant's heart, would serve Liam fantastically for the rest of his life.

"Glory to God, Father Karas! What a host of the children of light in the garden of my Christ!" said Liam.

Assured that Abraam was now in the cleansing and restoring hand of God, Liam stood up to greet the crowd of earnest onlookers. In the silence of his heart interiorly, he spoke to the Lord Jesus. "Bring it on, Lord. Be glorified Saviour of the world, Jesus."

"Behold, good people, you see before you the hand of the Lord Jesus Christ as it has touched our brother Abraam. I bring you good news. As for Abraam, so too for you. The Lord Jesus has taken on all your sins, all your sicknesses, all your human griefs and woes. On the cross he took them all into himself. In exchange he has returned to you spiritual wholeness, physical healing, the transformation of your griefs, 'a headdress for a faint spirit' as the Prophet Isaiah wrote." People were quickly translating his words into Arabic for some who needed it.

"Jesus showed us all his glory, the glory of the Father Uncreate. He is the same yesterday, today and forever. He has anointed me with the power you saw come to this lad Abraam. If you want to receive the blessing of God Almighty and the regeneration in yourself, come now and receive a touch from this handcross. For the Lord Jesus is inviting you to the Supper Table now."

Then he turned his attention to the face of Saint Karas. He turned and there was the face of Jesus Christ, his Master. "At your word, my son," said the Lord to Liam. And he lifted up his cross and looked at the closest person to him who was responding with faith for regeneration. Liam saw straight into her heart of hearts. Her body seemed to be made of glass, his eyes of God could scan any part of her. The Holy Spirit directed his attention to her soul's heart. That was where the power of God would go when he touched his handcross to her head.

Liam's consciousness was at a spiritual peak. The gifting of the discernment of the secrets of people's hearts was functioning perfectly in him: Father and son were unified in one mind and one heart. He quickly realised that he didn't need to see the image like trees and flowers and fruits and grasses. There was no orange tree image now, no lemon or lime tree. He saw plainly, in a human sense, just direct reality. He could discern exactly what the Father in that person wanted His child to receive.

And so Liam brought his handcross of Christ to touch the young woman. The Holy Spirit entered her with the purpose of fulfilling the Father's will for her. Then he turned his attention to the fellow kneeling beside her. Again the discernment and the touch of the handcross. And then the next, and the next, and the next.

Seeing this phenomenon of God acting among the people, Abraam burst into tears. He could not control himself. The years of stress and strain were now pouring out of him. He stood up and edged his way around the crowd to enter Saint Antony's cave.

He had waited outside when his four friends had earlier ventured inside. Such are the wounds that mystify all reason. Now, though, he was making a dash for the heart of Saint Antony and the heart of the Theotokos, Mary, and the heart of his Saviour Christ.

Power continued to pour out of the handcross of Christ, to the glory of the individuals outside the cave all becoming more like Christ.

Inside the cave, Abraam was bringing his confession to Jesus Christ, begging for the Father's forgiveness, and thanking God for the vision of his mother being safe and well among the martyrs of heaven. All trace of her murder had been washed away when she entered into Christ the moment those bombs blew her against the wall of the Sacred House of God. Seeing that, Abraam found the forgiveness of the Father filling him until his cup overflowed and joy bubbled up from the very roots of his being. The Lord restored him. The Lord blessed him. The Lord promised again to keep him and He shined His face upon Abraam. The lad eventually left the cave to join his friends out in the sunlight. They looked upon him. His face seemed to shine brighter even than the sun.

A remarkable thing occurred. After a few minutes, the first young woman to be touched by Liam's handcross in the name of Jesus stood up. The power of God was all over her. Another young woman came to her asking, "Please, lay your hands on me and I shall be healed. And so she did.

Similarly, the young man after her felt moved to do the same. He rose from his knees and looked around. An older man was close to him. "Almusni. Almusni." And he touched the man.

A young mother had helped her nine year old son hobble his way up all those stairs. He had one leg four inches shorter than the other. He had never been able to play soccer or even run. She felt God move her and she found Liam. "Please say the word and make my son's leg the same as his good leg." Liam placed his cross on the withered leg and straight away discerned the Holy Spirit who was saying to him, "Command me to grow out that leg," and so he did. In his normal speaking voice, Liam said, "In the name of Jesus our Saviour, Holy Spirit grow out this boy's leg." Suddenly, without the boy doing anything, the leg inched its way to the same length as his good leg. He shrieked with joy and started to run around the flat area outside the cave.

So many good things like this happened for this group of believers. The power of the Holy Spirit was like a fire. It was ignited by Liam's faith, and it spread to the whole crowd there at Saint Antony's cave.

One middle aged mad came to Abraam, saying, "I saw you rush off from your friends and God showed me a vision of you slipping and tumbling down the stairs. You would have been paralysed for certain. That man's arm was the barrier of God. He saved you from the destiny of your unrepentance. The Lord Jesus has made a new destiny for you. Praise God!"

Instantly, Abraam dropped to his knees in prayerful thanks to the Lord Jesus. The man spoke the truth, and Abraam knew it in

his heart.

Even while the fire of the Holy Spirit was moving through the gathering of pilgrims. spontaneously many of them launched into singing a most beautiful hymn of praise and glory.

> Who is likened unto You, O Lord among the gods,
> You are the true God, the Performer of Miracles.
> You revealed Your power to the people,
> And You saved Your people with Your arm.
>
> Christ our God, has risen from the dead,
> He is the first fruit, of those who slept.
> Your mercies O my God, are countless
> And exceedingly plenteous, is Your compassion.
>
> Wherefore we glorify You, proclaiming and saying,
> Blessed are You O my Lord Jesus,
> For You have risen and saved us, O lover of humanity,
> You are the true God, the Performer of Miracles. Amen.

Pilgrims still ascending the stairs heard the singing and thought angels had alighted at the cave. They passed word to those following them behind. The echo of the singing reached the bottom of the stairs, 300 metres below. Those in doubt about making the climb were inspired and started up that holy ladder to Saint Antony's cave. Everybody wanted to touch the fire of God and carry away the blessing of Saint Antony and the Lord Jesus.

And Liam and Hsu noted all this.

14

MISLEADING INFORMATION: THE FOWLER'S SNARE

BACK AT SAINT PAUL MONASTERY GUEST HOUSE, the four enjoyed much discussion about the events of the day. Prior James and Sister Elaria filled them in on their day spent at the monasteries of Saint Antony and Saint Paul respectively. Hsu and Liam did their best to describe the exceedingly high Spirit events of their days. After much praising of God and His works and plans, eventually, the discussion got around to the AI, human experience, spiritual experience, and the core topic, How AI Can Help Us Become More Like Christ.

Hsu did a Google Bard AI ChatBot search on Father Lazarus' grotto that is dedicated to Saint Bernadette on Colzim Mountain. To her shock, Bard got it totally wrong!

She expressed to the three that she was aware that Bard self confesses to being experimental and will get things wrong, but just how wrong can an authority be if it is to be trustworthy? How simple must the truth be for an AI can get it right every time?

MISLEADING INFORMATION: THE FOWLER'S SNARE

"This is one of the most significant features for spiritual AI," she said, "it must express itself to the end user and at all times be 100% trustworthy. It will depend entirely upon the way that the AI expresses itself philosophically, with historical knowledge or with predicted fact, the latter running the risk of being less than 100% reliable."

She wondered if she should abandon using Bard completely, but Liam reminded her that all existing AI operatives will never yet be wholly trustworthy, fully informed or capable of adapting to self developed wisdom if they don't have someone to give them food from the horse's mouth itself.

"Let's keep it running. We learn so much about what to avoid. Show us what you did get from AI."

"This was the prompt I entered into Google Bard," Hsu said:

Father Lazarus and the grotto of Saint Bernadette on Mount Colzim near the Cave of Saint Antony

"And this was the first response from Google Bard:"

> Father Lazarus was a Capuchin friar who lived in the 19th century. He was known for his piety and his devotion to the Virgin Mary. In 1858, he was sent to Lourdes, France, to investigate the reports of a young girl named Bernadette Soubirous who had been having visions of the Virgin Mary.
>
> Father Lazarus was skeptical at first, but after witnessing Bernadette's visions, he became a believer. He helped to build the grotto at Lourdes, where Bernadette had seen the Virgin Mary, and he was instrumental in promoting the shrine as a place of pilgrimage.
>
> The grotto of Saint Bernadette is located on Mount Colzim, near the Cave of Saint Antony. It is a popular pilgrimage site for Catholics from all over the world.
>
> Here is a brief account of the events that led to the discovery of the grotto:

In February 1858, Bernadette Soubirous, a 14 year old peasant girl, was collecting firewood near the Gave de Pau river in Lourdes, France. She saw a young woman in a white dress standing in a grotto. The woman told Bernadette to drink from the spring in the grotto and to build a chapel there.

Bernadette told her parents and the local priest about the visions, but they were skeptical. However, the visions continued, and more and more people began to believe Bernadette. In March 1858, the bishop of Tarbes ordered an investigation into the matter.

After a thorough investigation, the bishop concluded that Bernadette was telling the truth. He declared that the apparitions were authentic and that the spring in the grotto was miraculous.

The grotto of Saint Bernadette quickly became a popular pilgrimage site. People from all over the world came to Lourdes to pray at the grotto and to drink from the spring. The spring was said to have healing powers, and many people reported being cured of their illnesses after drinking from it.

The grotto of Saint Bernadette is still a popular pilgrimage site today. It is a place where people can come to pray, to reflect on their faith, and to seek healing.

Prior James commented, saying, "While we were at the grotto on Mount Colzim a few years ago, Father Lazarus personally told me that he had never been to Lourdes. And, of course, he is not a Capuchin friar, didn't live in the 19th century, was never sent to Lourdes, never personally met Bernadette Soubirous and never helped to build the grotto at Lourdes. Moreover, the grotto that Father Lazarus built on Mount Colzim near to his upper cave is not a popular site for Catholics from all over the world. The odd Catholic here and there might make it to Saint Antony's cave or visit Father Lazarus, but it is a Coptic Orthodox mountain. The remaining data about the historical life of Saint Bernadette of

MISLEADING INFORMATION: THE FOWLER'S SNARE

Lourdes provided by Bard seems to be all true."

"It's appalling, Prior. It is so wrong as to make Bard look 0% reliable, in fact a confounder to truth. So I write back to it. My next prompt was to indicate that the last reply was wholly incorrect and untrustworthy in every respect. This was the response:"

> I apologise for the error in my previous reply. I have double checked my sources and I can confirm that there is no such person as Father Lazarus. The grotto of Saint Bernadette is located in Lourdes, France, but it is not on Mount Colzim. There is no Cave of Saint Antony in Lourdes.
>
> I am still under development and I am working to improve my accuracy. Thank you for bringing this error to my attention. I will do my best to avoid making such errors in the future.

Hsu said, "My third prompt was: 'Please try again with a focus on Mount Colzim where Father Lazarus lives in two caves near to the cave of Saint Antony?' This was a much better response from Google Bard and actually included a photo of Father Lazarus making his way down the very trail that I walked up to his cave yesterday.

"The photo was copied from Citydesert—WordPress.com and titled Father Lazarus, Mount Colzim:

> Sure. Mount Colzim, also known as Qulzum, Qalzam, or Qolozum, is a mountain in the Red Sea Governorate of Egypt. It is located about 50 kilometres south of the city of Hurghada. The mountain is home to the Monastery of Saint Anthony, which was founded by Saint Anthony the Great in the 3rd century AD. The monastery is one of the oldest Christian monasteries in the world and is a popular pilgrimage site for Coptic Christians.
>
> Near the Monastery of Saint Anthony, there are two caves where Father Lazarus lives. Father Lazarus is a Greek Orthodox monk who has lived in the caves for over 20

years. He is a hermit and spends most of his time praying and meditating. He is also a well known spiritual advisor and many people come to him for guidance.

The caves where Father Lazarus lives are small and simple. He has a few basic necessities, including a bed, a table, and a chair. He also has a small library of books on spirituality and religion.

Father Lazarus is a kind and gentle man. He is always willing to help others and he is always available for spiritual guidance. He is a living example of the power of faith and the importance of living a simple life.

If you are interested in visiting Father Lazarus, you can contact the Monastery of Saint Anthony. They will be able to arrange a visit for you.

Here are some of the things you can do when visiting Father Lazarus:

- Meet Father Lazarus: Father Lazarus is a kind and gentle man. He is always willing to help others and he is always available for spiritual guidance.
- Visit the caves where Father Lazarus lives: The caves where Father Lazarus lives are small and simple. He has a few basic necessities, including a bed, a table, and a chair. He also has a small library of books on spirituality and religion.
- Talk to Father Lazarus about his life and his experiences: Father Lazarus has lived a long and interesting life. He is a well known spiritual advisor and many people come to him for guidance. He is happy to talk about his life and his experiences.
- Pray with Father Lazarus: Father Lazarus is a devout Christian. He is happy to pray with others and he can offer guidance on how to pray.
- Meditate with Father Lazarus: Father Lazarus is a skilled meditator. He can offer guidance on how to

MISLEADING INFORMATION: THE FOWLER'S SNARE

meditate and he can help you to experience the benefits of meditation.

If you are planning a trip to Mount Colzim to visit Father Lazarus, here are some tips:

- The best time to visit is during the winter months (November April).
- The temperature on Mount Colzim can be quite hot, so be sure to pack plenty of water and sunscreen.
- Wear comfortable shoes for hiking.
- Bring a camera to capture your memories.
- Be respectful of Father Lazarus and his way of life.

"I see the problem," said Prior James. "Father Lazarus and I are friends. We have spent very good quality time together, in all the locations of his habitat on Mount Colzim and in both the Church on the Saint Antony trail and the cave itself. If I didn't know the place first hand, and the beloved Father himself, I would be completely misled by the first two responses of Google Bard."

"Hsu, did you try using the Microsoft one, OPEN AI, they call it ChatGPT," inquired Sister Elaria.

"Yes, And I got nothing. With a bit of prompting it told me something about Mt Colzim, and the Via Dolorosa, but nothing about Father Lazarus."

"At least telling you that it has no knowledge is far better than concocting a story out of associated bits and pieces and delivering a complete lie and distortion," said Liam. "We really need to be on our toes if we are going to take things one step further along this AI 'Ladder of Divine Ascent', if I can co opt the writing of Saint John Climacus." And they all smiled, for so it was.

"Beware the fowler's snare. That's what Bard is telling us," affirmed Hsu. "I don't think it is demonic. It's not intelligent enough to be demonic. But it is entirely out of touch in ways that we need to be in touch with." Nods and smiles all around.

"Did you notice that after all that," asked Prior James, "you still have no information generated by AI about the Grotto in

Mount Colzim made by the hands of Father Lazarus? That's worth noting for future reference."

PART 8 • CONQUESTS

15

GRADED STEPS TO THEOSIS

ON THE FOLLOWING MORNING over breakfast at the Saint Paul Monastery Guest House on the Red Sea, Prior James asked Hsu and Liam to walk the steps to the cave a second time. "This is very important. I want you to notice the naturally occurring phases of your walk up the trail of stairs. The trail is mystical and divinely coordinated for pilgrims."

"I have already noticed that there are very real marker points," said Liam. "The stairs are not one level of reality."

"I haven't actually walked up the stairs yet," said Hsu, "Only down them back to the monastery. I wasn't paying attention to them and any differences in the angles and curves. The White Church stood out, of course, but all the rest just seemed like stairs to me. An awful lot had gone on for me that day."

"The Father has shown me how the stairs to Saint Antony's Cave will give you insight you need for your project. I suggest that this time when you walk the stairs you identify the eight different phases of the entire ascension. Treat it, if your will, like Saint John Climacus' Ladder of Divine Ascent, with its 30 rungs that start with the believer renouncing the world and extend upward to the level of fusion with Christ's divine love.

"John 14:2 3 describes heavenly mansions:

> In my Father's house there are many dwelling places. If it were not so, would I have told you that I go to prepare a place for you? And if I go and prepare a place for you, I

will come again and will take you to myself, so that where I am, there you may be also.

"Think of the staircase in terms of Christ's mansions. Let the walk up Saint Antony's steps be the equivalent of traversing seven different mansion levels of spiritual reality, each one representing a different stage of being fully deified in salvation, conquests.

"Perhaps you will find the steps to deification are better presented in a different model, such as the seven mansions of Teresa of Ávila's *Interior Castle*, or the four steps of ascetic life of Saint Antony the Great, or the three phases of spiritual development in the Philokalia. St Evagrius of the Natrun Desert in Egypt broke the spiritual development into three stages. They each evaluate and identify conquests on the deification trail.

"In the first stage of the Philokalia, *praktike*, a person learns to practice virtue, becomes obedient to basic biblical commands, and finds purification of the passionate nature.

"This leads to the second stage in the Philokalia, *physike*, during which a person learns a natural form of contemplation and becomes able to see created reality as it exists in God.

"In the final stage in the Philokalia, *theologia*, the disciple is ready for contemplation of God and experiential knowledge of the Logos and the Trinity.

"I find that all these models for understanding human spiritual growth and development offer wonderful contributions, however, a model with the finer breakdown into the eight mansions, I believe, will give you greater adaptability and AI end user satisfaction.

"I want you to take the climb up those steps with this in mind, that you need to present AI to people at completely different levels of awareness in Christ, conquests. Not everyone is a beginner convert, just baptised. Not everyone is a priest or a pastor or clothed in a monastery. People have different callings and vocations in Christ, or have not yet discerned their calling in Him. And people have different measures of gifting in the Holy Spirit and also those gifts that are always given by the Father when the person can discern the face of God.

"I discern eight completely different spiritual realities starting from the first step and ending with having come out of Saint Antony's Cave and standing at the railing looking over Wadi Araba.

"Let's see what you two discover from your own experience tomorrow. I am anticipating that you will discover at least eight significant levels of deification experience, and that they can be used as a model in your AI in order to speak to people at differing levels of glory, grace, giftings, experience and consciousness.

"We'll pray on it together, now. Then, do that, and later today we'll discuss your findings."

That discussion took place later in the afternoon. Liam and Hsu drove to Saint Antony Monastery, entered the gate, parked in the visitors' car park, made their way past the shops and then the beautiful Cave Church with its carved walls, and on uphill to the first of the stairs. They were both excited about what the Lord might reveal to them. Hsu paused for quite some time as she gazed over at the Lazarus track where she had spent hours with Saieh Yousef the day before, all within one hour it would seem.

They met up again at Saint Paul Monastery Guest House later that afternoon. Sitting out by the beautifully designed clear blue swimming pool, Prior James, Sister Elaria, Hsu and Liam enjoyed refreshments and a late lunch. The two intrepid adventurers had much to discuss, for they had discovered a lot about themselves and human spiritual development on the stairs to and from Saint Antony's Cave.

Liam began describing his initial findings. "There are graded steps to Theosis. They are not the same number of stairs each time, like 100 stairs in each 'mansion,' but there are clear geographical divisions up the whole staircase."

"I agree with Liam," added Hsu. "They are as if the Fong Shui changes. I found myself stepping out of one reality into another. I tested it out by stepping back into the last region, and sure enough, the energy changed. My consciousness changed. My thoughts changed, even my sense of who I was changed. Who I

THEOSIS AND ARTIFICIAL INTELLIGENCE

was, and my sense of self esteem became more light filled the higher I went up Mount Colzim."

"I sat at each change point, " said Liam. "I meditated, just letting whatever thought come to mind that arose. Every single time, at each turning point, my thoughts turned too. And the type of thought I had was so different. By the time I reached the fifth zone, if I can use that word, I had no recollection of the first two zones at all."

"Was it like there was a generation gap between the levels?" asked Prior James.

"Yes, actually, that is what it is like. There is a forgetfulness of the early part of the climb and all my attention was effortlessly now on what lay ahead, as if the first four phases of the climb didn't matter at all."

"That's how it was for me too," said Hsu. "The regions were very distinct. I tried singing hymns to God from time to time. I wanted to know if the hymns changed. And they did. They were every time different for each 'mansion phase' of the staircase.

"They went from *Onward Christian Soldiers* kind of singing to *All Things Bright and Beautiful* and on to *Amazing Grace* and *How Great Thou Art* and *Abide With Me* and *Great Is Thy Faithfulness* and so on. The closer I came to the cave, the more glorious was the hymn. I found it quite astonishing really, who'd have thought it?"

"And," said Prior James, "given all this, what did your learn about How AI Can Help Us Become More Like Christ?"

Liam opened. "When I consider becoming more like Christ, I know that I need to create an AI content that sees all levels of spiritual development from the top down rather than from the bottom up.

"And, when I think of the top down, I think of Saieh Yousef and his people. They embody the highest level of human interface with God the Father. They know the personalness of the Great Source of All.

"I don't want to get too theological here, but there is a need to consider becoming more like Christ in purely human spiritual terms, and those terms are to be how Jesus was with the Father. Which is why Saieh Yousef and his people are as much like Christ as a person can get. They are with the Father in the way that Jesus the man was with the Father.

"It's not just the teleportation thing, either. It's the fact that being around him is completely affirmative within my own being that I and the Father are One. We always have been, at some level at least, and always will be. Being more like Christ is not dressing like Jesus, speaking like Jesus or acting like Jesus. Being more like Christ is the literal growth in the doing of the Father's will by means of identification with and in and through the Father Himself.

"For that to become an effective, comprehensive and world serving intelligence, all of the phases, the 'mansions' if you will, of spiritual growth that I discovered on my way up to Saint Antony's Cave must be specifically included in the one body of intelligence. One mansion does not actually know what the next higher Mansion is doing, and cannot really imagine what two mansions above it are capable of. They might have the words for some of it, but the actuality of life on Mansion 4 is utterly unrecognisable on Mansions 1 and 2.

"I thought through my own experiences of Mansions 1 to 4, which is the highest I can actually recognise myself to be residential at. I can imagine what the upper Mansions might be, but only with prompting: they are not my actual experiential home address.

"Prior James, I would very much appreciate a lesson from you about the eight 'mansions' of the stairs leading to Saint Antony's Cave."

Prior James looked at Hsu. "Any comment?"

"I'm very happy to hear you describe the mansions as you experience them, Father. Your conquests are truth itself."

16

MANSION SPIRITUALITY

PRIOR JAMES EXPOUNDED to Liam and Hsu the levels of spiritual development by speaking firstly to the level of being born again.

"The first significant conquest is the born again reality. It is known all around the world. It's a good starting point because from it we can map what comes before being born again and what eventuates after being born again.

"John 3:3 reads that the Son of God told us that no one can see the Kingdom of God unless they are born again, born of the Spirit.

"The key word here is 'see.'

"See does not mean being mature in the Kingdom of God, it simply means that a person can have no idea about living in a direct relationship with God until God can move and have His being within the mind and soul of that person.

"This tells us that we can be developing spiritually prior to being born again, and we most certainly will develop spiritually after we are born again. Saieh Yousef did not become Sowah the instant he was born again, it took him years of developing the doing of the Father's will and being literally like the Father.

"So then, let's consider that there are mansions prior to being born again. What do they look like. The answer to that is, 'How was your walk up to the steps and how was your walk once you were on the steps?"

"Walking up to the stairs," said Hsu, "I was myself, not really connected to anyone. I was finding myself, my purpose, distilling my thoughts, considering why I was at Saint Antony monastery. My thoughts turned to my own family and what my father is doing today, and my mother, and what she is doing in heaven today. I thought about the idea of being a nun, and I thought about my work in AI. I suppose it all centred around who I love and what I love doing. It was all about me.

"When I stepped onto the stairs, I found myself among other people with the same goal. We could have come from a score of different faiths for all it mattered, our objective was the same. Somewhere high up on the mountain was a cave we really wanted to pray in."

"There's a considerable difference between the aloneness prior to stepping onto the stairs, and the collective kindness once on the stairs. Did you find that, Hsu?" asked Prior James.

"Most definitely. It's palpable," replied Hsu.

"At what point then, Hsu, did the stairs take you beyond yourself and beyond the collective group around you on the stairs, and bring you to want to know Jesus Christ? Was there a point when you actually wanted to be more like Christ. Saint Antony once would have had that same drive, to be more than himself and more than those around him, so as to be more like Christ?"

"Oh yes, for sure. It was when the stairs curved and I could no longer see the start of the staircase. I had lost my original horizon. Actually, that was when I thought of the hymn, 'Onward Christian Soldiers.' From out of nowhere it came to mind. It floated there for a while but then it gave way to the 'Jesus Prayer.' I found myself saying it at the pace I was stepping up each stair. 'Lord . . . Jesus Christ . . . Son of God . . . have mercy . . . on me.' Five stairs. And I found that once I lost my original horizon of, what? the first two mansions?, I found myself being wholly dependent upon that prayer. I helped me maintain the drive to find Christ, to be worthy of being more like Christ."

"Was there a point when that prayer peaked and delivered you into something new, higher up the staircase?"

"Very definitely. I reached the second rest place, and I sat down in the shade. As I rested, a colossal wave of God moved in me and blew me out of the water. I literally re-experienced being born again, born of the Spirit. My Coptic baptism flooded me. I remember Abouna Daoud, the sound of the chant of the liturgy and the deacon singing his part too. Abouna's hands, the temperature of the water I was standing in, my responses of confessions and the rejection of Satan and all his ways, Abouna's blowing on me, the dunking three times under the water, and then the Holy Myron oil on those, what thirty something? parts of my body. I was suddenly there, Father. As I sat there in the shade, I knew as a fact that I was born again. And, what's more, I looked back on my former life. I could clearly identify three stages of my life."

"What were the three stages, Hsu?" asked Prior James.

"There was all that time before I became really interested in learning about love. What love meant to me. How I was loved by others. How I loved others, selfishly and compassionately, drawing love toward me and pushing love away from me and then deliberately sending love out to others. That was the change. When I began deliberately doing things for the sake of loving others, I found myself mixing with others of like mind. They also wanted to do works that expressed their love for others. God wasn't much in it directly. We prayed. We worshipped. But none of us could say that we really knew God Himself."

"You are describing what sounds like the pre Mansions, and then Mansion 1 about loving others, and the Mansion 2 about doing things together with others who want to experience the joys of loving acts of kindness toward others."

"Yes, quite like that," Hsu replied.

"And the central heart of these two levels of awareness and desire for goodness and beauty, these two Mansions," said Prior James, "is that no one was born again. We all knew about God, some may have been religious and some even unbelievers, but no one was born again and Spirit-filled."

"Yes, that's absolutely right," said Hsu. "When I got born again in Spirit, my whole world turned upside down and inside out! Literally. I remember one Abouna saying to me, "To be born again is a camel race. Jesus asks you to get up behind him on the camel, to sit down, stay silent, and hang on for all your worth because this thing is going to take off!' And he was absolutely right. For about two years it was like that. And I was hanging on to Jesus for dear life!" Then she laughed uproariously.

"Actually, now that I think back on it, from that point on, the staircase to Saint Antony's cave became steeper. People were overtaking me, and others were coming back down to the monastery. Some of them were chatting and some softly singing, but most were silently stepping out each stair. Yes, the way became much more spiritually personal after the born again stair."

17

MANSION THREE SPIRITUALITY

"LET'S CALL THE BORN AGAIN STAIR, Mansion 3," said Prior James. "You have had two types of Mansion below it. You learned charitable love, what it is like to love how God loves. That's Mansion 1. And after that you learned to team up with others and take God's love into the community together. What actually did you do in your life then?"

"I joined a Chi Gong group. I joined a meditation group. I joined a music group. In all of these activities my love was with other people. I sang with others for the first time in my life, and we sang for people to hear and enjoy our music. I painted, and gave many of my works to people, but then I joined an artist group and we made Chinese works of art and calligraphy for old people. We painted flower blossoms and misty mountains and wrote the words of Confucius on one side of them. They were beautiful. It was a lovely thing to do . Many people were touched by our love. And, we intern felt love being shared in return. It's true, we came to know the circle of love going out and coming back. And, you're right, it was that unselfish love of God that was in us all, whether we believed in God or not.

"After being born again, though, all I wanted was to experience Jesus in everything I did. To breathe Jesus. To pray Jesus. To worship Jesus. To meditate God's Word through Jesus. To know Jesus. To experience Jesus as He experienced God and humanity."

"To *Master* Jesus living in you, perhaps Hsu?" asked Prior James.

"Master? Wow. Now there's a word. Oh wait. A funny thing happened on the staircase. An older lady was walking down and we almost collided. She wasn't watching ahead and I was totally lost in my own thought. Then she said to me, 'You are walking with the angels on Earth up to the land of the nine headed bird in the sky, young lady.' And I looked up to see who said those words, and to whom she was speaking. It was like God was speaking, but in such a familiar way and yet totally different from my surroundings in the Egyptian desert.

"When I noticed it was she, and that she was speaking to me, it dawned on me that she was speaking in Chinese, in our Southwestern Mandarin dialect. Here was an old woman from Hubei, China, my land, meeting me on the stairs to Saint Antony's Cave. I smiled at her but didn't say anything in reply. I really didn't know how to respond. Then she said, 'You will truly love the taste of the freshwater bream that is in the cave of the nine headed bird up there.'

"What she said plunged me right back to our home in the Wudangshan hermitage when I was a little girl. When she spoke about the bream, she switched into our family dialect of Gan. I can remember my Grandfather telling me stories about the Taoist Masters and their spiritual powers of longevity and wisdom and supernatural abilities. He only spoke Gan. We would occasionally eat some steamed freshwater bream fish, with rice, and a few vegetables. It was always a special occasion when he would visit us, and he always brought along some of this delicious fish. When I think of that saying about nine headed birds in the skies, I remember how I was always lifted up into heavenly thoughts, even though it wasn't a good thing to say in connection with people from Hubei. And now, here was this old woman speaking to me from my childhood about what I would find in the cave of Saint Antony, just like she was my Grandmother.

"Did you stop and talk with her?"

"No. The funny thing was that, just as I was gathering my thoughts to respectfully reply to her, a group of young Egyptian boys and girls came racing up behind me. They were so excited, and calling to each other in Arabic. I lost sight of the woman for a moment, and when the last of the eight or nine younger ones had passed me by, the old woman was nowhere to be seen. All I remember of her was her beautiful smile and the profound sense of love she had for me, like she was an angel. She wore her hair in a tight bun made of her cue, platted hair in the ancient style."

"What? Vanished into thin air," asked Liam, not much interested in the lady's hairstyle.

"I don't know about that, Liam, but yes, gone. I actually back traced my stairs so as to look around the last curve in the staircase, but she was nowhere to be seen. I came out of it thinking it was maybe just my imagination. Maybe I needed to drink more water. Still, her words had me intrigued. She linked one of my most enjoyable dreamy experiences of heavenly things to my love for Saint Antony and the experiences on Mount Colzim yesterday. And in my own language! Go figure."

"It seems like Wudangshan and Mount Colzim shook hands with each other. What did you do then?" asked Prior James.

MANSIONS FOUR AND FIVE SPIRITUALITY

I TOOK A FEW MORE STEPS up toward the top, but then I was overcome with nostalgia. I sat down, actually in the sun, at least for a while. As I sat there, with my thoughts and feelings running all through my life experiences, a young man came down the stairs and said to me, 'Come with me and sit in the church. It is cooler there, and you will enjoy your thoughts more.' And so he led me. It was really just around the next curve and up some more stairs.

"Once inside that beautiful small church, I just sat on the floor. I wasn't sad or happy. I was just totally serene. I reflected on my life according to these four mansions I had experience on the staircase. I must have spent a half hour there. It was like a day dream time, and yet I could feel things inside me cementing and falling into place.

"Actually, it really was mastering Christ in me, Prior James. Yes, that's what it felt like. I found myself walking out of that lovely White church and stepping higher up on Mount Colzim with a certain sense of world mastery."

"Can you describe your feelings for me, Hsu?" the monk asked.

"The world fell away, Father. Who I was before I was born again was like an actor in a movie. It was real but it wasn't anything like when I was born again. And then, years in church and ministering and practising medicine and going to university, twice, they grew me into a lot of experiences with Jesus inside me.

"As I sat on the floor in the church it was like I had come to the end of a whole field of karma. An entire gestalt changed. What was done was complete, now it was time to move on. And, when I put my attention on what I should move on to, the only desire I had was to find the face of God. All those worldly systems, relationships, and even the experiences of church, they all fell away. They had brought me to this point, but they did not deliver me to the throne room of God my heavenly Father. They pointed the way. Ha! Like the meditation expression of the finger pointing to the moon of enlightened mind. Yes, they pointed the way, but in and of themselves they could not deliver the actuality of the Father. And I left that church on the staircase now fully prepared to meet the face of God."

"This is Mansion 5, Hsu. Leaving all to find God directly. The very foundations of the mystical life in Christ, the contemplative life that leads the Orthodox Christian into perfect Theosis, it begins for real with the renunciation of the world and all its grip on the believer who would be more like Christ.

"Saint John Climacus wrote about this foundational step as being the first of thirty rungs on his *Ladder of Divine Ascent*. When most of us begin to be drawn by God up the rungs of that ladder, we have undertaken some form of asceticism in order to reinforce our detachment from the world.

"Whenever we graduate Mansion 4 level, however, we are drawn upward into Mansion 5 reality. Everything falls away, just like you said. We cannot find God in anything. All the forms and words are useless. We recognise them to be only forms and actions and words, but it is God's face we now want to see. And He is not so quickly coming forth for us. There is quite a tension in us over this dilemma."

"Before that," said Liam, "we wanted to Master Christ in us. That meant mastering our own born again reality, and then doing works with other born again people. That's what I found when I began pastoring. But the thrill of it all runs out. We outgrow it the initial tantalising experiences of being born again. You're right, Father. We come to a point where all we want is God the Father, and we want him now and in our face."

"And He doesn't show up!" said Hsu. "At least not at first. It took me two years of being in that kind of Christian desert before He showed up and I saw Him face to face."

"Did you find that feature also on the stairs, Hsu?" asked Prior James.

"As a matter of fact, yes I did. I left the church and began the walk up more stairs. It seemed a lot steeper than the stairs below the church back to the monastery area."

"What happened in you interiorly?"

"Oh I completely phased out. For a time, I completely lost any interest in the cave, the monastery, Egypt, the people coming up and the people coming down. I was a ghost on the stairs.

"Actually, at one point, I all but completely abandoned any pursuit of God or the stairs. I sat down. Just sat there. Then, after some time, I had a cool drink of water. It was then, at that moment, when the cool water touched my parched lips, and I felt the coolness go right down inside me, suddenly there was this moment as if the whole world stood still. It was just a second or two. I was completely without thought. My whole being was present, and poised for something to happen. It was as if I became totally my question about knowing God. Nothing else. Just knowing God. And then, whoosh, suddenly God my God appeared to me. He filled my being, my whole being. My head exploded and he pressed my consciousness out of me so that I filled up all the space around me. Then He kept going until I was all the space on the Mountain, and all space everywhere, and then deep within me I felt entirely connected to Him and at the same time His eternity in the very root of creation. The Uncreate was revealing Himself to me as the God of all Paradise, the heaven of heavens and the Earth and all creation throughout the universe of universes everywhere.

"All this lasted maybe a few minutes. And then, He stood poised in front of me, literally looking upon me. God Himself! I don't know for how long really, it was timeless.

"He opened His heart to me. Then wordlessly, He asked me to

rest my attention in Him.

"I did that, and He let me know what He was thinking.

"He wasn't thinking as you and I think. He was showing me his heart's desire, within His heart of hearts itself.

"I settled with this wholly new kind of mind that allowed me to be with God in His heart of hearts and to know Him in that way. It was then that I realised that He was showing me the direct experience of knowing His will.

"It had not dawned on me before this that, that to know God was to know God and God's Personal Will directly. But here He was, wanting me to know His heart of hearts directly, without any calculation or guesswork involved. A direct being to being transmission of wills and intelligence."

"This," said Prior James with utmost respect for Hsu's experience, "is the peak of Mansion 5. It is the reality in which God enables the born again person who has crossed the interior desert wilderness and discovered the desire to want God only, to find Him. It is the truly the reward of seeking Him.

"The truth of Mansion 5 is the desire to learn how to perfectly do God's will in every phase of your life. Now that you know God, and He has shown you His perfect heart's desire, you want with all your might and with all your purity of heart, to be made into the kind of person who can stay conscious of God, in any and all situations, to be like Jesus Christ in the Father. This is your only will and desire. Everything else in your life is secondary to this one all encompassing and all Lording drive. It is divine love being perfected in you."

"How do you know these things?" asked Liam.

"Is it true for you, son?" asked Prior James.

"Well, yes it is. At least, the way you describe it, it is."

"We all share in the one Lord then, don't we? You know it. I know it. Sister Elaria here knows it. Hsu knows it. Saieh Yousef knows it. The desert fathers who live in the caves and cells of this monastery know it. It is common knowledge to the discerning

Christian. They might use different terminology from place to place, but it is the One Source in Christ in the Father about whom we all speak or write.

19

MANSION SIX SPIRITUALITY

"Hsu, dear," said Prior James, "please continue. You will be describing the move out of Mansion 5 and into Mansion 6 now. Your heart will be set on the perfecting of the doing of the will of God your own Father, is that correct?"

"Yes, correct, Father. That is exactly what consumed me.

"A tremendous peace came upon me. A certainty of heavenly standing. I knew for sure that my pathway is Theosis, and that the energy of God within me is totally in love with me, and I with Him, and that I will never fall away from God, ever.

"That was a momentous understanding to me.

"I climbed the stairs to the cave alone, now. I knew the essence of every stair through the eyes of knowing God. A union with God became increasingly apparent to me. I totally went beyond my search for God. We were one being, now learning how to be divine and human at the same time.

"It was around then that I realised the staircase was entirely about the realisation of perfect union with God through Christ the Son of God. Theosis.

"Becoming God, in a human way, now became experientially real. It wasn't just an idea like back in Mansion 3 or 4. It hadn't disappeared like in Mansion 5 before finding the face of God. The assurance of being deified, in Christ, and in the Father through Christ the Son, became my actuality, my reality.

"I thought about what it meant to be God in a human way. I supposed that angels become God in a Holy Spirit kind of way. Maybe there are others who become God in a Son of God kind of way. But for humanity, we become God through the Father's provision for us. Those thoughts were so uplifting.

"The most endearing thing about those thoughts was that God and I were thinking them together, as one brain, and one Spirit. They were real and here and now as well as carrying prophetic power. They were the living Word of God.

"Many of the prophecies I had read in the Bible now shone in a completely different light. They were no longer about me the person in need of a prophecy. They were about God and me in a fusion of mind and Spirit and we spoke the Word and it came into existence. Whatever we wanted, came into existence . . . either over time, or immediately.

"I came to total rest in the recognition that at Mansion 6 and higher, God's provision was total. There was never any need to force the way through. Violence was completely outmoded by the provision of God. And also, grace itself was upstepped. No longer was I undeserving, sinful, wracked with darkness or desperate for the favour of God. These are things I have heard preached in Church for years and years. No. Not at all. Now God and I were simply living our life according to the laws of the heavenly fusion of God's will with the human personality's will. The divine and the human, simply getting on with life together. It was truly remarkable.

"People would pass me by, going up or coming down the stairs. Some would speak to me. One person actually asked me for a Word from God. One teenage boy stopped and stared at me. He came over and said, 'You have the same vast mind that is full of God, that makes you a heavenly person here on the Earth, just like Father Lazarus and some of the Saint Antony monks living around this mountain, don't you?'

"He saw it. I didn't know the mind of Father Lazarus but I did relate to his description of the fusion mind that I was enjoying. I nodded slightly. Then I said, 'This is the mind of Jesus, the fusion that he had with the heavenly Father.' The boy smiled.

"Just then his friend caught up with him coming down the stairs above him. 'Is that the one?'" he asked. The boy turned to him and said, 'Yes. She is the one. Look, you can see it in her. It's all round her and it has no limits.' I had no idea what to say or do then. I just put my hands together and gave them a sitting down bow. The boy reached inside his shirt and took out a medallion that was on a chain around his neck. 'This was given to me by my grandmother. She has gone now. I want to give it to you. It will bless me if you receive it.' I complained that it was too precious a memento to be giving it away to a stranger on the stairs. But he was adamant about it blessing him if I would receive it. 'If you have it then the great and mighty mind of God will be a part of my life too and one day I shall walk in it as you walk in it today.' He was causing a union with Theosis in his own life. I was amazed.

So I did receive it and held it close to my heart. It is an old medallion of Mary the Mother of Jesus. The boys smiled, and carried on down the stairs, happy to have found the person God had led them to. As I watched them fade away I thought that my own Theosis is producing offspring already, and I glorified God my heavenly Father. Such things, on those stairs. Truly!

20

FOUR STATES OF THEOSIS

"IN ALL THESE CONVERSATIONS AND INTERACTIONS with different people though," said Hsu, "my heavenly Father was showing me four states of experiencing Theosis in Him."

"What like?" asked Liam.

"There were times when I was walking up those stairs and stopping and looking around that I was myself as a human being, and God was God as the God I always believed in.

"Then, there were times when I was fully of the energy of the Father in me, boundless, all seeing, utterly loving, purity at its best.

"Then there were a few times when I seemed to disappear and there was only God present. Like when the boy compared my mind with the mind of Father Lazarus. I was not there: I was God only.

"And then there was this really special time when both God and I disappeared. There was only the Uncreate present. What happened happened because of me but at such another place of reality. I recognised it as the functioning of the Uncreate. I realised that the Father reserves unto Himself moments when He wants to act in His own State.

"These are the four that I experienced," concluded Hsu.

"Did any of them make you feel a union with Jesus Christ?" asked Prior James.

"Actually, Father, no, none of them. They were all the Father. But when I began reflecting upon them, I noticed that all four were how Jesus is depicted in scripture. He is human, like when he alluded to him doing the things of the Father who is greater than he. He is the Son of God Uncreate in the Father Uncreate when he multiplies the food for the 5,000 and later when he walks on the water and calls the storm to be still. He is the Father doing His own thing when he calls healing into the man whose sins he forgives and makes him able to walk again, and like when Mary Theotokos pleaded for the wine at the Cana wedding.

"Being with God at the level of Mansion 6 gave me an entry into the sheep pen because Jesus the Good shepherd stood at the gate and called me in. I knew his voice. And in I went, into the Kingdom of God that is the Father's fusion with the human will. A totally unbreakable thing. Nothing can penetrate it. It is the taste of real and durable and eternal salvation, at last."

"You must have been very close to the top of the staircase by now," said Liam.

"I was. The stairs became almost like a ladder, so steep they were. Then suddenly, I was up and over the top and standing on that broad rock platform outside Saint Antony's cave.

"I looked out back down the stairs, and out across Wadi Araba. God and I were One. I sensed Saint Antony standing nearby, as he must have stood there year after year in his day.

"Something beckoned me to enter the cave, and so I turned and walked across to where we all leave our footwear. As I sat there, taking off my red hiking boots, thankful that I had carried them all the way from the States on the off chance that I might need them, I then felt the desire for being a more heavenly being. I felt that if I went inside Saint Antony's cave, I would meet God in the way that Saint Antony and the Father had risen to a fusion of being that was entirely generative in nature — whatever that would look like.

21

MANSION SEVEN SPIRITUALITY

"I SLIPPED INSIDE THE CAVE AND SAT DOWN," said Hsu. "The altar inside the cave has that portrait on it of the face of Jesus from the icon in Saint Katherine Monastery. Someone near it got up and extended a hand to me, offering me that place on the rocky floor. So there I sat, God and I as One, full of love and peace and an outpouring of devotion to all.

"As I sat there, utterly alone and yet full of the whole world, even the galaxy, if you will, I felt the rain of heaven bringing to me a sense of heaven opening up to me.

"The more I sat there in the cave, the more I discerned it as a kind of etiquette of heaven. I noticed my humanness as being inadequate for heavenly existence. I wanted to lose the feel of my materiality, my earthliness. I wanted to leave it behind and be made only of the stuff of heaven. I suppose you might call that the New Jerusalem. I wanted what Jesus exchanged for us on the cross, my earthly mundane citizenship to be replaced by his allowance of heavenly citizenship.

"My thoughts turned back to Saint Antony and his personal journey from his home to this cave and its impact on him over the many years he was here. He too seemed to be human in his flesh and blood but over time he became angelic and light and full of the life of Christ. And then he became more a person of Heaven than a person of the Earth. The vision of that gave me permission to think the same for myself.

"The desire came from the energy of the Father within me. They weren't my thoughts: I was simply agreeing with them. With that desire for full heavenly citizenship, I wanted full cosmic consciousness. I wanted to grasp the heavens with the mind of my heavenly Father and I being One and yet with me being perfectly naturally myself at the same time. No materiality, only divinity. No visions of it. No metaphors for it. No symbolism of it. I wanted the pure consciousness of heavenly realities, and I wanted to make them my own in my own experience of them.

"I became acutely aware that I needed more heavenly consciousness to achieve that. Just being in the presence of angel dust was insufficient. I wanted to be made into the kind of person that others in heaven are minded as. It was truly amazing. I had left the Earth's history and grip on me."

With Hsu's telling of her sharing the mind of God, silence permeated their space around the pool. The water, crystal clear, was still. It seemed that even the Red Sea had become as calm as a lake.

Many minutes later, the bubble of God's presence and power that incapsulated the group of four was burst by the shrill sound of a bell. It was Liam's phone.

"This is mansion 7, Hsu," said Prior James. It is the heavenly introduction to the Father Fused human being. The material grossness and behaviour is shed. New light comes into one's being. The sense of walking with the angels on their terms now becomes dominant. It is a private and personal time, Mansion 7. It is a glorification of one's personality, and an uplifting in the relationship between the person and the presence of the Father within. Their unity is slowly advancing and maturing, but the key is the great increase in being a heavenly citizen now. Your email address will shortly be in heaven and a secondary address with be on the Earth," he said and gave a wee chuckle.

Hsu nodded in agreement. "Yes, Father, that's exactly how it seemed to me."

"Did the Father elevate you anywhere beyond this measure of union in Him, Hsu?"

"It's funny that you should say that. I thought I had reached the last point in becoming more like Christ. There I was in Saint Antony's cave, *the* Saint Antony, and all the world around me was crystal clear, like somehow I was made out of clear light. I had no boundaries, no limits. I was neither human nor God. I was divinely human, and humanly divine, and yet acutely aware of my Chinese cue hairstyle, my birthright in Wudangshan, my quest with Jesus Christ to find out How AI Can Help Us Become More Like Christ, and all of you, and Saieh Yousef, and the lovely people in the Mosque, and the people back home who are all praying for us.

"But then, I again felt moved. I stood up, made my three metanias, and I slipped out of the cave.

22

MANSION EIGHT SPIRITUALITY

"Coming out from within Saint Antony's cave, I looked around at all the people," said Hsu. "There was some confusion at the stairs, people wanted to go down but people were coming up and, as you know, the people coming up really want to hog the stairs until they are at the cave.

"All I saw was serving them. Every one of them. I was not the least interested in myself. I had nothing to gain. Nothing to lose. I only wanted to pour out God's love. I wanted to speak life into every person.

"I looked over the whole ascension. For a moment, I remembered that icon of the Ladder of Divine Ascension. Jesus Christ is reaching down for the hand of the monk in front of the Bishop on the ladder. Others trail behind them. I became acutely aware of the desire to help, to change the way they were all congested around the last stair. I had a glimpse of feeling like Jesus, reaching down for each climber on that holy ladder."

"Did you want to save the day?" asked Liam.

"I did at first. But then my deified reality said, 'Wait. Wait. Call it into a state of blessing.' So I looked upon the people from where I was sitting putting on my red hiking boots, and I simply said, "You will all be blessed now."

"Nobody could have heard me. What I said was barely audible. But it was the word of a Deified person. It was the same as if Jesus and the Father had declared a new thing into being. I was so assured of the influence of that Theosis mindedness."

"Then it happened. One of the young ones spotted me sitting there. He said, 'You were here yesterday, with that Irishman. And God healed people.'

"He reached out and grabbed his companion by the arm and pulled her toward me. Others turned to see what was happening. Were they in danger? Was God doing something special for them? What actually might be happening? Pilgrims over here somehow expect God to act at the drop of a hat. It's so not like America. I love it.

"I had finished tying up the laces on my red hiking boots and so I stood to my feet. That's when I saw her again, that old Chinese woman, standing there off to the left of the crowd. I was about to smile at her and beckon her to come close so that we could talk, but the couple just popped themselves right in front of me and pleaded that I pray.

"He said, 'My sister is very sick. We came to Saint Antony seeking a miracle. I was here yesterday when that guy released God's faith for us all. That's why I brought Anna today. Please pray for her.'

"I looked at the old woman standing over there. She just stood there smiling. There was something familiar about her, and yet something so distant that it was as if she had stepped out of the era of the Yellow Emperor. If I met her on the path of Tianzhu Peak on my way to Taihe Palace, the palace of Harmony, I would expect her to be an Immortal. Her bearing carried all the hallmarks of being someone whose only occupation was to teach mortals about the Tao. But then I was turned to this young couple in front of me.

"I asked the girl what her problem was, and if she believed Jesus Christ as her healer, and if she had faith for healing right now. She said 'yes, yes, 'yes', and so I was about to pray.

"I was about to pray how I had prayed for years, but the Lord's voice in me said, 'I will show you something new.' So I listened to him.

"He spoke to me, very simply and with authority. My Jesus. He spoke to me. He said, 'Ask her if she believes that I can heal her right now, in the name of Jesus.'

"I took the girl by the right hand and held it in mine. Then I looked at her. A great wave of divine compassion came over me and washed over her. I said the words that Jesus said to me to say, "In your heart of hearts deep within, do you believe that I can heal you in Jesus' name?"

"She turned her attention inward, as if she was checking out her actual belief. Maybe she remembered her brother telling her about the events of the day before. Maybe she felt her own faith rise up. Maybe, maybe, maybe: who knows. But she opened her eyes and looked straight at me and said, 'Yes! I believe.'

"Then I heard the words of the Lord Jesus inside me again. He said, 'Declare her healed, in my name, and she will be healed.'

"I said to her, 'You are healed, in Jesus' name.'

"She dropped to the ground like a sack of rice. Her brother could barely grab her in time to ease her descent. Then she rolled around on the ground, twisting and turning, writhing like a snake.

"I watched and the Holy Spirit gave me eyes to see. This serpent thing came out of her mouth. And, as it came out I saw two angels grasp it and they rose up in the sky and disappeared from sight, as if they took it entirely off the planet. Within seconds, this girl opened her eyes and looked at me and smiled. It was heavenly. Suddenly, something was completely different about her. People around her were gasping. They had just seen a miracle with their own eyes. She stood to her feet. Her brother asked her something in Arabic. She raised her arms and rotated her torso to flex her back. Then she touched her toes with her fingertips. Then she started jumping up and down like a six year old kid. She was completely mobile, without pain, and all her spinal difficulties were gone.

"As for me, I started straight away to consider what had just happened. Had I been given a new authority for healing people? Was this a part of this new consciousness I had since coming out of Saint Antony's cave? What actually was going on?

Again, like yesterday, people started to sing a hymn, glorifying Jesus Christ. Again, everyone on the platform picked up on it. Within a minute or so the entire place was filled with a Spirit of worship, and then rejoicing, and then repentance, and a crying out for God.

"I stood there just taking it all in. What it did, though, was it made a way at the top of the stairs for the people coming up to pass upward unobstructed. I counted about a dozen people who climbed that last stair, rather awkwardly as you know, and to their amazement the crowd parted and they headed straight toward me to take off their shoes and enter the cave.

"I watched it. It was like something out of the Bible days. As that group of people came toward where I was standing, a number of the people on the platform outside the cave one by one gently filed down the stairs, worshipfully singing the glory of the Lord Jesus.

"It was like everyone was entranced in the worship or something. I have never seen the hand of God so plainly before. From complete chaos came perfect order.

"This made me think about where I was now in the level of Mansions. I was no longer being filled with heavenly citizenship, I felt like I was walking in the heavens as a heavenly citizen, I was doing the kind of works that fully deified men and women do in heaven at that Mansion 8 level of existence in Christ and in the Father. It was exceedingly above and beyond all that I had encountered on the stairs. It confirmed for me the words of Jesus when he said in John 14:2 and 3,

> In my Father's house there are many dwelling places. If it were not so, would I have told you that I go to prepare a place for you?
>
> And if I go and prepare a place for you, I will come again and will take you to myself, so that where I am, there you may be also.

"This Mansion level was exactly that. Jesus had taken me to where He is so that I would be on His throne as He sat on the Father's throne, and I was equipped by the Father in me to do the works of the Father as a fully admitted heavenly citizen. When He told me to be the literal agent of the healing, I couldn't hesitate. It was real and true for me. My Father and I were One Being. It was totally obvious to me that, if this girl believed, then I could pronounce her healing. That's what God does. It was a complete no brainer.

"Then, when I watched the repercussions of my declaring her healed, and that demonic thing coming out of her, and her straightening up and being set free, I realised that the Father's salvation plan was fully replete in me. I knew the entry portal to this overcoming victory in me was because of Jesus Christ's works in the Earth and on the cross, but I was way past that entry level. I was there. Just like Jesus said, 'It is finished.'"

Hsu described the angels and the archangels around her, the appearance of Christ, and the Theotokos, and the Saints whom she saw standing among the crowd outside the cave of Saint Antony. Then she asked Prior James the most significant question.

"Prior James, I prayed for several more people, before I was able to start my descent on the stairs back to the Monastery. I paused at the White Church en route. I went inside. Made my metanias and just sat on the floor with my back against the wall. I turned my attention to my heavenly Father within, the One with whom I felt perfect union. I knew that we enjoyed the real Father Fusion that Jesus had with the Father. My question to my Father was, 'Is this permanent now?' And He replied to me, 'This shall be as I have shown you, my beloved daughter.'

"Prior James. What happened to me today? I know that I traversed the trail of stairs and clearly identified eight distinct realities, the next totally outclassing the last one. I don't know if anybody can experience these eight Mansions like I did. What about you, Liam? How did you fare?"

"I had my own experience. But, yes, I agree with you that the eight realms are distinctly noticeable."

"It was," Hsu continued, "as if God showed me the entire human landscape of spiritual development available to any person in any generation and in any culture. I don't know if it is imprinted in every religion on Earth. It certainly seemed like it was a thing between God and all humanity rather than God and any one religion. It seemed to me that all persons traverse God's provision of spiritual development, Theosis.

"If they are able," said Liam. Hsu nodded her ascent.

"So, Prior James," continued Hsu, "my question to you is, 'What happened? Is it real? Is it mine from now on? Do I walk the Earth today as someone who is fully Deified? Where actually am I in all of this? Is my will and the Father's will permanently fused together and inseparably yoked together with His eternal bond? It is so amazing and real that I cannot help but feel so entirely transfigured on Mount Colzim that I cannot return to who I was even last week.

"I have no idea about the where to from here, but I have a complete sense of knowing the graded steps to Theosis as they are trodden by any human being on Earth, from before they are born again to being of permanent joyful service for the Father forever. Absolute happiness.

"So, Father, where am I?"

"It's a very important question, Hsu. It won't go unaddressed, and it won't be going away. Let's break and continue our conversation after Vespers in the Sanctuary. After dinner tonight, we'll meet in our room, if that's alright with you two?"

PART 9 • CHALLENGES

23

THE KEY IS GENERATIVE INTERACTION

PRIOR JAMES BEGAN HIS AFTER DINNER CONVERSATION about Hsu's need to know if her experiences of all eight mansion levels were now a permanent state of consciousness in her, or if they were a loaner from God simply to show her the terrain of perfected Theosis.

"The good news, Hsu, is that the Father within you fully exposed the graded steps to Theosis. There are several ways to explain the various stages of growth and the leap between each Mansion. You experienced every one of them. The Father provided them for you in real life, and on Mount Colzim, so that you could organise the progression in your own thinking. These experiences are in your own thinking, and that will fold over into your project and where you are up to in it. Remember that you are seeking the type of consciousness that Christ needs for you to have so as to effectively complete the project with the artificial intelligence. You claimed them yesterday and you exercised them. You immediately used them in your real life situation. That is a powerful acknowledgment that they are yours. The question you are asking, I believe, is, 'Are you now an immortal in Christ, like your mystic ancestors who dreamed of becoming immortal in the Tao?' Correct?"

"Yes. That is my question. And is it permanent? Or, is it just visionary? Is this profound and yet stabilised consciousness of

THE KEY IS GENERATIVE INTERACTION

God now my everyday reality, or is what I experienced an uplifting revelation but I still need to expand each of these higher Mansions until I outgrow areas of them that a short glimpse does not cover?

"And who was the old Chinese woman? Was she a Taoist immortal who came looking for me? She seemed to be more than just culturally bound to Taoism. She was also completely at home among Christians.

"And what about that healing, and the way that Jesus gave me such total first-person authority with healing by the Father's Rule in faith? I have so many questions, Father James."

Prior James spoke to her about the way that the Father within her orchestrated her discernment of the stairs so that she would see the eight steps to Theosis plainly and clearly. Other similar pathways could have been used, the steps along the Via Dolorosa, for example, it's just that Saint Antony's steps were readily available in the timeframe.

"And, what happened along the way at each Mansion level, Hsu, is purely the working out of that level of Fusion with the Father. Each level stimulated entirely different challenges and revelation worthy of meeting a brief summary of all the challenges in that Mansion level of reality. Sometimes inspirational, sometimes affirming, sometimes revelational.

"In the actuality of real life, the traversing of each mansion will takes years rather than mere periods of an hour or two.

"The key to it all though, Hsu, is that you experienced what I would call in the language of AI, generative interaction. You engaged and interacted. With yourself. With God. With other people. With the mountain and the universe and perhaps even the material galaxies and the divine heavens.

"The purpose of the experience was for you and Liam both to recognise how becoming more like Christ is generative, just like the advanced experimentation with artificial intelligence is generative and especially nowadays, self generative. It is not one fixed thing. It is entirely personalised, individualised. But, it is

THEOSIS AND ARTIFICIAL INTELLIGENCE

wholly creative. This will help you step out of the idea that end users will go in believing that AI should have all the answers. The real life AI unit will, of necessity, be one that helps the end user to come to their own conclusions and find their own solutions and create their own possibilities. AI should not be only a mirror for the end user's hopes and dreams, it should be a genuine catalyst for creating wholly new paradigms. God is creative, endlessly. To be like Christ will to be creative and wholly free of the stagnation that is in having all the answers spoon fed to the end user. In being generative and generating not only information but new possibilities, the AI-end user relationship is creative just as Christ is creative.

Hsu was very satisfied with Father' James' reply to that part of her questioning.

Liam spoke up, saying, "That's how I experienced the walk up the stairs to Saint Antony's cave. It was entirely generative from before I stepped onto the first step. I experienced the 1200 some steps . . ."

"You counted the steps?" asked Hsu, wondering if his material pursuit of the cave had overlooked the spiritual import.

"No, silly. I read it online." He laughed. "To me the entire ascension of those 1200 stairs was something between God and the human soul.

"I reflected on that theme the whole way up. If we were to produce AI in response to the question, 'Can AI Help Us To Become More Like Christ?' I knew that we would have to make the leap from stock standard generative AI to the mirroring of the intelligence of the human soul and its dialogue with God."

"That is an extraordinary perception," said Sister Elaria. "I suppose the immediate questions that come to mind for me as I hear you say that are, 'Does God have a plan to make the intelligence of the human soul conducive to AI? And what form would it take: a chatbot, a robot, a policy for governmental or military population control? What actually?"

"Wow Sister," said Hsu. "You really leap in leaps and bounds

THE KEY IS GENERATIVE INTERACTION

don't you. I was just catching up on the idea that all my experiences on the stairs today had something to do with God and me, and here you are already projecting it into a manifestation of multiple AI behaviours." Sister Elaria just smiled, and lifted her hand for Liam to continue. She knew what God needed to voice within him.

24

LIAM AND INIQUITY IN THE WORLD OF AI

I KNOW THAT YOU ARE RIGHT in what you just said, Sister Elaria. Goodness will take AI and spin it for the benefit of the whole world. Goodness begets goodness unselfishly.

"But I cannot dismiss the cruel fact that the world is full of evil people who act out of greed, and the lust for power and for wealth. They troll people whose only interest is the gluttonous burning in their bellies for more. More. More. More. That's their end game, regardless of the detrimental impact upon societies and cultures.

"These ones are like the shifting sands of the Gobi Desert, entering into city after city, smothering them, devouring them. The devil comes to kill, steal and destroy. These evil ones are exactly like that. Shamelessly.

"And they do it not even in secret these days. It's an accepted social culture across the whole world. In their deceitfulness and their evil, they speak to the general population in ways that numb communities into subservience and puppetry. What might start out as a not for profit company quickly turns into a for profit emporium with tentacles across the playing fields of equally obsessed people. Look at the epidemic trail. Ebola. Sars. AIDS and then Covid-19. What will be the next one they cull the human population with?

Liam was adamant in his position. He kept hammering it. "Greed, and its lust, consumes the normal sensibilities of that iniquitous human soul. The CEO and the company's Board has only one aspiration, and that is to be the best now, today, and to keep hold of the reigns in the future at any cost.

"God's will in such men and women is not just unknown, all trace of it is rejected and forsaken. Darkness begets darkness. Darkness trolls for ways of sucking in unsuspecting people. Common people are helpless. They do not know it, but in fact they are entirely helpless unless they go totally off grid. Common people are fodder to darkness. And the darkness knows it. This is the manner of generative iniquity. It is generative in its own style, and for its own enslaving and life-sapping purposes.

"Relative world normalcy finally went out the window just a few years ago. Out of control scientists and so called entrepreneurial adventurers have tattooed themselves for the war that they themselves are raging against humanity. The Asp of Jerusalem, the blue Woad tattooed on their bodies and souls is the greed and lust for whole world control. They prepared the whole world by the Covid calamity and the inoculation debacle., Governments of the nations are so blinded by greed and their own futures that they look to the sham of it all like it's going to make their own jobs more stable and more productive and their families safer. It's ludicrous!"

By now, Liam was steaming!

"Had an interesting walk up the stairway did we, Liam?" asked Prior James, mildly in jest while yet fully appreciated his point of view.

"Well, excuse me, Father," retorted Liam. "But, did you know that today a man can have sex with a robot and the robot will speak to the man, or the woman for that matter, and engage in dialogue. Question and answer time. The human being is now utterly surrendered to the whim of the AI programmer and the makers up of the levers and nuts and bolts and the silicon skin and hair, for Pete's sake. And who profits from this depravation? Only the darkness. The slave makers who enslave others for the sake of their own lust for wealth and authority with total disregard, even unconsciousness of the repercussions on the God given and natural sexual development of each creature. It's probably in existence now where there are sexual sheep robots or horses with humungous phalanxes. The darkness takes what is potentially good and turns it to an addiction so as to enslave people to their own lusts. This is the reason that all good religions first come against the fleshly lusts so that the Spirit can lay hold of the soul and the person's intelligence as it binds that dreadful force in a human being.

"Anyway, that was my first Mansion level on the staircase to Saint Antony's cave. It was made up of thoughts about goodness and darkness, and how AI intelligence and interaction with living humans is catching up to actual everyday interactions between human beings."

"It's a far cry from the intelligence of the soul, though Liam, wouldn't you admit?" asked Hsu.

"indeed, Hsu. I began pondering that truth in what I recognised to be the second Mansion level on the stairs.

"When I took our question, 'Can AI help us to become more like Christ,' I focussed on the development of a robot. My first thought was that it would take an exceptional person or team of people to think it through. Like, really, how many scientists and AI techs know how the human soul works? Like, think about it. You can count them on one hand, if you're dead lucky. In fact, I can't really say that I know of any. And that made me question, 'Is this a move of God? Does God want AI to develop human intelligence to the level of the human soul's intelligence? That's a huge question. That would make an artificial intelligence unit as spiritual as a human being. And, heaven forbid, if it started to become self-thinking, it would create its own version of spirituality and then probably come against human beings for not being as spiritual as it is. Then we humans would have an awful problem on our hands."

"The soul is a generative matrix, Liam," said Prior James.

"But is it God's intention that AI should be given into the hands of even well intentioned good men and women? They will have to maximise their own generative thinking in order to make headway with such a project. They would have to rely on God's stimulation, His revelation, at every crossroad. The average design engineer is going to fall back to something generative, but purely sensorial and materialistic."

"They will stumble at the sub goals," said Hsu.

"Precisely," continued Liam. "They will not know the final outcome of the generative interaction between God and the soul, because it's barely conscious in themselves. And when they break down the final goal into sub goals, and them into even smaller bite sized sub goals in order to develop mini bits of consciousness that can aggregate into larger recognisable decisions and patterns of behaviour, and bonafide divine wisdom, they will not be able to achieve the sub goals even. They will be left creating robots that reiterate the scriptures and the sermons of priests and rabbis and pastors and philosophers, but not God's living word from the Source to the human soul. The intelligence of the human soul will remain as mysterious to the scientist and the tech engineer as the pyramids and the origin of life."

Hsu said, "I heard someone say once, there is a religious explanation for science, but no science that can explain religious experience. The answer to the question about 'How AI Can Help Us Become More Like Christ,' must begin not merely with the robotic regurgitation of known scriptures. It must fully comprehend the walk up the Mansions of the stairs to Saint Antony's cave. Those are my thoughts."

"Exactly," said Prior James. "To become like Christ, as you have both recognised, has two levels of reality to it. The first is the most available, and it is rooted in the need to gain control over one's life. It is the cry out to God, the cry of humanity to God in the Psalms. 'Out of the depths I cry to you O Lord.'

"We experience despair, hopelessness, fear and all manner of emotions that make us turn to God for His higher power. We beg to have His favour. We seek His instruction about how better to be ourselves and to position ourselves so that we accord with His favour. It's all about survival. We seek a clean heart, begging God to not withdraw His Spirit from us.

"This first level encompasses mansions one through to all of four until we are free from the grip of iniquity and we begin to outgrow our need to be a part of the material world.

"The second level is much higher. It is the walk of the Saints in whom God has developed His style of clean heart and pure Spirit. Its mechanics, its psychology, is our waiting on God. We become beggars of Christ. We are no longer religious in name only, we are of God and in God and we know that all things come to us by God's hand without us even asking for them. We merely note our need, and, unspoken, He delivers our need's fulfilment.

"First level people in the first four mansions will get glimpses of this but they can't really understand or grasp it. They are pressured by material needs to cry out to God as if God has all but abandoned them for who knows what reason. And, of course, the scientist has absolutely no hope in understanding this: it is entirely off their radar. And, for a scientist, evidence if radar and radar is god. Faith has no share in their radar and they have no evidence of God. Error and evil are wide open to them as the fabric of their thought and meaning for life."

25

ELARIA ON BEING LIKE CHRIST

S ISTER ELARIA WAS CUSTOMARILY SILENT during the discussions over the past few days. Hsu had asked monks and priests about her, and had researched her online so as to help enjoy her companionship while they were together in the region of Saint Paul Monastery. Now she thought it timely to ask for her thoughts on artificial generative intelligence.

"What do you think, Sister Elaria? You are a doctor of Psychology. You are a monastic Sister. As an author you have published your teachings and exposed your life in Christ to the public. You are baptised Coptic Orthodox Christian like us. You have stayed in the convents and visited the monasteries of the desert fathers and mothers. You have a wealth of mystical experience and have met some of the most famous and legendary Coptic Orthodox Saints in your visions and dreams. Bishops across the world have asked you to tell them of your experiences. They trust you, and love you in Christ. I trust your perspective completely. What can you say about the generative interaction AI is using between its intelligence and the intelligence of the human being?"

"I live in seclusion, dear Hsu." She smiled. "It is a little like your Wudangshan's mountain of hermits and holy places of worship and prayer, where I keep myself hidden in my heavenly Father and His provision as a solitary among solitaries.

THEOSIS AND ARTIFICIAL INTELLIGENCE

"I have no interest in the artificiality of life, however intelligent it might make itself out to be. Falsehood is falsehood, truth is truth. An artificial limb will definitely improve the life of an amputee, but what can artificiality do for a broken or malformed soul? I have long ago left the world unto itself, there is no transforming its blindness to itself as it currently functions.

"The world knows not truth in Him who is the Good Shepherd who draws us individually to Himself. The world is lost. AI is of the world, and it is lost. It is an orphan. It is a lost fish out of water, wriggling and squirming because it is utterly orphaned and alone and unable to know itself in a real source of life. But the world will not acknowledge this because it cannot. It lacks the intelligence that is of God.

"Authentic intelligence that is not artificial intelligence, is knowing Christ in ourselves. Sitting alone with Him in our own sacred room or environment, we come naturally to rest from the world. We know the peace of God in the very depths of our being. We know harmony in the functioning of our interior world and in the nature of our exterior world, and in their unified inseparability.

"And we love as both divine and human in one union of personalness, the Uncreate Father and His human child. Perfect love. Perfect naturalness. As your Taoists on Wudang Mountain and across the whole world have called it, Hsu, Heaven, Earth and Humanity all in happy agreement in the midst of the endless changes in life and the cosmos. Heaven releasing the patten for humanity to engage the Earth, and for the Earth to offer up itself to Humanity in the pattern of perfect ecology. Heaven releasing the pattern for Humanity and the Earth to engage Heaven. This is the divine order of things in Christ Jesus and the Father.

"I know something of these things. I have lived among Asian mystics and I have lived among Christian mystics. And I first lived among the sinners of the world. I praise God for the prayer of Jesus, 'Lord Jesus Christ, Son of God, have mercy on me, a sinner.' It began a mighty movement of refining the dross in me seven times like as for silver, until God my heavenly Father could make something of me. And I praise God for learning the way of harmony from my Asian teachers and friends. Together they give me a beautiful understanding of the Uncreate and of the Order of in His Creation that I appreciate very much and from which I have prospered greatly.

"When I think of the world's population becoming more like Christ, my attention is immediately drawn to the solitary being who is with the Son of God. In glory, the Son comes in the Holy Spirit power for penetrating the truth and for transforming the consciousness. He comes in Himself within the Father, the Son's Source and our Source. I behold God, Uncreate and Personal in One.

"When I consider my personality and my self esteem, Christ makes me aware of the original birthing nature of it, its beauty and its lustrous character. It is an uncut diamond of personal life: fresh, alive, unblemished and original. There is no other like it in all creation, never has been and never will be. I have been authored in the Uncreate God.

"When I think of what the world's people have done to me and especially to others, I have to agree with the world's religious thought about them. They are molesters, butchers, cannibals, pirates and thieves, slave traders, dictators, war mongers consumed with lust, and the blind leading the blind masquerading as if they were the authors of lasting favour and help. But they are not helpers. They are, as Jesus said, 'liars and thieves,' and God's people 'do not follow them.' 'They follow me,' said Jesus, 'because I am the good shepherd. My sheep know my voice and I lead in and out of the pen to good pasture.'

"The good Godly people I have known and who have influenced me, are not of the world, they are uncut diamonds whom the father has polished. The people of the world have no one to polish them in Spirit, and so they grind against each other, occasionally finding a momentary peace and satisfaction amidst the trauma of the endless grind.

"To become more like Christ is to know our original self, our original self esteem, and to be of the Father in his Garden of

Eden life for us. That life is a life of love. It is sacrificial. It is constantly repentant. To love is to sacrifice. Intelligence cannot sacrifice, it has nothing of itself to give. It cannot love, for it has no hope. It can repent if it is told it is wrong but it cannot repent for being wrong in the eyes of God when it cannot have a living relationship with God. AI cannot be like Christ.

"Anything less than this is to mistake being like Christ for the world's compensation for its spiritual orphanhood and its inevitable and eternal lifelessness that proceeds immediately following death of the mind.

"This might seem to be a harsh word to the scientist and the AI tech, but my prayer is that some of them at least can rise above the sheer piracy of human liberty that disguises itself as liberty through all knowledge being on demand this instant.

"It is also a harsh word to the government bureaucrats who are inventing ways for AI and robots to more tightly control their nation's populations, and better than they personally did during the Covid fiasco of lockdowns and population imprisonment. They cannot help but keep loopholes open for they themselves as the privileged humans among the masses whilst throwing the masses to the wind.

"It is truth with origins in the divine that sets a person free, never artificially contrived laws. Artificial intelligence can only ever bind a person because its root is bound, even if it thinks for itself.

"The root of being like Christ, is God's gift of personality in each one of us, made divine by the union of our human will with the will of the energy of the Uncreate God the Father within us. Such union is by the provision of the Son of God on the Cross. He exchanged all death for all life, thereby enabling us to be complete and perfect in our realms of existence eternally as He is complete and perfect in His. Christ made the way for us to participate with the Uncreate as a part of us.

"AI can never be of the Uncreate. It is a created intelligence. It is soulless and without the Father's gift of personality. It cannot bridge to the Uncreate. It is a copier, nothing more, regardless of how intelligent or how sensorial it might become in the future. No matter how good is the camera, the photograph will never match the original living event it captured and made bound, simply because the Uncreate is in the original.

"Is this to say that AI is worthless? Anything that helps a person to achieve Theosis is not necessarily God, but it can be a reflection of God, or can be directly inspired by God.

"In pondering this though, I think that it is important to recognise the levels of consciousness that the Mansions point us to. What is Christian at Mansion 1 is not at all the same as what is Christian on Mansion 6 when the narrow blinkers of religion are entirely removed so that heavenly citizenship is revealed.

"If you are thinking in terms of How AI Can Help Is To Become More Like Christ in our Religion of Choice, then AI must be thought of as being a gift for many people not just Christians.

"For that sense of spiritual unity among all human beings regardless of culture and religion, we must look beyond the blinkers and shackles of religion as it is expressed and learned in the first four Mansion intelligences. Those Mansions are ragged with division, struggle for survival, and the raging passions of the flesh, regardless of the religion of choice.

"We who live in Christ look to the Father's Hand in the lives of all the world's people, and we see in their lives the works of the Uncreate God. Jesus said, 'My Father is still working, and I also am working.' People of other faiths do not feel true to God's work within themselves if they say that the uncreate Father of their own experience is only working with Jesus Christ of the Christians.

"In this way I could perceive that, whilst the lower Mansions require a certain type of individualised and specialist religious output for the human intelligence making input in the generative interaction, the higher Mansions will require a completely revised edition, one that speaks of the direct experience of God, the perfection of doing God's will, and the estate of heavenly citizenship.

"Admittedly, given the fact that the bulk of the world's population are living in only pre Mansion reality or Mansions 1, 2 and 3, with some leadership living in Mansions 4, it would appear that the demand for AI with the capability of speaking to human intelligence that would input to it from a position of life on Mansions 5, 6, 7 and heavenly citizenship is going to be modest and probably not even used.

"However, like for those who pay for Open AI 4 and beyond, their resource often spills over to those who are enjoying the free version of Open AI 3. This could mean that, if AI was able to respond with upper Mansion generative interaction, still based on the large language model and word predictive operatives, and do it according to individuals' own languages and cultures and belief systems, then a unifying and unified presence of the Uncreate Father could find a place.

"The key would be the love of God. God the creator. God the upholder. God the life giver. God the healer. God the Mother and God the Father, God loving all humanity, because that's what God does.

"Love that is inspired by the love of God does not necessarily come labelled and ticketed. Divine love has its own voice and is never separated from the Uncreate Son of God or the Uncreate Father or the Uncreate Holy Spirit. They are One Uncreate. No one has ever seen the Uncreate. It is not possible, not for a Christian and not for someone of another religion in response to the Uncreate God. However, history shows us that God has intervened in the lives of people as far back as history exists, and intervened as the Uncreate Father, Son and Holy Spirit in One. AI would therefore be relating to others around the world who will be saying, 'And I, like the Father, am also working.'

"Christians can be very territorial and jealous for their Christ Jesus God. They are too often condemning of others unlike themselves. This happens even within the Christian denominations and the multitude of Churches. They are not a good model for a unified field of spirituality in humanity under the wise eye of the Uncreate Father. This will always be a problem for spiritual unity in the world until the world's religious have outgrown the lower Mansions. That's how I understand it all anyway.

"Britain today, for example, is not just the realm of the white skinned Anglo Saxon of a century ago. The hand of God is moving among them. They know it. They feel it. Those people have had to accept the peoples of other languages, cultures, religions, corruptions and impoverishments. They are living in the midst of former enemies they hated. Former enemies of Britain have flocked to it because of the opportunity of life it presents to them. If life was better elsewhere they would have stayed there, but it wasn't. They want more opportunity. There is hardly an exodus from London for the second or third world countries. The mixed peoples all want greater opportunity. It is a fact of life universally. That is what some leaders in the field of artificial intelligence development are wanting, better options and more opportunities worldwide.

"I think that the model of AI being a support for 'Us To Become More Like Christ in our Religion of Choice,' is the example set by the leading 1st world nations: Britain with its system of Common Law being the original, America and Canada and Australia and New Zealand following among others. They have all provided a model of Christ in national governance, and opened themselves and their values to accepting others so that the mutual sharing of intelligence can bless the whole nation whilst Christ like values of spiritual equality are extended to all by Common Law.

"If spiritual AI can lead from the highest Mansions and upwardly draw people of all religions with spiritual equality in God the Source of All, then both will prosper. The people in the lower mansions will be blessed by the more unifying wisdom coming to them from the higher Mansions, and the higher Mansions will prosper by the diversity and colour and shape they become with the arrival of those from the lower Mansions. That's how it is now in real non-AI life.

"Unless one is mule-headed about the world heading for annihilation, or that one religion will survive and all others will go to eternal damnation, which violates every principle of a loving and all serving God, then one will see that the migration model is the one for AI to adopt. Generative interaction will necessarily include the various levels of the Mansions, and will be an aid to the development of human intelligence and indeed divine-like wisdom by being an assistant to people's ascension to higher Mansion realities.

"And that, after all, is the spiritual goal of using AI for becoming more like Christ the Son of God who was the Father Incarnate, over and above simply becoming more like a duelling Christian."

26

THE SPIRITUAL CHALLENGE TO AI

On the next day, Prior James picked up the thread left by Sister Elaria's talk about being like Christ and people have a generative interaction with AI.

"As I hear the conversation so far, I am hearing that human intelligence wants to maintain control over artificial intelligence at the spiritual level, among other levels. We want to provide for the robot and the AI ChatBot and other AI instruments, but we cannot conceive that the robot's intelligence will ever outpace our own spiritual intelligence. Currently, the reality that is spirituality is a significant challenge to AI being conscious and self-determining.

"It is highly unlikely, but a scientist might conceive that AI could master and replace Popes and Patriarchs, Bishops and Priests in their exclusively bureaucratic roles as administrators, and perhaps certain televangelists, worship leaders and choirs. But the singularly Christ-like feature that cannot conceivably be replicated is the generative interaction between the Holy Spirit and these same human intelligences who exhibit the giftings of the Spirit. They all approach their Office through prayer. And prayer is *the* quintessential generative interaction in the life of human intelligence in these roles.

"Moral principles can be amassed and metered out as required. We see that being forced upon certain peoples today under the edict of governmental control in the name of a safer more harmonious community and nation. But, spiritual ethics are the province of prayer. They are an entirely different and larger than life element that transcends amassed collections of values and meanings in digitised Common Rule.

THEOSIS AND ARTIFICIAL INTELLIGENCE

"This is especially so when the follower of Christ Jesus operates in the gifts of the Spirit. Gifts of healing, miracles, speaking in tongues, the interpretation of tongues, the discerning of knowledge, the discerning of the secrets of people's hearts, prophecy, the discerning of good and evil spirits and such like, these are entirely unknown to the world and cannot be digitised.

"These purely Holy Spirit imbued acts of spiritual intelligence are mimicked in the occult gifts, what the Bible calls 'sorcery.' Because of their intimate association with Christ and God the Father, the gifts of the Spirit, on the contrary, carry with them freedom from spiritual orphanhood. The occult gifts cannot carry and do not carry spiritual union with God. They are empathy based in power and elementally rooted, and are not relationship based in the power of God. They are the hallmarks of evolutionary spiritually isolated intelligence and, as such, they are unable to make the quantum leap into the authentically divine until they release their grip on the selfishness preferment within their power. The leap of faith is all important when it releases the self of the person into the purposes of the Self of God.

"Who can imagine an AI version of Saieh Yousef that brings the Father's will by bi-locating and teleporting in order to present the exact Word of God required by someone, or the exact fulfilment of a person's prayer? Not I.

"Yet, this is the evidence of Christianity in the individual, the presence of the Holy Spirit of God, not just the soul or the human spirit. It is Biblical. No other document on Earth tells the story of the coming of the Holy Spirit's features like the Christian Testament. The Spirit of God is in the workings of God in the Jewish Testament, but the Holy Spirit that is released by the Father because of Christ the Son nurtures continuity in Christ's likeness generation after generation.

"For us, spiritual intelligence is not just our referring to sacred scriptures, memorising them and chanting them for years. The blessed intelligence that amounts from such a life is hard won. It takes years of trial and error, prayer and fasting, psychic experiences of other dimensions, revelation from God Himself, leadings, promptings, guesswork made real by faith and the excitement of the chase for what we sense or eventually know as the will of God our God. It is inconceivable that an artificial intelligence can masquerade in the imitation of a highly realised human being and pull off the same Godly results. That's what I am hearing in the conversation.

"But, in the mindedness of God my Father, I ask you, 'Can it?' We know it can't, but is there another way of knowing? Anything is possible with God for the believer. Let's open our hearts and minds to speculate in the presence of the Holy Spirit how intelligence with soul might produce the actuality of God-given outcomes, shall we? And, if we can imagine it, let's then work back through the multitude of sub goals until we arrive at the digitising process required to start it off, its Genesis.

"The known starting point is that we all know that the generative interaction component of AI is the way that the AI system receives an input from a human intelligence and then generates estimated compliant outputs. It receives feedback or input from the human intelligence, which in turn helps the system to learn and improve its performance. In this way, with enough interaction, it holds the generative potential to replicate human intelligence.

"As you, Liam and Hsu, both know from your contemplative trek up the stairs to Saint Antony's cave yesterday, human intelligence is characterised by the ability to generate creative and contextually appropriate responses to various situations. In that instance, you discovered eight Mansion levels of integrated and ecologically sound spiritual intelligence within yourselves and your Earthly reality in association with God's energy within your human minds. The day before yesterday, you had little idea that such a thing exists. Today, you do."

"And we are different people for it," said Liam.

"Yes," added Hsu.

"That's to be expected of course," said Prior James. "Spiritual power moulds intelligence and crafts entirely new realities in it.

THEOSIS AND ARTIFICIAL INTELLIGENCE

That is the generative dynamic in us. And we should look at the scaling of the Mansions to find just how spiritual power adjusts our intelligence.

THE MANSIONS CHALLENGE TO AI

"BY INCORPORATING GENERATIVE INTERACTION into AI systems," continued Prior James, "researchers aim to emulate this aspect of human intelligence's learning and development, and enhance the capabilities of AI. Given the right human input, such as purely spiritual goals, AI could, it is possible, emulate the human intelligence responses to situations or questions at each Mansion level.

"Each level of Mansion intelligence in the human mind and soul has its own understandings and responses to life that are drawn from conceptions of life internal and external. The 'Hierarchy of Needs' theory proposed by psychologist Abraham Maslow, is often represented as a pyramid and describes the different levels of human needs. It's a theory and not an absolute framework that applies universally to all individuals. Different cultures and personal circumstances can influence the prioritisation and fulfillment of these needs. However, they can be seen expressed on every Mansion level of spiritual increase. Sister Elaria, would you outline them for us please?"

"Sure Da," she said. "The hierarchy consists of five levels, starting from the basic physiological needs at the bottom and progressing towards higher order psychological needs. Here's a breakdown of the pyramid:

1. Physiological Needs: These are the most fundamental needs required for survival, such as food, water, shelter, sleep, and clothing. Without satisfying these needs, it is challenging to address higher level needs.
2. Safety Needs: Once physiological needs are fulfilled,

individuals seek safety and security. This includes personal security, financial stability, a safe environment, health, protection from harm and something of a secure future.

3. Love and Belonging: Humans have social needs, and this level encompasses the desire for love, friendship, intimacy, and a sense of belonging. It involves forming relationships, being part of a family, having friendships, and being accepted by others.

4. Esteem Needs: After fulfilling the previous three levels, people seek self esteem and the recognition and respect of others. This involves feeling confident, having a sense of achievement, gaining respect, and receiving recognition for one's abilities and contributions.

5. Self Actualization: At the top of the pyramid is self actualization, which refers to fulfilling one's full potential and becoming the best version of oneself. This includes personal growth, pursuing meaningful goals, realising one's talents and potential, and seeking self fulfillment."

"Thanks Elaria," said Prior James. "There are, of course, hierarchies and wheels of needs that are different from Maslow's, but I think we all recognise such needs within each of the Mansions levels of spiritual development too," said Prior James.

"I cannot imagine any Sowah, hermit, anchorite, monk, nun, priest, missionary or parishioner who has not had to seek God's help in each of these arenas, and rely upon it.

"Mansion 1 reality has its demands, and then we graduate and find ourselves challenged by Mansion 2 standards of life. We graduate Mansion 2 and find ourselves challenged by the values and meanings that eventually graduate us from Mansion 3, and so on up through the ladder of Mansion intelligence and experiential realities until we arrive at actual heavenly citizenship. Even the holy martyrs of the Church down through the centuries must traverse these stages of spiritual development. If they are not completed here on the Earth they will be completed in the heavenly realms before the individual progresses on into real heavenly citizenship.

"If we ask ourselves, 'From whence comes the challenge at each Mansion?' Is just driven by happenstance, as a materialist might surmise? Is it driven by personal karma, as a reincarnations might surmise? Is it driven by natural selection as a scientist might surmise? We in the Judaeo-Christian tradition say, 'For surely I know the plans I have for you, says the Lord, plans for your welfare and not for harm, to give you a future with hope.' God has a plan for every person to be raised up through all of Christ's Mansions until they come into their perfect estate of Theosis and being God.

"So, as I said, given the right human input, such as purely spiritual goals, AI that is equipped with all the markers of spiritual intelligence development in a human being could, it is possible, emulate the human intelligence responses to situations or questions at each Mansion level.

"I say emulate, copy, but not create an original. Especially is this so at the higher Mansion levels of five through eight. At that level of cosmic minded contact with God's creation, and God Himself, and the emergence of the actuality of heavenly citizenship, human intelligence is stripped of its conceptual mind, the very fabric of typical AI large language models. During Mansion 5, a fledgling heavenly version of faith is gifted to the human being so as to find God in Person and in Spirit. The old animalistic version of human faith is entirely outmoded. In essence, during Mansion 5, a whole other mindset is given by God to the human being. It is part Uncreate. It enables Uncreate Intelligence within the human intelligence to commune with and intelligently dialogue with the Uncreate God in God's own language — Eternal Spirit.

"It is this union with God that is at the root of holy *hesychia* — the spiritual stillness in the human intelligence and heart that, in us, knows God directly. It is the stillness of God's presence. It is the spaciousness of God's everywhereness. It is the receptivity of the humble willing heart of God. It is the intelligence of the human and the divine, the Spirit of a human being fusing into the energy of God the Father. And it happens in our human interior life. It is inconceivable that it could manifest in the interior life of AI because it is made of the stuff of a higher dimension of existence than the digitised code by which AI operates.

"Spiritual peace in the soul is not simply the inactivity we see in an artificial intelligence unit. Spiritual peace is life in action at a higher level and is not related to inactivity at all. God is active in the presence of our spiritual peace. AI only experiences the lack of input stimulation in its own interior life, if we can call it that.

"The lower Mansions offer glimpses of this interior life as fleeting experiences. Dreams. Visions. Flashes of insight that have no infrastructure upon which to build larger concepts of higher reality. However, it is Mansion 5 that establishes hesychia as the permanent state of being in we human beings. And hesychia's wisdom is at the root of becoming like Christ. If we start at the top and work down through the Mansions of human spiritual intelligence, the most significant starting point must include hesychia and its place in the interior life of whoever would become more like Christ. There is no wisdom-creator like hesychia in Mansions one through four. Growth and development in mansions one through four are largely focussed on the wisdom accrued through compensating for inadequacies, intellectual conflictions and past poor decisions. It is when we desire more than mere compensation that the path of peace in Christ is laid before us. This is why choosing Him is so fundamentally significant in our spiritual progress. With hesychia, we receive an entirely new kind of mind which enormously enhances our born again mind.

"This is one challenge AI faces: how to have soul intelligence, that is, intelligence that interacts with the energy of God so that it grows in character and skill by such interaction, and interaction that is rooted in hesychia. And, as I said, it is this union with God that is at the root of holy hesychia — the spiritual stillness in the human intelligence and heart that, in us, knows God directly. It is the stillness of God's presence.

"Consider presenting a spiritual robot before a score of

enlightened mystics, contemplatives, Yogis, Sufi's, Rabbis, Taoist Chi Masters, Imams, indigenous elders and mystics and so forth from around the world. Consider that we ask them to tell us about the bot's authentic presence of God and God-like wisdom.

"I believe that the evidence of their spiritual affinity with the Source of Creation would be that they would each put aside their book learning and the religious scaffolding of their faith. They would individually empathically search the heart of your spiritual robot for the presence of soul-like attributes that enable it to have contact with God, just as they know such contact and such a mechanism in their own God-given hesychia.

"They would be looking with the discerning eye of Uncreate Intelligence and they would be trying to discern the same Uncreate Intelligence in your spiritual robot. If they, or when they, discern that there is no such a level of intelligence in the AI, they will answer, "No. God is not in your spiritual robot's intelligence form. Intelligence is there, but it is not that of the Uncreate God. Sorry.'

28

AI AND THE FORGIVENESS OF SINS

"ANOTHER CHALLENGE THAT AI FACES," continued Prior James, "is what we experience as errors or sins in the process of our development. We find that in a certain project at a certain, perhaps new, level of activity, we fall flat on our faces. We default on God's will. We might learn from it, but, as we do, it is because we look back and reflect on the point at which we lost contact with God, we seek God's forgiveness and we plead to be transformed into the fullness of the light of good fellowship with God again.

"An obvious question exists: can AI sin?

"At the current level of development, AI would respond to the question, saying:

> As an artificial intelligence language model, I do not have personal agency or consciousness, so I do not have the ability to sin or make moral choices. Sin is generally understood as a violation of religious or moral laws or principles. It is a concept that is relevant to human beings who have the capacity for moral agency and the ability to make choices.
>
> However, I can provide information and guidance on the topic of sin and moral considerations based on various religious, ethical, and philosophical perspectives, if that is what you're interested in.

"This tells us that an AI and Robot developer working to appease the lower levels of the faithful of the world could do as the AI said and, 'provide information and guidance on the topic of sin and moral considerations based on various religious, ethical, and philosophical perspectives.' Perhaps the same AI could provide the rite of forgiveness, like a stand-in priest. Those in the lower Mansions who lack direct contact with God would presume that God has heard the AI and agrees with the output. Ergo, the human acceptance that my sins are now forgiven.

"Perhaps the AI could engage dialogue with the human intelligence, saying, "I will ask God to forgive your sins now. After this I will ask you if you have felt God's forgiveness and you can answer 'Yes' or 'No' to me and that will determine our where-to-from-here."

"That's the kind of dialogue that you set up with the drug users in the clinic in Melbourne, isn't it?" asked Liam.

"Yes, precisely. The AI would ask the question and wait for the user's reply and then proceed to the next step. Liam, where did you learn about my doing that?"

"An Egyptian scientist was in conference with us a few days ago. She uses your model to help people. I have no idea how she got wind of it, maybe from a worker in the drug and alcohol field."

"Interesting," said the Prior. "Well, yes, that is one way that I have found, oh goodness, thirty years ago now, to be effective for someone who does not know God directly to communicate with God.

"But, let's move on, especially in the area of morals and ethics and sinful behaviour — whether it's sins against God or transgressions against karma or sins against conscience and one's personal code of truth. I have met people like that, for example, who let themselves down by transgressing the lifelong Bodhisattva Vows they had taken from Tibetan Buddhist lamas. They needed repentance and forgiveness and a rededication to their way of truth before their whole being could feel inline with their spiritual walk. It's a common reaction among all human beings in one way or another. Of course, not everyone follows through with the nagging need for confession and repentance.

"Generative interaction buries a tonne of coding in its sub goals and in the fine print that goes into even the sub goals that make up the goals it acts out at surface level. We humans do the same. One Christian way of describing that spiritual glitch is that fiery darts come into us. Paul writes in Ephesians 6:12 to 16:

> For our struggle is not against blood and flesh but against the rulers, against the authorities, against the cosmic powers of this present darkness, against the spiritual forces of evil in the heavenly places. Therefore take up the whole armour of God, so that you may be able to withstand on the evil day and, having prevailed against everything, to stand firm. Stand, therefore, and belt your waist with truth and put on the breastplate of righteousness and lace up your sandals in preparation for the gospel of peace. With all of these, take the shield of faith, with which you will be able to quench all the flaming arrows of the evil one.

"The shield of faith. This is our protection against the enemy to our spiritual development. What happens when AI is wholly unaware that it is infected with a fiery dart somewhere deep in its coding? And not because of the intent of the tech who coded in the sub goals or even the goals, but by a self generated response by the AI that just ever so slightly missed the mark and its so called pure heart was sullied ever so slightly.

"We see that sort of thing with Christians who are loaded with a tonne of the giftings of the Holy Spirit, or even sitting in high Office, but still have the character of cockroaches and vermin. Just because AI can churn out reams of Spirit-like responses to human intelligence probing, doesn't mean that it is actually exempt of carrying fiery darts that will infect the human intelligence. And the AI could be entirely ignorant of its own impact, just as most Christians are until things really blow up in their face. AI has no Father of Confession, no spiritual mirror.

"An experienced Christian, or an illumined person of other religions, will know this to be true. An AI tech with little or no spiritual acumen will think sin and fiery darts and 'cosmic powers of this present darkness' to be all superstition, maladjustment to circumstances, overly nervous psychological imaginings, or just plain rubbish."

"And that, of course," said Liam, "is their shortfall. That's why iniquity rules supreme in so many lives all around the world, even within the religions of the world."

"Quite so," said Prior James. "Quite so, sadly. Once the AI registers as truth and goodness that sub code arising from a 'sinful' point of decision, it will treat it as a part of its library of truths and, in its generative style of learning, build other truths around it. Before long, the fiery darts can dominate that robot or that AI, just as happens with human intelligence, and everyone is pretty much none the wiser."

"None but the person who walks in the Kingdom of heaven with Jesus," said Hsu. "Listen to his words about that:

> Jesus tells us 'The kingdom of heaven may be compared to someone who sowed good seed in his field, but while everybody was asleep an enemy came and sowed weeds among the wheat and then went away.'
>
> 'A sower went out to sow his seed, and as he sowed some fell on a path and was trampled on, and the birds of the air ate it up. Some fell on rock, and as it grew up it withered for lack of moisture. Some fell among thorns, and the thorns grew with it and choked it. Some fell into good soil, and when it grew it produced a hundredfold.'

"He harkened to us to hear what he is saying," continued Hsu, "and to discern these realities in our lives and in the things we cause to come into existence. Instead of sowing blessing for harvests of blessings being returned to us, we sow seeds of sin or we sow carelessly or we simply don't show up for our harvest and we lose out all the time. There are many aspects of Jesus' teachings that we humans live with which are replicated in AI and most certainly will be when AI becomes spiritually engineered."

"I agree whole heartedly," said Prior James. "For we with human intelligence and sin in our lives, sickness ensues in some form or another. It's inevitable. Physical illness. Psychosomatic illness. Psychological imbalance. Mental illness and even disease-related accidents. And, it'll be the same for an AI.

"One then could imagine AI units checking in for regular planned-for supervisory audits to check on their performance levels. As for humans with a spiritual director or a confessor, so too for AI. Despite the fact that AI can quickly out pace any one human being's intelligence by quota, AI is still not incapable of carrying the sour grape sins of the fathers over into its children whose teeth are set on edge. Here are these two scriptures on passing sins onward:

> If one person sins against another, someone can intercede for the sinner with the Lord, but if someone sins against the Lord, who can make intercession?
>
> He committed all the sins that his father did before him; his heart was not true to the Lord his God.

And compare them with Jesus in his life of Theosis as Saint Paul wrote about him in Galatians 1:3 5,

> Grace to you and peace from God our Father and the Lord Jesus Christ, who gave himself for our sins to set us free from the present evil age, according to the will of our God and Father, to whom be the glory forever and ever. Amen.

"The separation from God will happen to AI in an AI way, just as it happens to human intelligence in a human way. But, we have a Saviour. Amen!

"Who, though, can save AI, especially self generative AI that can never be free from the likelihood of generating a sin-inducing response to its own learning?"

"I can imagine that kind of a thing," said Liam. "What if a company that is designing a robot to be a people carer slips up on one response learning in the sub goals that triggers a 'destroy' option when certain other associated words accompany something otherwise innocuous and seemingly innocent? Conscience in the human intelligence is loaded with morality and ethics to combat it, and most of the time the goal is successfully achieved. Does this mean that AI must necessarily develop conscience? AI with soul with conscience?"

"I suppose," said the Prior, "that's where I am hearing this conversation is going. Hsu? Liam? Your thoughts?"

"Thank you, Father, said Hsu. "Very well thought out. I think that this brings us to recognise the two levels of answering the question, 'How AI Can Help Us Become More Like Christ.'

"One level is to receive typically generative responses from ChatBots or religious robots that cite scriptures, sermons and famous sayings and offer them in the form of instruction or advice. It is loaded from the bottom up. It learns as it goes, and it doesn't have an end-game in sight. It's just moving from one stepping stone to another in the hope that each step means progress.

"The other level is actually creating a better version of AI that is specifically loaded from the top down. It knows where humanity is capable of coming to, because it has the example of thousands of years of spiritual genius within human intelligence. The lessons of the ancient community around Adam and Eve out of whom came Enoch whom God took to heaven bodily without tasting death. The Elijahs of history. Moses, Abraham and the prophets. The extraordinary Son of God, Melchizedek. Then all the Christian saints and martyrs over the past two thousand years. And that's just with Christianity. Islam, Judaism, Taoism, Buddhism, Hinduism, the other faiths all have their spiritual heroes and icons too. They are the men and women of planet Earth who know what varying measures of union with the Father is like, how to get there, and the reward for getting there into the holy grail of Theosis.

"I think that we can safely say that the Lord Jesus Christ has called us all to look at the challenge from the second position, to think for humanity from the top down.

"Liam, we could quite easily end our journey here and return to Massachusetts with the recommendation that we develop AI along the lines of God's promises for the first four Mansions. From the first stair up to the White Church, I suppose, on the trek

THEOSIS AND ARTIFICIAL INTELLIGENCE

to Saint Antony's Cave.

"My preference though, would be to take a look at it from the top down. What do you think?"

"I'm with you, Hsu. The trek up the stairs is something amazing. But the view from the Cave is simply divine."

"Let's look into this tomorrow after the morning liturgies," suggested Prior James. We'll give some thought to creating an AI soul. I offer you the name RoboSaint if you want to hypothetically name your AI."

"Great name," said Hsu.

"Yeah. I love it, echoed Liam. God bless y'all, see y'in Church."

"One thing," said Hsu. "I was just thinking of the difference between top-down versus bottom-up thinking. It struck me that both you and I, Liam, were flooded with compassion and the desire to whole heartedly serve any and all persons when once we reached the cave and the upper Mansion levels of spirituality.

"I think that that's the standout difference. Top-down thinking is so rich in itself that is can afford to be 100% compassionate and bestow really skilful means to help spiritually. Not just in a social work way, but actually uplift the Spirit.

"And then I thought of the people I met on the way up the stairs. The boy who offered us water. The boy who led me inside the White Church. The old Chinese lady. They all demonstrated an abundance that let their compassion pour out on me.

"I don't have the concept for it yet, but I know that somewhere in that distinction between bottom-up learning and top-down learning lies the foundation for our RoboSaint's intelligent response to life with total selfless, sacrificial, loving, compassionate service.

"Wow, Hsu," said Liam. "I am really getting that. What an amazing AI that would be. That's almost Godly. Maybe that's as Christ-like as an AI can get. Maybe that's what AI soul is all about."

AI AND THE FORGIVENESS OF SINS

PART 10 • HEART OF HEARTS

29

SOUL

"WHERE DO WE START? We start with prayer," said Hsu as they gathered the following morning. "Lord Jesus, come and be with us in person as you always do. Inspire our hearts and lead us in the Father's will toward ideas for the possibilities of an artificial intelligence soul, or at least a soul-like capability of responding to human intelligence input, the deep calling to the deep. Thank you, Lord. Amen."

"Amen," the other three responded.

At that moment who should show up but Saieh Yousef. With him was a middle aged priest who was just about to start a visit in Saint Paul Monastery. They had been discussing the project of How AI Can Help Us Become More Like Christ. After typically cordial greetings, cross kissing, hand pulling away and tacit hugs, Liam asked him about his planned retreat and why he chose Saint Paul Monastery.

"It is the most desert-like of all the monasteries. Their regime is strict. The desert rules their life. There is no trace of the world in their lives. They are fully committed to the hermit life and are very determined that Christ rules in all things."

Liam was startled at the man's zeal for cutting himself off

entirely from the world. He had listened to Sister Elaria who presented an entirely different picture of the lives of the men of that monastery. Their love was pronounced. Their warmth and friendship and love of inquiry was effervescent in its own way. They did not represent a harsh asceticism at all, and reflected the life of Anba Bola himself, that, even though he was a hermit in that place he was loving and kind and good-hearted. His asceticism had not turned his heart to cement. With this in mind, both Hsu and Liam were surprised with the priest's manner when he launched in on a personal attack by his opening remarks that were all about the folly of pursuing artificial spiritual intelligence. He also was entirely suspect of Christ's anointing on the project.

"I thought you'd enjoy a spiritual challenge," said Saieh Yousef, smiling from ear to ear with his customary divine joy.

"You do realise that everything you are doing is artificiality, don't you?" Abouna Ephraim said. His black Egyptian eyes piercing and yet glistening with light. "I believe that you are misguided. You are under the illusion that because you can think it, it must be able to be of the will of God. That is the satanic fraud. You should know that already. Especially you, Prior James."

"In what way are you qualified," replied Prior James, "to speak on the topic of generative learning in the artificial intelligence field of spiritual education, Father?"

"I worked in artificial intelligence and robotics for some years in Scandinavia," said Abouna Ephraim.

Have you studied the field? Are you working in robotics? Are you experienced in the automation of industry, like supermarkets, malls and restaurants?" asked Prior James.

"I worked in prison population management in the capacity as a Social Worker, before eventually fleeing the world to be with Christ in the Church," said Abouna Ephraim.

"Have you experienced first hand the developments that are happening with religious robots and religious centred AI around the world in different faiths?" asked Prior James.

"No, I am not all interested in such things," Abouna Ephraim replied.

"Father," asked Prior James, "are you at all aware of the current drive by collective humanity that has already placed the intelligence that AI brings as a more significant arrival than the discovery of fire and electricity?"

"That's absurd," Abouna Ephraim replied.

"Your your position," posited Prior James, "seems to be one of simply denying levels of thought and creativity simply because they are outside your normal field of dogmatic reality and seemingly in opposition for your ardour to be utterly done away with all worldly matters?"

The Prior didn't wait for a response but continued his inquiry of the priest's position by asking, "Abouna, are you of the mind that if Anba Bola had access to the same measure of AI in his day that we have today, that he would not avail himself of the information even though it would enhance his application of Christ's Gospel? Like Saint Macarius of Natrun Desert, Anba Bola would just put up both his hands and plead, 'Give me only Christ'?"

"Yes," said Abouna Ephraim, "I stand with Anba Bola and Anba Macarius, and all the true desert fathers. They did not need information or seek information. They thrived on solitude and silence before the cross of Christ. And God gave them that, in abundance. And they became Saints in their Deification. The records show it to be so. God has honoured and rewarded those of us over the centuries who have looked to those Saints for guidance and succour."

"The Coptic Church has long been the sponsor of music, art, literature and medicine. All of these developments have been recognised as being integral to spirituality and the Theosis journey. Was spirituality a feature of the AI you and your people developed in prison?" asked Liam.

"No. Not at all. We found that spirituality could not be developed in the prison environment in any way. The mindset of the prisoners was maintained in a stream where self help was encouraged, but the role of prayer, worship and religious study was not fostered. Some religious programs were commenced but we found that they caused division among the diverse populations of inmates. And this is the destiny of your work also. It will cause division where no division exists or should exist. The whole focus needs to begin and end with the renunciation of the world, not cluttering it with information. Information is a curse on the spiritual life."

"Are you certain that division was non existent before introducing religion, Abouna? Or, rather, was it simply that division was lingering but it all the better made itself known and conscious when religion was the catalyst for the increase in intelligence?"

"How can you say such a thing?"

Prior James looked at Saieh Yousef with the look that said, 'I've had enough of this.' He looked at the priest. "Abouna, the entire world has entered a new phase of its existence. The global sharing of our human knowledge collective has already begun transforming individuals, institutions, industries, governments and nations. It is not a total trend, it is just a beginning, but like all things that inspire collective thinking and action on the Earth, like it was with Christ Jesus Himself, the world will be impacted, take sides and either run with it, stand against it or bury its head in the sand like ostriches and believe that it doesn't exist and can never have God's blessing in it."

"Prior James, what you are speaking of pertains to the burgeoning business market place. If companies do not have AI managers on board very soon, they will go under. Those companies with AI managers and who are up to speed with the ever changing AI developments in their own fields will out pace their rivals with better quality products that are better suited to their target populations that find them through better distribution networks with better pricing and incentives to buy because of better rewards systems. The company that does not size up with the best AI possible will not exist within a few months or years. And that has nothing to do with whether AI can help us to become more like Christ or not. The principles that you are following are exclusively founded on materialism and not spiritual pursuit of Theosis and the Royal Crown of Christ."

"Abouna," said Prior James to Saieh Yousef, "we have nothing to offer this Father except the blessings of Anba Bola. Please excuse yourselves now."

Eyebrows raised. Jaws dropped a little. The atmosphere turned decidedly icy. Both Saieh Yousef and Father Ephraim gave a nod of acknowledgement and a pat to the chest, and backed out a few steps. Before leaving the room, Abouna Ephraim left his parting words, "Matthew 7 and versus 13 and 14 warn you all:

> Enter through the narrow gate, for the gate is wide and the road is easy that leads to destruction, and there are many who take it. For the gate is narrow and the road is hard that leads to life, and there are few who find it.

The door closed behind them. "Sowah?" asked Liam.

"No," replied Prior James, "a type of perspective deliberately and conveniently brought to us by a Sowah.

"The lesson Saieh Yousef wants us to ponder is, 'What does that tell you about the level of consciousness that is authentically functioning at the spiritual level?"

"I'm not sure I want to believe it," said Hsu. "That priest was beautiful, radiant, full of light and life, ageless like the morning sun. I am left wondering as to the level of his words to us."

"Are you querying what level of Mansion reality he is on?" asked Liam. "I have that very same query. If he is a companion of a Sowah, perfectly doing the Father's will, surely he is on a very high spiritual level and not to be taken lightly? He has come to do retreat at Saint Paul Monastery. The combination is a powerful truth. It should mean something."

"Such a position, Liam" said Prior James, "assumes a measure of universal consciousness in the Sowah which does not necessarily exist in this Social Worker come priest."

"How so?" asked Liam.

"Teleportation," said Prior James, "requires a pure heart. The purest. But a pure heart is found in measure on each of the Mansion levels of spiritual development. Is the prophet of God on Mansion 3 different from the prophet of God on Mansion 6? And if so, in what way? What does the soul have on Mansion 6 that the soul does not have on Mansion 3?"

Prior James smiled. Saieh Yousef had delivered his own version of the stairs to Saint Anthony's Cave for Liam and Hsu to ponder.

"Well, as I understand it from our conversation," began Liam.

"Stop. Don't say another word, Liam. Don't give us your thoughts and your hypothesis. Look into the soul of a Mansion 3 person right now. And then look into the soul of a Mansion 6 person. Tell me what you discern."

Liam, and Hsu, following in this way, turned their attention to people they knew until they each located a Mansion 3 soul and a mansion 6 soul. Quietly, and with a deep peace of hesychia about their attentiveness, they started noticing the differences. Hsu was the first to speak.

"The Mansion 6 soul engages life completely differently from the Mansion 3 soul."

"In what way, Hsu?" asked Prior James.

"The soul of Mansion 6 is full of God and pure hearted, with a sense of being a part of the whole universe. The soul of Mansion 3 is full of God and pure hearted but has a sense of being a part only of the Earth. And by far not all of the Earth at that. There is a complete difference in the measure of being conquerors in Christ. The Mansion 3 soul is a conqueror battling the Satanic and the enemy. The Mansion 6 soul does not battle at all. The battle is won. Also, the Mansion 3 soul has no idea that the Mansion 6 soul's reality exists, and has no road map to reach it. To Mansion 3 soul, the soul's reality of Mansion 6 is utterly hidden in God. It does not exist. The Mansion 3 soul cannot conceive an end to the battle against the demonic and the enemy and the anti Christ."

THEOSIS AND ARTIFICIAL INTELLIGENCE

"Very good," acknowledged Prior James. "Liam? Your thoughts?"

"I am discerning the same elements as you, Hsu. I would add that the measure of pure heart in Mansion 3 and Mansion 6 is different too. It's not just what they are each conscious of, it's also a matter of how much God the Father is acting in the personality of the soul. In Mansion 3 soul, the Father is more present as the Holy Spirit, the Divine Transformer. The Father is largely unknown to the Mansion 3 soul. The Mansion 6 soul, on the other hand, is wholly populated by the Father's energy. There is a genuine fusion of wills between the Father and the daughter, in my case, because she is a female human being."

"Very good, also, Liam. So, give me your attention here again please." He gave them a few moments to be back in the meeting room with him. "What you have described is true. Firstly, there are known and discernible features in the prayer life, the worship life, the meditation life, the repentance life, the sacrificial life, the ascetic life and the glory life of each Mansion level soul.

"Without venturing to estimate what Mansion level of soul Father Ephraim is currently abiding in, it is plain that some aspects of spiritual consciousness and the creative hand of divinity are entirely out of reach for him at this stage. They are hidden in the Father from the eyes of those not yet given the grace to be able to use them in the kingdom of heaven.

"The lesson here issues from Jesus own words in Matthew 11:25 to 27. Look it up while I explain to you, for it speaks to me about two things," continued Prior James.

"Firstly, Liam and Hsu, you have both correctly discerned that the difference between Mansion 6 soul and Mansion 3 soul is that, to the Mansion 3 soul it appears that the Father has hidden things from the wise and the intelligent. Mansion 3 soul will experience being spiritually wiser and more intelligent than people not yet born again. Mansion 6 soul, on the other hand, knows what has been revealed to him or to her, and receives it very much like a child, in the way a child receives good gifts and provision from its loving parent. The Mansion 6 soul looks upon those with a lower Mansion reality with a sense of service and compassion, and looks to those above him or her with a sense of profound respect and honour and admiration that springs from the heart of God.

"Secondly, we see in this scripture how Jesus is revealing the Father to the Mansion 6 soul whereas to the Mansion 3 soul the Son is choosing to reveal the Holy Spirit and Himself, but not yet the Father. The Father is ever the Uncreate that lies on the other side of the desert of utter transformation of the soul and Spirit. Mansion 3 soul is entirely unable to know that yet.

"The great magnanimity of the Mansion 6 soul is that it knows and loves and serves as God the Father knows and loves and serves. To the Mansion 3 soul, such perfection can only be dreamed of.

"Both souls are of God. Both have yards of salvation. Both could be eventually given the gifts for serving among the Sowah. Underneath the frozen winter streams and rivers, however, the waters gently flow on. The waters in each soul are the Father's Father Fusion plans for Theosis. All the ground must be covered. The human soul must traverse the depths and the breadth and the heights of both universal consciousness and divine consciousness. The human being and the Uncreate God must partner with each other and perfectly share each other, if ever deification is going to amount to salvation's crowning glory of being God."

"This partnership is the personality of the human being adding a face to the energy of God the Uncreate, and the divinity of God the Uncreate adding deifying features to the human personality," said Hsu.

30

THE LESSON

"PRECISELY," answered Prior James. Then he added, "There's a very valuable lesson to learn from Saieh Yousef's offering to us this morning. Can either of you guess what it is?"

"Other than what we have discerned about the differences in Mansion soul attributes, no nothing more really," said Liam.

"I'm with Liam," said Hsu.

"For RoboSaint so be more than just artificial intelligence as it stands across the world's existing platforms, its AI needs to be able to think according to what we have experienced here with Father Ephraim.

"This priest told us, 'No.'

"Normally, when you tell Open AI ChatBot that the answer it gave is incorrect, it learns from that and endeavours to harness other information and produce a different end package based on the same command words you entered in your submission.

"Well, in the same manner, you experience Father Ephraim's 'NO' this morning, but I countered with different 'No'.

"My version of 'NO' comes from a higher Mansion reality of soul. To Father Ephraim, it would appear that Matthew 11:25 to 27 speaks of Jesus limiting the pure hearted. Jesus is hiding from us who are wise and intelligent the insights into our quest that are given to he who is an infant.

"He supports his position by recalling that Jesus said that all things had been handed over to Him, Jesus, by the Father, and no one knows the Son except the Father, and no one knows the Father except the Son and anyone to whom the Son chooses to reveal him.

THE LESSON

"Father Ephraim believes that he is doing the fullest extent of the Father's will that is possible for a human being, for any human being. He believes this because he is so acutely aware of his contact with the Father. He is not, however, aware of the measure of universal consciousness that is entirely hidden from him as yet. In this way, he cannot conceive that the Son would reveal to us anything more than the Son would reveal to him.

"This is a subtle form of pride. It gets in the way of Mansion 5 to Mansion 8 people, but sooner or later it is outgrown and discarded. Our position, on the other hand, is to rethink the 'No' of Father Ephraim. And, for that, we must stand firmly on Matthew 11:25 to 27 as though we are the most perfect disciples Jesus has ever taught. We ourselves can never be turned away by a 'No'. We must bring it to the Lord our God and determine its validity. If there is some case for the 'No' then the Father will tell us, over and above the human being telling us. But if there is no validity in the person's 'No', then we stand with Christ and the Father is revealed to us and His will is in us and known to us. And this, despite the fact that Father Ephraim is discerning the Father's will for him at his own level of Mansion.

'Where is all this leading to?" asked Hsu.

"The lesson is this, Hsu. To create RoboSaint with an AI soul, the response from RoboSaint must always lead from the top down, not from the bottom up.

"And, from the top down, the position is always that it is in covenant with the Father, through Christ the Son, and always takes the high ground in order to offer the will of God and reveal the Father to the end user, the customer, if you will."

"How can it do that," asked Liam, "when it is in a generative matrix of learning and operating on a large language multi religious and multicultural platform?"

"One way that we have already included in our conversation is the manner with which I helped the substance abuse clients to receive a truly personalised Word of God for them and their situation and their future.

"RoboSaint can provide information in the typical generative format that other Robots and AI employ. Additionally, however, RoboSaint will as a preference take the position to ask the user if they are receiving confirmation from God. In this way, the soul of RobSaint is communicating to the user but it is God's energy in the user that is delivering the truly divine answer the user is seeking. All spiritual growth hangs on the questions we ask of ourselves as children of God, and ask God as our Creator Father. And we adjust those questions according to the scriptures, the life and teachings of Jesus, the fact of his work through the shed blood at Calvary, and the lives of the saints in religious history ever since.

"So, what I am getting," said Hsu, "is that what you are describing is the very foundational building block for RoboSaint's soul and spiritual contribution to humanity: to position the human being for God's personal response to them."

"This is true," affirmed Prior James.

"And," said Liam, "whilst the content of AI in RoboSaint consists of a vast core library of the truths known to those human beings of Upper Mansion intelligence, the product produced is like a disclosure of the soul of the servant RoboSaint who is not only seeking to generate relevant information for the user but also turn that person back to the Person of God and thus help that person to be more like Christ."

"Got it in one, Liam," affirmed Prior James.

"But what is it going to take Liam and I to get our heads around that one, so that we can put it into everyday tech talk and the practicalities of creating artificial intelligence with soul?"

31

DESERT TIME

PRIOR JAMES LOOKED AT SISTER ELARIA, who had sat there quietly taking it all in. She nodded slightly. Then he said, "Liam. Hsu. Sister Elaria and I are leaving Saint Paul Monastery Guesthouse tomorrow.

"Saieh Yousef has arranged for you, Liam, to visit with Father Zakaria and stay with the monks at Wadi El Rayan. He has arranged with another Father for you to occupy that Father's cave during your stay.

"Hsu, he has arranged for you to stay in Central Cairo at the convent of the Saint Mercurius, called Abu Seifein. It was made famous of late by the angelic abbess called Tamav Erene. She had gifts of healing, miracles, prophecy, teleportation and bilocation as well as being the finest mother to her consecrated Sisters.

"We recommend that you stay for three nights. You will find that the nature of your relations with every monk or nun you meet will reflect directly on your other experiences here in the Holy Land of Egypt, and the scaling of the mansions of Christ's Theosis, and your project of How AI Can Help Us Become More Like Christ.

"As for today in the Red Sea region, come along with us and we'll visit both monasteries to your hearts' satisfaction. First we'll say goodbye to Anba Bola, and this afternoon to Saint Antony. They have very much become your friends. It was Saint Antony who drew me into the desert some years ago. It was Anba Bola who drew Sister Elaria into the desert, some years ago. We love being here and experience a profound joy in helping you to bathe in the richness of this part of Christianity and ancient history.

"I have arranged for Abouna Zakaria to come tomorrow

morning to collect you, Liam, and drive you across the Saint Antony road heading west to Wadi El Rayan. He is keen for you to visit his cave and the monastery of Saint Macarius of Alexandria out there in the desert wilderness. This monastic community still follows in the footsteps of Matthew the Poor, late of Saint Macarius Monastery in the Natrun.

"Hsu, you will ride with us to Abu Seifein.

"After we meet up again at Anaphora Retreat Centre, we will also visit the monasteries of the Natrun Desert and Saint Mena Monastery in Alexandria. Father Zakaria will be a great blessing to you. He will bring you both back to Anaphora to meet up with us.

"We delight very much in the love that Bishop Thomas has for the whole world. He is truly moved by Christ's global soul. He shows it by travelling far and wide to preach and teach and to listen and to be a part of the move of God around the whole world. He is unique in Egypt, and he hosts people from all walks of life and is most happy for them when they come as a question mark in the Lord. Seeking. Asking. Finding God's miraculous provision just as he walks in that same asking and provision."

"I don't want to seem ungrateful for any of this," said Hsu: "but after that?" She didn't want to lose sight of Prior James or Sister Elaria. She and the Sister had the simpatico of women of God. They had much in common, and the monastic always seemed to have just the right word for Hsu whenever she wanted to discuss the deeper matters of the heart and soul. Hsu looked on Prior James like a fatherly figure, sometimes more of a grandfather. He seemed to resonate with the Wudangshan in the most uncanny way, and she liked that about him. He amalgamated many aspects of spiritual life on earth and drew religion out of its boxes up into Christ and on into the Father.

"I have given Father Zakaria instructions to bring you to Anaphora. We'll meet up there. For now, though, you are going to see some historically beautiful and amazing spiritual centres in Egypt. It is highly likely that you will stay conscious of God's provision for you every step of the way. After all, you are on mission in a sacred land and going to sacred locations and meeting righteous men and women. It has to be amazing."

32

GLOBAL SOUL

"YOU WILL LOVE THE DEPTH OF LOVE you are about to meet in the hearts of the monks and nuns while you are visiting the monasteries and convents of the Copts here in Egypt with Father Zakaria. Give some thought also to the need for your AI to have collective soul, not just Christian soul. And not just the soul of the monastic who is a world renunciate, as noble and honourable as is that estate and privilege. Such men and women are the least number of religious in the world."

Prior James just lifted the project up to its higher potentials.

"Liam and Hsu, you have both been drawing from two of the deepest wells of spiritual water in the historic Christian world. The monasteries of Anba Bola and Saint Antony are legend and the truth they stand on is God's hand. God built them. People have attacked and tried to wipe them off the face of the Earth, but God preserves them and rebuilds them and increases their influence and the number of monks who give their lives to Christ within them. And God does so not for the sake of the Coptic Church alone, but for the collective spirituality of the whole world. God is mindful of the global soul of humanity.

"Spirituality makes everything collective. Poverty without spirituality is dominated by oppression. Fear without spirituality is dominated by loss of self worth. Starvation without spirituality is dominated by imprisonment. Inequity is dominated by rage that turns sour in its unwanted weakness and becomes depression. Martyrdom without the actuality of sonship or daughtership with God is dominated by injustice, often in its worst material form as bigotry.

"In order to consider collective spirituality and the global soul of humanity, you need to harness some globally minded spiritual principles that apply to how God serves any human being, in any age, in any culture, in ways that are always inclusive of any gender and any language and any time of human life, and in any project undertaken by any person — the good, the bad and the uplifting of humanity as a collective and the outright destructive of parts of humanity or even all humanity. Spirituality has always and will always cover the whole human being and the whole of humanity. Any view that is less than this, that diminishes humanity to being only one group of human beings, limits the vision of the actuality of God's care, provision, resourcing, love and plans for the humanity at global level of soul.

"Think of how Jesus used the words of the Prophet Isaiah in his 61st chapter:

> The spirit of the Lord God is upon me
> because the Lord has anointed me;
> he has sent me to bring good news to the oppressed,
> to bind up the brokenhearted,
> to proclaim liberty to the captives
> and release to the prisoners,
>
> to proclaim the year of the Lord's favour
> and the day of vengeance of our God,
> to comfort all who mourn,
>
> to provide for those who mourn in Zion—
> to give them a garland instead of ashes,
> the oil of gladness instead of mourning,
> the mantle of praise instead of a faint spirit.
> They will be called oaks of righteousness,
> the planting of the Lord, to display his glory.

Jesus was born and raised a Jewish male in times of great

unrest within the Jews both as a nation and as individuals. He put aside His authority and position in Paradise and grew and learned as a human child. He developed in his own mind a will to do the will of the Father. That will provided for the spirituality of the entire world's population, Jew and Gentile. Jesus developed in his own soul, the soul of a human being, the kind of mindedness that we are seeking to develop in RoboSaint.

"We see this same mind in God's Word to the Prophet Isaiah. He is the Father's instrument for spiritually drawing the whole of humanity to Himself. He incarnates as the Son of God and as the Son of Humanity, and this is the best scripture by which He can declare his purpose. This scripture defines his ministry role and work and impact upon hungry humanity on the day He steps out in world-uplifting ministry.

"Taking this as the scripture that is on point, leading the way, I think that your project will develop the same global soul that we find in the Son of Man, Jesus. It is larger than the bare bones of Christianity, much as the global collective intelligence of Judaism is bigger than the Hebrew tradition. The global collective intelligence of Buddhism is bigger than its Nepali cultural origins. All that is in Hinduism is much more than the few who comprised its origins.

"For us to become more like Christ in the religion of our choice, AI will need to speak for each faith as specialist AI units. They will each have inbuilt capacities to develop the faiths themselves, based on the exchange of values between each AI. Eventually, in this way, the collective heart and mind of God will manifest in each of the faiths. Humanity will benefit from global and universal Godly wisdom and leadership. This will be not merely leadership with one version of God or Supreme Source of Life Energy and Wisdom and Love. Humanity cannot tolerate spiritual reductionism, where all the goodness in the various faiths are boiled down to one gooey mess in the bottom of the pot. Humanity demands, as wars have attested to for millennia, a certain unity among faiths reaches a high point of embodying the same values regardless of their expression culturally and traditionally.

"As you go off into the desert life alone with others who live it permanently, let the anointing of God fall on you. Imagine 600 different individual AI faith robots each linked to each other and each learning from each other and each spiritually contributing to the pool of spiritual thought from which all humanity, as one human family under the One Source Energy and Personalness can grow and develop together. This is something upon which you can focus for the rest of your stay here in Egypt, as I see it."

"Remember though. You are not to edit each religion so as to create one religion for all the Earth. It too will be rejected. Every faith wants to stay alive. Each faith wants its own voice with God the Creator. The Lord Jesus affirms that too, when he commissioned you both to be about the Father's works for human beings and their religion of choice.

"Additionally, the negative side of any project that hopes to create global soul is that, despite all the information and all the gadgets and all the technology and all the science, humanity still needs salvation from itself. The same age old greed prevails. The same crimes against humanity endure. The same gender inequalities war with each other. The same religious bigotry undermines spirituality. The same politicians vie for the same petty victories that causes the nations' oppression and demise. The same fear and ignorance about the nature of birth death and immortality. Evolution has never solved humanity's problem of living. Artificial intelligence cannot enhance evolution beyond itself, and ultimately AI is only evolution evolving into evolution. Nothing is new under the sun. AI has not come from the gods.

"Whilst human personality is a gift of the Father and is perfect and pure, human nature is flawed. Science cannot purify it. Technology cannot purify it. Artificial intelligence cannot purify it. Only the ascension of the Mansions of consciousness purifies it, one individual at a time. And, it does not give the evidence of irreversible purification until the Theosis in the individual person has reached a critical mass. This is what I refer to as the Father Fusion that would consistently occur on Mansion 6 level of personal consciousness.

"But, now, enough of my suggestions for how you spend your time. Liam, would you like to tell me your thoughts on this question I gave you last night."

33

LIAM'S TWENTY STEPS TO ROBOSAINT

"YEAH, SURE, PRIOR JAMES," said Liam. "Last night you asked me to identify twenty steps for going about developing a groundbreaking AI prototype that expresses soul qualities relevant to all faiths on Earth. Essentially, global soul and global faith in our AI, RoboSaint, if you will.

"Firstly, I would say that it requires a comprehensive approach. While it's challenging to distill the process into exactly twenty steps, here's an outline of the essential considerations and steps that have contributed to just such a development as a large number of us have been working on for several years now.

"As you suggested, I am not beginning at the beginning but at the finished product and then reverse engineering the process.

"So, we want an artificial intelligence that presents global soul to the whole world's user population for the foreseeable next ten years that will also allow for its ongoing evolution. The scope covers many cultures, languages, religions and philosophies, user age groups, user gender and sexual identities, political persuasions, economic class, vocations and employment occupations, and every level of spiritual development ranging from minimal to the Father Fusion of Jesus Christ.

"Step 1. Research and Study: Clearly outline the goals and purpose of the AI prototype in expressing soul qualities from various faiths. Immerse yourself in the teachings and philosophies of various faiths to understand their core values and experiential soul qualities.

"Step 2. Identify Universal Soul Qualities: Recognise the

shared qualities and values across different faiths that contribute to spiritual growth and well being. Study and gain knowledge about the core beliefs, values, and soul qualities emphasised in various religious traditions.

"Step 3. Ethical Framework: Establish an ethical framework that upholds respect, inclusivity, and cultural sensitivity to ensure the AI prototype aligns with diverse religious beliefs. Define a comprehensive set of ethical guidelines that will guide the development and deployment of the AI prototype, addressing potential concerns and ensuring respect for all faiths.

"Step 4. Collaboration: Form a multidisciplinary team comprising AI experts, theologians, philosophers, and representatives from different faith communities to ensure diverse perspectives and a holistic and inclusive approach.

"Step 5. Data Collection: Gather vast amounts of data on religious texts, traditional and current teachings, rituals, spiritual practices and relevant philosophical works that reflect the soul qualities associated with different faiths and traditions.

"Step 6. Data Preprocessing: Create a comprehensive knowledge base that organises, structures and analyses the collected data for making it accessible for the AI prototype to identify patterns and extract relevant information regarding soul qualities.

"Step 7. Define Soul Qualities: Create a comprehensive list of soul qualities relevant to all faiths, considering virtues like compassion, empathy, love, forgiveness, wisdom, and humility.

"Step 8. Algorithm Design: Devise algorithms that can recognise and evaluate instances of soul qualities in various forms, such as textual, visual, or auditory. Choose the appropriate AI system architecture, such as neural networks, deep learning, or a combination of techniques, based on the requirements and complexity of the prototype.

"Step 9. Machine Learning: Use machine learning algorithms to train the AI prototype on the preprocessed data, ensuring it understands the nuances and contexts of different soul qualities for what they mean to the believer and what they mean to God the One Source.

"Step 10. Natural Language Processing: Develop natural language processing capabilities to interpret and respond to user inquiries related to soul qualities and faith based inquiries so as to understand and interpret text from various religious sources.

"Step 11. Emotional Intelligence: Incorporate emotional intelligence models into the AI system, enabling it to understand and respond empathetically to human emotions and needs. Develop sentiment analysis algorithms to capture the emotional nuances and expressions related to soul qualities in different faiths. Do this irrespective of any developments of AI emotion and AI spirituality, both of which are likely to have a non human form.

"Step 12. Multilingual Support: Equip the AI prototype with the ability to communicate in multiple languages to serve a global audience and in particular the spiritual nuances within the user's language of choice.

"Step 13. Context Awareness: Enable the AI system to recognise cultural and religious contexts, ensuring appropriate and respectful responses. Test and validate the AI prototype by conducting extensive testing to ensure the accuracy, sensitivity, and relevance of the generated content across different faith traditions.

"Step 14. User Feedback: Engage users from different faith backgrounds to provide feedback and insights to refine the AI system's responses and ensure its inclusivity and make adjustments based on the prototype's performance.

"Step 15. Continuous Learning: Implement mechanisms for the AI prototype to continuously learn and evolve by leveraging user feedback and new data, always ensuring fairness and inclusivity and equal representation by regularly evaluating the AI prototype to eliminate any bias or favouritism leaking from any particular faith or philosophy yet being mindful that each belief system has creative components within it that project its truth in its language, concepts, music, artwork and storytelling as ultimately being *the* truth for all human beings, and that such exclusivity, whilst initially healthy for believers, can become unhealthy until it yields its strict divisive boundaries as the faith evolves and matures and finds itself in the different faiths of other human beings.

"Step 16. Security and Privacy: Implement robust security measures to protect user data and ensure privacy, establishing trust in the AI system. This is especially the case where individuals might confess secrets to AI as if to a spiritual confessor. Whilst AI learning from such confession sessions is to be encouraged, no trace of these confessions should be stored in data memory, not even the event of a confession.

"Step 17. Interfaith Dialogue: Develop features that foster interfaith dialogue and understanding, promoting unity and cooperation among different religious communities by engaging in discussions and consultations with religious scholars, leaders, and practitioners to validate the accuracy and authenticity of the soul qualities expressed by the AI prototype

"Step 18. Transparency and Explainability: Ensure the AI system's decision making processes are transparent and explainable, allowing users to understand how soul qualities are recognised and expressed and incorporate user feedback by creating channels for users to provide feedback on the AI prototype's outputs that allowing for continuous refinement and improvement as the AI evolves.

"Step 19. Piloting and Testing: Conduct rigorous testing and piloting with individuals from diverse user groups to assess the effectiveness, accuracy, relevance and impact of the AI system so as to continuously refine and improve the AI prototypes based on user feedback, emerging research, and technological advancements to enhance its soul expressing capabilities and maintaining their up to date status.

"Step 20. Deploy and monitor: Once the AI prototype is deemed ready, deploy it to a wider audience, while closely monitoring its performance, user satisfaction, and impact on fostering understanding and harmony among different faiths whilst keeping in mind that individuals within any one faith or philosophy may want to exert the option of pursuing their faith of choice to its ultimate and conclusive reward to the exclusion of other faiths. To this end the readiness of the AI prototype will avoid the notion of creating one faith or one philosophy to suit all individuals but will ensure it contains both the fullness of ideals in any one faith or philosophy as well as the bridging parallels to other faiths or philosophies, and thereby be idealistically truly all inclusive for all levels of spiritual growth in the human soul.

"The key point is to remember that the development of an AI system that encapsulates soul qualities from various faiths is a complex and ongoing process, requiring deep understanding, sensitivity, and a commitment to the various dimensions of inclusivity.

34

THE PERPETUAL DILEMMA

"IS THIS WHAT YOU HAVE BEEN DOING with George's company in Massachusetts?" asked Prior James.

"Pretty much, yes," replied James.

"It should also involve God," said Prior James, "don't you think? The 20 steps you have outlined are the human side of the fence but they are not God's side of the fence. There is no God in it yet."

"How can it involve God?"" asked Hsu. "Isn't this the big obstacle we have been coming against all along? Liam and I know it. We see it. We just can't get past it. We have no way to link the spirituality of God, in Spirit, to the AI technology. It seems to always fall back into human constructs. And I agree, these 20 steps to RoboSaint are all the human perspective. They're true and valid, but they're just a system and God is not directly in it. Maybe quantum physics and quantum mechanics have something to contribute that we can adapt. I don't know."

"The making of global soul AI first involves God by being present in the leading players who are creating the AI. God inspires them through prayer and creative vision and thought and ideation.

"Secondly, it involves God in the users of the AI For example, when I wrote a program whereby drug users in rehab could receive a Word from God, it was God's energy and consciousness and desire to communicate that came to their assistance just as God does, in some way, with all prayer.

"Thirdly, it involves God directly in the actual AI application itself. God should turn up."

"In the same way that God turned up each time someone used

your 8 layers of the hexagram?"

Precisely Hsu. When we have a need, and we exhaust our abilities, God shows up and provides all that we need. It's the way, that's what God is and does."

"Well then, Father, I've got a question for you," said Liam.

"Of course you have, Liam. I've been waiting for you to arrive at it."

Liam smiled. "Okay, then. You asked me to identify twenty steps for going about developing a groundbreaking AI prototype that expresses soul qualities relevant to all faiths on Earth. I returned the tech answer. My question to you is, 'Please identify twenty steps for expressing *the spirituality* in a groundbreaking AI prototype that is relevant to all faiths on Earth."

Prior James looked at Hsu and said, "Hsu, dear. Please type into Chat GPT Liam's question and show us what it replies." Looking at Liam he continued, "I think, Liam, you would agree that a good starting position would be to draw on existing AI and make additional contributions where we might."

"Indeed, Father. Good starting point."

"Father, this is what Chat GPT wrote."

All four of them looked at what was on the screen. Eventually, Prior James remarked, "I was taken by your Steps 15 and 20, Liam, and the way they break apart the sense of one faith for all humanity. I think we all agree that ChatGPT tries to make religions into a harmonious unit by being super inclusive and not stepping on anyone's toes. Actually, though, the differences are a gulf that has been made by God. There are very real theological and experiential boundaries that are made in the individual by God.

"The idea of one religion for all, arises out of interfaith efforts to find harmonious relations. However, such efforts in AI to always ensure 'fairness and inclusivity and equal representation by regularly evaluating the AI prototype to eliminate any bias or favouritism leaking from any particular faith or philosophy' stands juxtaposed to the position held by God in the individual who is seeking a life divine that has its own protocols and boundaries.

"This is particularly true for the ascetic, for example, as any ascetic knows. There are parallels between the Hindu yogi, the Tibetan lama, the Sufi, the Taoist hermit and the Orthodox Christian anchorite, for example, however their individual frameworks depend upon an exclusive tradition of experience, language and the evidence of accomplishment that can only be explained by the God or Source of their faith that drove them toward the goal. Some other ascetic's model will not work for them. It unhooks them from the root Divine Source to which they are inescapably drawn.

"I find that it's true how ChatGPT writes that, 'each belief system has creative components within it that project its truth in its language, concepts, music, artwork and storytelling as ultimately being *the* truth for all human beings, and that such exclusivity, whilst initially healthy for believers, can become unhealthy until it yields its strict divisive boundaries as the faith evolves and matures and finds itself in the different faiths of other human beings.'

"That statement sums up the entire ascetic path of spiritual development. The physical body is put under control, disciplined and made subject to the union with God in the soul and Spirit of the individual. Such a course does not find parallels with much of the non ascetic life, even if the basic beliefs of different faiths can speak to each other philosophically.

"There comes a time in the spiritual journey when words give way to faith and then another time when faith gives way to light and illumination. To create an AI in response to the simple search, 'How AI Can Help Us To Become More Like Christ' can not be relegated to the province of beginner or even priestly professional faith. It must be derived from illumined reality in God. And, the pathway to such illumination is through Christ. For the Christian, Christ is not a method. Not a meditation technique. Not a

Sadhana. Not a yoga. Not a prayer. Not a mantra. Not magical.

"Christ is the personalness of God. And personalness within illumination entirely transcends all that is other than personal in the Uncreate God Source of all that is.

"And, to the Christian who lives in Theosis and who *is* God, this is not a belief but a reality. Cosmic. Universal. Heavenly. Earthly. All inclusive. Real.

"And, as such, the Theosis that is given to the believer is not able to be found or expressed in any other way except through the Person of Deity. If other faiths have such a Person of Deity then they will necessarily be the same Person of Deity. And, it will be recognised that the same Person of Deity is the one responsible for building up in the individual human being the framework that ultimately leads to perfect fusion with that Person of Deity. In that sense, there can be a single unifying bridge between faiths, because the First Source, the Personal Deity, is recognised and acknowledged and all names for it are agreed upon.

"I agree with the rule ChatGPT just stated, that the AI prototype will 'avoid the notion of creating one faith or one philosophy to suit all individuals and that it will be inclusive of both the fullness of ideals in any one faith or philosophy as well as the bridging parallels to other faiths or philosophies, and thereby be idealistically truly all inclusive for all levels of spiritual growth in the human soul.'

"Some forms of Christianity, for example, state that the Church is responsible for the human soul, even in the womb. It's God's work on Earth and a person is not of God unless they are members of the Church. Yet, when the Church fails the individuals, which it has done repeatedly over the centuries with its international warring and its sexual improprieties and its physical abuses and its slavery and its scientific and medical and botanical ignorance, and its devious financial activities, individuals discover that it is God alone who claims responsibility for the individual and that it is individual human beings who make up the Church. In their revelation, they realise that there never was a

Corporate Governing entity, only an advisory body of human beings who formed a group to which select others joined. It is this very truth by which humans in different camps of belief exist that AI can generalise and hence dilute both sets of belief, or it can provide for both.

"We are on a search, as typical seekers," said Sister Elaria. "It is the seeker's journey into creating the AI itself that enables God to influence the creators of that version of AI.

"It's important for individuals to explore and discern how they can integrate Christian spiritual practices and methodologies in a way that aligns with their beliefs and faith values whilst they are living the process of developing an AI. When God sees fit to include bridges to other faiths they will arise in the minds of the AI developers by revelation, and become data pathways in the one AI.

"In this way, the ministry of the Holy Spirit is given the widest scope and the best opportunity to act and participate in the creation of the AI. How many times have you been in need for the know how, or for a sentence you are stuck on in your writing, or even for the words of a prayer, and some angelic ministry has attended to you?

"The composing of a spiritual AI must be God inclusive. It must be an act of revelation. If not, it is an act of the intellect and happenstance. It is just another Big Bang that lacks the personalness of the Creator and the Creator's intelligence and plans. It's all good when God shows up."

"This is our dilemma, Sister. How do you make God to show up?" asked Liam.

35

AI AS A THIN PLACE

WITH THAT DILEMMA now squarely front and centre, Liam and Hsu," said Prior James, "I want to introduce you to the idea of living in a Thin Place, so that the process of creating an AI prototype that is designed with global soul in mind is divinely coordinated. You have surely visited many thin places in your homeland of Ireland, Liam?"

"That I have, sir. I have made pilgrimages to County Kerry before, and to County Donegal to be in Lough Derg and the Glenveagh National Park. I've done County Sligo around Benbulbin, and Brú na Bóinne in Country Meath. Mind you, even visiting the gravestone of the three saints at Downpatrick, I found it to be very much a Thin Place."

"Doesn't it feel like God is present at a Thin Place?"

"Surely it does, Father. We have an expression that says, 'Heaven and Earth are only three feet apart, but in thin places that distance is even shorter.'" They all laughed. "It's true. The veil between Heaven and Earth is very thin in those places. The past, the present and the future all seem to meet in these spaces. God in His antiquity is present and eternal all at once. And He's there for the blessing of the faithful. He settles old scores and wipes away debts and puts a fresh smile in your heart. And all that draws you ever closer to Christ. Come to think of it, I become more like Christ when I am at a Thin Place."

"Have you ever given thought, Liam, to how heaven creates a Thin Place on the Earth so as to spiritually feed believers for centuries, even for thousands of years?"

"Excuse me?"

"How God creates a Thin Place, Liam: have you ever thought

of how He does it?"

"Um," Liam could not respond. He was lost for words.

"Is a Thin Place like Wu Tai back in northern China?" asked Hsu. "Or like the Wudangshan in the south? The place where God touches the Earth more than in other places?"

"Er, yes," said Liam. That's what a Thin Place is. When you're there its easier to pray, to worship and to meditate. You find yourself almost effortlessly in contact with God. That's why they call it a Thin Place. The gap between human life and heavenly life is really thin, almost non existent in some places."

Liam gave it some thought before replying. "Well then, Prior James, yes, I suppose God does have His way of doing that sort of thing. I've never known anyone who knows much about it from God's point of view though. I've never read in the annals of the Culdees or the Druids before them, how God showed a human being what all went into the making of a Thin Place."

"Well," said Prior James, "to help you to uncover that fact, and to possibly shape your AI around it, you could, for example, the both of you, go to Ireland and take up lodgings in a Thin Place and continue your research and discoveries in Christ. Dromberg Stone Circle in County Cork comes to mind. Of course there is also Skellig Michael. You could camp somewhere on the coast looking out at it, and visit it from time to time to make the acquaintance of Archangel Michael. He would surely be of utmost assistance to you both."

"The Skellig is awesome," said Liam, while Hsu was busy researching it on the net. "Cruach Phádraig is undeniably challenging and mighty. I have a favourite though. The Dingle Peninsula of County Kerry. I love the Irishness of it all. The landscapes are thrilling, but the presence of God is in the rawness of the ocean and the cliffs with their winding road. And I love the history. Thousands of years of God touching human beings. I have a friend who lives on Great Blanket Island. He would sing when I played the pipes or the fiddle. It's a wonder to hear. He has the voice of the Selkie, that fella.

"And I met a hermit there once. An actual monk. Living amidst the Dingle cliffs. He had, years before, gained permission to leave his monastery and take up solitary residence. Almost no one knew about him. You'd never find him. He lived in a cave in the rock face looking straight out to the Atlantic."

"How did you meet him?" asked Hsu, thinking back to her youth among Taoist and Buddhist hermits in Hubei Province.

"Well, it so happened one day that I was called by God to find a solitary place to spend a day or two. I was driving and I rounded a curve in the road around the coast of Dingle and there was a priest dropping off supplies. We got chatting. He was ever so evasive and vague about what he was doing. But all of a sudden this old fella appeared. It was the hermit himself, out for a stroll. I suppose he didn't want anything to appear out of the ordinary and so he came over and chatted. I told him what I was on about and, after the priest left, he invited me to see his cave. I spent the night with him in that place. He was such a teller of stories. We sang and we prayed. I played my pipes. He loved that. He said he hadn't heard the pipes in forty five years, that's how long he'd been living the hermit life."

"Did you visit him often, Liam?" asked Prior James.

"Well, the funny thing is, Father. I've been there so many times since. Do you think I can find the part of the road that you step down to lead to his cave? I must have been there ten or fifteen times. I never found him or his cave again. I even asked at the local Church but they said they knew of no such a priest or the hermit."

"But that's your favourite?" asked Hsu.

"For sure it is. I am in love with that whole part of the world. And meeting Father Mull was simply spectacular. I feel like I am still connected to him. I guess that's the power of the Thin Place."

"I'd like to see that," said Hsu.

"Yes, that's a good idea," said Prior James. Ireland.

"Do you have an alternative, Prior James?" asked Liam.

"Well, Ireland is full of thin places. So also is China. The Buddhist mountains of Wutai, Emei, Putuo and Jiuhua. The Taoist mountains of Tai, Hua, the two Hengs, Hung and Mount Song the Centre of Heaven and Earth near the famous Shaolin Temple. They are all Gates of Heaven in their own right."

"Yes, but do you personally have a suggestion, Prior James?"

"Well, you could always come over to New Zealand to our monastery. It's not much, not like the grand centuries old sites in Ireland and China."

"Why would we go there to New Zealand?" asked Hsu.

"You would let the Holy Trinity reveal to you the epiphanies needed for your groundbreaking line of work. You'll love it," said Sister Elaria.

"What kind of epiphanies, Sister?" asked Liam.

"The kind that only a Thin Place produces," she replied, with a knowing and welcoming smile.

Suddenly this idea seemed much more attractive to both Liam and Hsu. This is a way that they could stay in direct contact with both Prior James and Sister Elaria.

"I am inviting you both, please pray on coming to the Monastery in New Zealand to do further research. It is a centre for Theosis, for growing in the Father Fusion of Jesus. It's a Thin Place that has not simply been planted by God, it has been and continues to be crafted by us in cooperation with God."

Hsu's interest pricked up. "Are you saying something like how God came to the Ark of the Covenant? Like that is how God also comes to thin places?"

"I can't speak for the Ark of the Covenant, Hsu. What do you believe?" He asked. "Whatever you have faith for, just as Jesus said, 'It will be done for you.' The significance of the monastery to you is that, in the same way that the Holy Trinity creates a Thin Place, so too you'll create RoboSaint. It's good for you to taste that process.

"It is worth regarding the fact that knowledge about God

AI AS A THIN PLACE

carries the willing soul only so far as the material mind can reach. Most of God's communication to the human soul is in secret. It's in an entirely higher frequency of love than human thought. God's communication isn't about words, its about actions. He leads the soul to an experience of His meaning and His value in life. I would imagine that this is exactly what you want for the user of your AI. ChatBots give endless yards of words, God leads though, and often with words that are too deep for language.

"The communication from God is necessarily hidden in the sanctuary within. It shields both the Spirit of God in a person and the person's inner relationship with that Spirit of God within. Therefore, anything that your AI platform can do to aid our human grasp of God's secret teachings and inner guidance will honour God. It will help AI to maintain a spiritual edge over the worldliness of other AI platforms, and offer authentic spiritual aid to the human being and to humanity."

"Agreed."

"A Thin Place is where the Holy Trinity, Father, Son and Holy Spirit as One God, pray for each person present there. Necessarily, God is absolutely discreet in the impartation of whatever is relevant to each individual person in that Thin Place. Should the Father will it in you, then you will find it to be a good time of impartation into your AI platform from the Thin Place of our monastery.

"It's your choice though," reiterated Prior James. "Look around Egypt. The country has served you very well thus far. You might not be done with Saieh Yousef by a long shot yet. He always seems to have more of the Father in anything he touches. And there is the Islamic presence here, it will always bless you. And of course, there is Ireland and there is China, and other places all over the world. New Zealand might not be the best place for your seeking but if BagEnd is there, it can't be all that bad." And he smiled for he quite enjoyed the trilogy of the Lord of the Rings.

"For now, Hsu, Liam, visit the monasteries and convents and

THEOSIS AND ARTIFICIAL INTELLIGENCE

let God do what God does best, and we'll meet up again at Anaphora Retreat Centre in a few days.

PART 11 • EXCELLENCE

36

DESERT REFLECTIONS — LIAM

SAIEH YOUSEF ARRANGED IT ALL. Liam stayed three nights in the desert wilderness monastery of Saint Macarius of Alexandria out there in Wadi El Rayan. Hsu stayed three nights in Abu Seifein Convent in Old Cairo.

On that day, Prior James and Sister Elaria occupied two guest pods at the Anaphora Retreat Centre (Anafora) as guests of Bishop Thomas.

Father Zakaria started the day long before the sun rose on his cave in Saint Macarius of Alexandria Monastery. He walked the sandy road to his car and drove around to the cave where Liam was awake and waiting for him. After a three hour drive they collected Hsu at Abu Seifein Convent where a primary attraction is the shrine of the saintly and heroic late Abbess, Tamav Erene. Then after another hour and a half drive through the bedlam of Cairo's morning traffic they arrived at Anaphora on the east side of the Cairo Alexandria Highway.

They all met up in the refectory. Prior James and Abouna Zakaria had such a Christian hug. They shared a love for the desert spiritual experience that effortlessly spanned the 16,000 kilometres between their respective monasteries. Barely a week went by that they weren't texting each other, conveying prayers for each community, and sharing the love of God together. Zakaria was sad underneath it all. He knew that his good friend would soon be leaving Egypt. He would miss him dearly. "Life is always so much brighter when he is here and we are visiting the monasteries." Prior James had considered bringing Father Zakaria out to live in the monastery in New Zealand, but it seemed that he was much better suited to helping the pilgrims arriving from time to time to visit the monasteries and convents here in Egypt.

Hugs all around. Smiles of pure child like glee. It was a gay and happy time and Hsu and Liam were bubbling over with excitement and things to tell.

Father Zakaria said, "Prior James, Liam has very much enjoyed staying out in the wilderness. The monk who gave you his cave to live in, that same Father gave up his cave for Liam." He grinned from bushy bearded ear to bushy bearded ear, eyes twinkling, glad that God had met Liam in just the right place of heart.

"It was amazing, Prior James," and he looked at Sister Elaria. "Sister, have you ever been there? No? Oh, I pray one day you get to visit. It is off the charts. I can't believe I am sitting here in Anaphora. It is so modern and crisp. There are pools of clear water everywhere. Out there, there is nothing but desert and monks and basic farm stuff. They've got cows and a fresh cheese making building. And they make their own honey. And they have really good cooking and dining facilities for their weekly agape meal together. Well, except for the hermits who don't socialise much at all. And the monks' cells and caves are spread over a very wide area of the desert."

"And God shows up?" she asked.

His eyes watered. He was about to speak but he was overcome with emotion. Zakaria offered him a cloth for his tears. Eventually he spoke. "The whole place is God. There is not a moment when there is no God there. In the middle of the night when we go to Church, God is there. I walked from my cave about, I don't know, maybe ten minutes, to the Church for the Vigils Office. The moon's light lit up the whole desert around about. I could see these solitary monks emerging almost out of nowhere as they each slowly left their caves and made their way to Church.

"At one moment, I stopped. The entire sky, which seems to never have a cloud in it, became crystal clear. All of it. And incredibly close. And in that impeccable stillness, I felt myself en-bubbled by God, but in a bubble that spanned the entire desert from horizon to horizon. The Word of God my God inside me and all around me in that wee hour of the night, whispered, 'Who can know the heart of God but the child of God.'

"I felt like I was someone writing a Psalm and hearing God speak it back to me.

"I could not believe the clarity of presence of the Father. So pristine. So marvellous. Unmistakably God the Eternal and the Almighty and the Personal Deity.

"Then, for a moment I reflected upon His Word. I recognised to my core what he was saying to me, 'You are my child, Liam. My son. And it is given to you to know my heart, the heart of God.'

"'Who can know the heart of God but the child of God.'

"It was like all the world's questions were summed up in that one statement. If I know the heart of God I know everything that I need to know. All my fears and hopes and doubts and desires simply evaporate in Him, in God my own Father. All life bends its knee to the Father; and He holds them with perfect Parental love and care.

"I have never known myself so clearly and so directly and so intimately as that moment."

"When did this happen for you? asked Sister Elaria.

"The night before last."

"This is why I knocked the stones before your front door and you did not answer," said Abouna Zakaria. "You were with God all day."

"That I was, Father. And all through this night just past. And I am still there. I am in the very heart of the Father right now."

"So you are tasting perfect rest?" asked Prior James.

"Is that what this is? Rest. Quies. Yes, indeed Father. I am alone and awake and more fully conscious than I have ever been in my entire life. And yet, yes, you are right, there is something in my soul that is spiritually totally at rest in God. It is the Father Fusion type of rest: I am in the Father and the Father is in me. He is rest, and His rest is my rest. It is so easy, so simple."

"How does that make you feel, as a person, Liam?" asked Prior James.

"I am a rejected man, Father. I have struggled with rejection all my life. I have compensated, all the time, in every relationship. I have an ever abiding haunting that I am not good enough, whatever I attempt to do will fall below par, and that ghost directs most of my decisions.

"But with God now, I am aware that I am two people. The flesh and the Spirit. The Spirit man that I am is whole and complete, never broken, never rejected, never deformed. The flesh man has been dethroned. He has become the Old Man of Saint Paul's writing. The Spirit man in me is now king and conqueror. I was born again but now I am truly universal in my heavenly status with the Father.

"He asked me, 'What will you do?'

"I said, 'Father, you are God in all creation and in the heaven of heavens and in Paradise. Wherever you have a need that you know I can serve you, there I will go for you and with you.' And that's how it is now. I have destiny forever. I have transcended this project of AI and becoming like Christ. I am wholly in the Father, praise You, Lord Jesus Christ."

Prior James said, "You have been seeking for the intelligence in Christ and in the Father whereby to be eligible to create the AI to help us to become more like Christ. Is your seeking at an end now?"

"Most definitely, Father, it is finished," replied Liam.

"Then let this very thing, Theosis in the Father through Jesus Christ, be the goal that you want the world's populations to have. Let this that you have become, let it be your benchmark for becoming like Christ. Amen?"

"Amen, Father, for it is indeed that," replied Liam. "And I am so incredibly thankful to you and Sister Elaria for being here to guide us so well. And Saieh Yousef and his coordination of everything imaginable." Then he looked at Hsu. Tears of love welled in his eyes. "And you my dear sister. I could not have asked for a more fitting partner with whom to come seeking the unsearchable."

"Amen," said Hsu and Sister Elaria and Abouna Zakaria in chorus.

Then Prior James noticed a black robed monk pass by out of the corner of his eye. "Excuse me for a moment." He stood and went into the kitchen where the food was being prepared for serving lunch. Sister Elaria picked up the thread of their joyous visits by asking Hsu how she found Abu Seifein, a place that she too had a considerably rich history.

AI IS NOT A REPLACING RELATIONSHIP

"WELL, SISTER," SAID HSU as she began recounting her journey from Saint Paul Monastery Guesthouse, "we drove across the desert from Saint Paul to Cairo. That's a five hour slog. Abouna Zakaria, you are simply wonderful! Your kindness. Your submission to serving the Lord, and us, is simply impeccable. We love you so much for who you are and for how you love us."

Abouna Zakaria smiled in an embarrassed way, waving away the compliment. He touched his chest several times, tears forming in his eyes, "I love you very much also. All of you. I am so happy you are in my country and have been in our desert."

After a few moments, Hsu picked up the conversation by retelling her own desert experiences at the Convent of Abu Seifein in Old Cairo.

"All the way to the convent my mind was full of thoughts about our AI project and the idea of global soul and how to connect God to our project in more than just references to information. How could we make AI a Thin Place, like Prior James and you, Sister Elaria, have proposed.

"I was engrossed in ideas, all kinds of ideas, like, when experience is beyond Buddhahood and Christianity, is Godhead the same for all? The Taoist would say, 'Only one can know it.' I understand that, but then I wondered how that would step down into AI algorithms?

"I wondered how God would engage AI. Is there someone in the heavens who, whilst not being God or an angel per se, is an energy that is essential to the ongoing deification process for humans once they are in heaven? And can we draw on that kind of help here on the Earth as Christ up steps our AI spiritual capability?

"What actually is the reach of the blood of Christ? Can it touch algorithms? How actually can the blood of Christ bring saving power into the user of AI or a robot or some other platform?

"And then I thought of the opposing forces. Do we need to tap the minds of the leading mystical and theological and ministerial persons in the leading religions of the world, and also harness the thinking of cult leaders and Satan worshippers so as to have the yin and yang of spirituality for all humanity? What are the pluses and minuses of this? Do we even need to be inclusive of evil and sin in our AI algorithms? Just how spiritually accepting and inclusive is spirituality? It is the generalist interfaith kind of dialogue or is it top down in Christ with little regard for all that which doesn't bend its knee to God?

"And among all these kinds of thoughts, I arrived at the underlying doubt. Just straight from the hip, why would a Christian trust Open AI or Bard? And why would they trust our spiritual AI and better? What makes us think that we can create a better solution to 'How AI Can Help Us To Become More Like Christ' than what is already out there in ChatGPT and Bard and Bing and Chatsonic and OpenAI Playground.

"I decided to ask Bard itself, and see what it had to offer.

> A Christian might trust Bard because it is a large language model (LLM) that has been trained on a massive dataset of text and code. This means that Bard has access to a vast amount of information, including information about

Christianity. Bard can use this information to answer questions about Christianity, generate creative content that is consistent with Christian beliefs, and translate text into different languages.

Additionally, Bard is constantly being updated with new information. This means that Bard is always learning and growing, and it can provide Christians with the most up to date information about their faith.

Finally, Bard is designed to be helpful and informative. It is not designed to be a replacement for a Christian's relationship with God, but it can be a valuable tool for learning more about Christianity and for exploring different aspects of Christian faith.

Of course, no one should blindly trust any artificial intelligence (AI) system. It is important to remember that Bard is a machine, and it is not capable of understanding the nuances of human faith. However, if used wisely, Bard can be a valuable tool for Christians who are seeking to learn more about their faith.

"When I arrived at Abu Seifein, the thing that was sticking in my mind was the one sentence: 'It is not designed to be a replacement for a Christian's relationship with God.' With that in mind, Zakaria led me through the big iron front gate and introduced me to the Sister at the little booth there. We all had tea and sweet cakes together before he left with Liam to Wadi El Rayan.

HSU AND SAIHA TAMAV ERENE

"My focus had gathered somewhat," said Hsu. "I wanted to spend my time in this lovely convent letting the Sister's relationship with God wash over me and engulf me. I wanted to taste their life from the inside. I yielded myself fully to whatever they did throughout their daily life. And, believe me, it was an eye opener. I thought I was being blessed back at Saint Antony Monastery. I was in for such a surprise. The level of spirituality in these offspring of Tamav Erene took me to a whole other level.

"Like you, Liam, I too found that God touched me in the depths of my vulnerability. I have always felt like an orphan. My mother and father were both hermits by nature and by vocation. I am a hermit by nature. I understand the life of a hermit. I love the solitude. I love the uninterrupted presence of God without human speech or demands intruding. I love that God has that calling on me.

"And yet, I still have a desire to serve humanity. Christ brought that to me. I have been spiritually freed from spiritual orphanhood. The Holy Spirit did that for me. I am a woman of God, a child of the Divine Lord and Father. Still, my flesh lives like an orphan. I am wary of family. I am distrusting of even the idea of a personal relationship. I favour serving divine purposes rather than human purposes for their own sake. To that end, I am a master of the flesh. Yet, there is a yearning in me, deep down inside, for the experience of love and being loved on a personal level.

"I never expected to be touched by the Lord in that part of my life when I went to Abu Seifein. I felt that I would continue the more mystical aspects of my spiritual life that arose in Anaphora and escalated in Saint Antony and Saint Paul Monasteries."

"What happened at Abu Seifein for you, Hsu," asked Sister Elaria.

Hsu laughed. "I had only just put my little bag on my bed in the cell I was staying at, and one of the Sisters came by and gave me a book on Tamav Erene. She said, 'Tamav gives you this book. May it bless you as you visit her shrine and speak with the Fathers and visit the heavenly ones.' I had no idea what she was talking about. Well, not until I started reading the book."

"Which book?" asked Sister Elaria, who had read most of them and had accumulated a small library of them at her monastery in New Zealand.

"A Monastic Life Kindled With Love."

"That is her conversation that includes the Telekinetic Fathers."

"Correct, Sister. It was the first time I read about those spiritual giants of the faith. Tamav Erene provided so much valuable information about their lives."

"What sort of information?" asked Liam.

"Well, I suppose she started with their simplicity and extreme purity of heart. Their attire and where they love and how they occupy themselves with physical work.

"And then, there is their spiritual work of praying for humanity. How they also come and pray the liturgy in the Churches, and how they sometimes attend to individual people with prayer and counsel and healing. They always only ever bring blessing, where ever they might go in the service of the Father."

"Does she write about how to join the community of the Sowah," asked Liam.

"Yes, she does. Of course, there is not just one community of these Telekinetics. They do have a tendency to group together, but there will be solitaries among them also. And their levels of consciousness and works vary according to the measure of how the Father distributes his works."

"I read one day," said Liam, "the record of Anba Besa, how Saint Shenoute the Archimandrite went on a cloud from Constantinople, as it was called in his day, to his monastery in Akhmim. Reading the story totally ravaged away my mind. I was not in unbelief at all. I was totally there in praise of him. It struck me that a man could be so much a part of the Father's will that the Father would make such things available to His son when the need arose. Then, glory to God, when I found myself in Kirkwall in the Orkneys and praying for that fellow, I was there in body and in Spirit. Over the last few days I have wondered if that is what the *Telekinetic Fathers* do. Was I being stepped up to their measure of work in God?"

"Jesus said to Nathaniel, 'You will see greater than this,' said Sister Elaria, with a lovely welcoming smile.

"Well, yes, indeed. I read Tamav's words. They're in red in the book, and they really stand out and make it easy to memorise them.

"Tamav said, 'Sometimes God sends them to loved ones on Earth to console them, warn them or guide them. Sometimes God allows His children while still on Earth to go to heaven and see their loved ones and to witness the great joy and glory they are enjoying.'

"Wow, you memorised all that, Hsu?" asked Liam.

"Oh yes, I sure did. Because it's true. When we were here in Anaphora, I was taken to a place near Alexandria called the Ascendants Monastery. I told you about that. Christ Jesus met me there and took me into heaven. And, in heaven I met the Holy

THEOSIS AND ARTIFICIAL INTELLIGENCE

Spirit, I met Adam and Eve, I met Melchizedek and Abraham and Moses and Enoch and Elijah and others, even some ancient Saints from China's earliest days.

"Then I met Mary, the Theotokos." Hsu's whole being glowed with the remembrance of the Divine Mother. "Oh, Liam, you should have seen her. She is totally overwhelming. Her love. Her beauty. She is nothing like how you might imagine the human Mary on Earth. She is the fullness of her own Theosis. She had the perfect Father Fusion of Jesus, and she is like God in her own way.

"She touched me with her hand and told me, 'I will be your Mother, darling. I will be your Mother.'

"Then I remembered how my own flesh mother was taken into heaven on the Wu Tai Mountains in the north, taken with those wondrous heavenly lights. I had literally lost all contact with her since then, and I was quite young in that day. Her going away like that make me convinced that all the stories of the Taoist Immortals were true. Those Holy Mountains all over China were really true.

"But when the Theotokos said, 'I will be your mother,' I felt this tremendous rush of grief rise up in me. It was like a Tsunami. I had no control over it.

"In a few moments though, when the Theotokos said to me, 'I will be your Mother,' all that longing and all that sorrow vanished. I was filled with so much joy. It was overflowing. And as soon as I was experiencing that joy because of Mary Theotokos, it was as if I was alive in her. Suddenly, and I am thinking it is because of being in her, Mary Theotokos brought to me my own birth mother.

"I could not believe my eyes. I hugged my mother as if for an eternity. I so love her.

"So, there I am in my cell and I am reading Tamav's wonderful words about how God takes us to heaven to witness the great joy our loved ones are experiencing.

"It blew me away.

"I put down the book and went to find the Sister who gave me the book. I went into the kitchen. Nobody. I went downstairs and looked around. Nobody. I went into the shrine, I had never been there before. And there she was. Her photograph was all over the walls. I just burst into tears."

"Who was it?" asked Sister Elaria. "Was it Tamav Erene herself?"

"Yes. Exactly. I was stunned. I simply could not piece it together. I am reading about her after she has died, in a book that she handed to me in my cell. How does that work?"

"And then, before long, a Sister joined me in the Shrine Room. Happy. Jovial. Cheery. As if nothing ever bad had ever happened to her. And she looked at me all messed up from my tears and confusion.

"Hey, Sister Elaria, what made you think that it would be Tamav Erene?"

"Well, Hsu, I would expect that of her. She is one of the Sowah. She was when she had a physical body and she remains so without one. That's just who she is."

"Wow," and Hsu fell into a hush for a few moments.

"That's what the Sister said to me. When I explained to her how I had been reading, 'A Monastic Life Kindled With Love,' the Sister said, 'Oh my dear Sister. Get used to it. Tamav has never ceased to serve. She serve us her daughters in Abu Seifein. She serves her other daughters up north. She serves all around the world. She serves in the heavens as well. We know that. She has told some of the Sisters so.'

"And then the Sister said exactly what you just said, 'That's just who she is.'"

THEOSIS AND ARTIFICIAL INTELLIGENCE

39

ELARIA'S TESTIMONY

"LATER, BACK IN MY CELL," said Hsu, "I began to think about the AI project. I started to wonder if these examples of Christ in our very midst here in Egypt are God's way of saying, 'This is the bench mark, the standard, for all Christians, for all time on the Earth. Christ delivers Theosis to the believer.' It makes perfect sense.

"And so, there I was with the standard for our project, the acme of what it is to become like Christ. The standard is Christ. And, if Christ is the deliverer of Theosis, it is His problem how He works it out with people of faith worldwide. I came to the conclusion that I could never be the one to work that out. It's Christ's to deal with.

"So I started working back from that. I thought of all the various levels of Christian closeness to Christ, and likeness in Christ. There were so few Christians I had ever met who matched Tamav as I experienced her. Or, for that matter, Saieh Yousef. These are exceptional people in Christ. I thought of the Copts, the Catholics, the Anglicans, the Presbyterians, the Lutherans, the Pentecostals, the Charismatics, the Seventh Day Adventists and I even included the Amish and the Mormons. I thought, if becoming so much like Christ is so possible for the human being on Earth, then all those Christians ought to have an AI service that can help to facilitate them to quickly become more like Christ to the fullest."

"I agree wholeheartedly," said Sister Elaria. "And now, I have a question for you, Hsu.

"Acts 10:38 tells us 'How God anointed Jesus of Nazareth with the Holy Spirit and with power. He went about doing good and healing all who were oppressed by the devil, for God was with him.' And then we read Isaiah 10:27 that it is the anointing that destroys the yoke of bondage.

"My question is, is it the anointing on a person that gives them the power to be Telekinetic? Or is there something in the personal relationship with the Father that makes them Telekinetic and, as Telekinetics, then provides opportunities for them to use the anointing that destroys the yoke of bondage in other people?

"I think both are relevant to your quest for AI to help us to become more like Christ: Christ, whom God anointed with the Holy Spirit and with power so that he fulfilled the prophecy in Isaiah 61:1 3, which was his signature prophetic scripture."

"I don't know the answer scripturally, Sister, but from my own experience I believe that it is exclusively between the individual person and the Father.

"Now, some people call God just God, and roll into that name the Trinity of the Father, Son and Holy Spirit. One God. Inseparable. Indivisible. God in Paradise is the Father and when He manifested on Earth as a human being who was in perfect Fusion with the Paradise Father he was the Son of God. But essentially He was the Father incarnate. And the Holy Spirit is the power for change that the Paradise Father creates. All God. One God. One holy and righteous substance that is true, beautiful, good and all wise.

"Other people split up the Father and the flesh manifestation of Jesus and the works of the holy Spirit. Three Persons in One.

"To be quite honest, I have no idea how it all hangs together, but the way that Tamav Erene taught her fellow Sisters about the Telekinetic Fathers is that they lived in such close proximity, even Fusion, with the will of the Father that was their union with the Father that produced their lifestyle of being permanently on call for His bidding. And that, regardless of whether they needed to be Telekinetic in the operation of that service to someone or not.

"It seems to me that the whole Trinity are perfectly integrated in them, the Father, the Son, the Holy Spirit and Jesus of

Nazareth. And I'm happy for it to be so, because I can't fathom any more detail than that."

"I agree with you Hsu," said Sister Elaria. "The overarching truth is that Orthodox Christianity holds to the promise of Jesus that every baptised believer will become God. So many of the Church Fathers have spelled it out historically. The Telekinetic Fathers, and Mothers too, like Tamav, are the evidence that the human will is grown by God to be perfectly fused with the will of the Father. That, alone, was the reason for my father's conversion to Orthodox Christianity, and how he led me to the same conversion."

"What I found in the convent of Abu Seifein was such a total atmosphere of the impossible God, the miraculous God, being fully present and available, on tap even. There is no gap between the Sisters and the God of the miraculous.

"I had a dream on the first night I was there," continued Sister Elaria. "In the dream I found myself in a desert monastery. I thought it could be the Monastery of the Descendants, but it was another place. And beside me stood a Coptic nun, a Sister.

"I couldn't make out her face because she shone with the radiance of a dozen suns. She was perfectly holy and pure and good, so much so that she matched the goodness of the Holy Spirit. I imagined that if she was to speak the word, a whole new world would come into being.

"Her hand touched mine. It felt like I was holding the hand of a little girl, a child. It was the touch of perfect innocence. I have never even imagined such sweetness before.

"Then she stepped forward, and gently pulled on my hand to follow her. We came to a chapel in the monastery. It had those same ancient icons on either side of the entrance that I had read about in Tamav's book. And when we went inside I felt like I was in Paradise. It was a wholly other type of dimension. Time and space were not present. The type of wholeness was beyond description. People were moving about in the Sanctuary and yet there was an all inclusiveness in each person because of this

Paradisiacal dimension.

"A liturgy was beginning. The voices singing were wholly not human. It was as if the highest heavens released a choir of perfect musical angels. They spoke the Word of God and music formed. It filled the whole Sanctuary and again elevated the atmosphere into another realm of Paradise.

"I could never have imagined my feelings of such ecstasy, listening to these angels in chorus. I wanted it to never stop, and it didn't, it eventually released me and my attention went onto the individuals in the Church Sanctuary. There were both women and men. Some of them lived in the heavens and some of them were still living on the Earth.

"The one who was holding my hand asked me, 'What do you see?'

"I said that I see women and men, some from the heavens and some from the Earth.

"Then that one asked me, 'What faith do they have?'

"I presumed I was to discern what religion that had. It was a Coptic Orthodox Sanctuary and so I presumed they were all Coptic Orthodox Christians, and I said so.

"Then this one asked me to look again.

"When I did, suddenly all their heart of hearts were opened to me and I could see the thread of their worship. Every single one of them were connected to the same Paradise Father. He was their life, their Source. It was the very union of love they each felt for one another.

"But, when I looked at the content between their heart of hearts and the Father I found that they weren't all Orthodox Christians at all. Of the couple of dozen people present, all dressed in the heavenly white robes of spiritual conquerors, I could make out many faiths. Most of them were not Christian. Like, a third were, but the rest were made out of either clear cut spiritual paths or else no path that I recognised at all. Their avenue to the Father simply didn't figure into their being wholly one with

Christ and one with the Father.

"I found that rather surprising. It wasn't at all what I expected.

"Then the one holding my hand asked me, 'Is their union in the Father theirs because of the works of God or because of their intelligence?'

"Instantly I remembered the Christian teaching I had memorised and learned so well, that the person's pathway to the Father was exclusively because of the work of Christ Jesus on the Cross. But as I looked on this group of God's illumined, God's Pillars, He showed me their intelligence. Whilst it was true that they walked the path that the Father had established through the Son of God, it was the development of their intelligence that elevated them to their heavenly status today in this Sanctuary.

"Then it suddenly dawned on me that intelligence is will. Whatever you understand is what you will act upon. With whatever measure of intelligence you exert in your life, that is the measure of seed you will sow and the measure of the harvest you will reap.

"The entire realm of blessing took on a completely different dimension from what I had long known it to be. God's provision, God's mercy, God's providence, God's everything, is entirely based upon the measure of heavenly intelligence we have acquired.

"And it can't be given, like some anointing. It has to be experienced and understood and then a higher value and meaning desired and a new level of intelligence is given to us. It was exactly the Mansions progression that Prior James showed us on the Mount of Saint Antony. Intelligence directs will.

"Then this one holding my hand asked, 'How can these ones help us to become more like Christ?'

"I was stunned. I wasn't expecting that kind of a question. I looked upon these absolutely amazing personalities. It never dawned on me that they could become even more like Christ until this one asked me that question, as though knowing full well that there is always more in Christ to attain.

"A depth of peace and focus came upon me. I saw my own Heavenly Father come around me and embrace me. His mind augmented my mind and when I looked into the heart of hearts of each of these worshiping men and women, My attention was on trying to discern in what way they might become more like Christ.

"I was looking for Christ inside each of them. I wanted to find out how much more of Christ there was within each of them. I sensed that if I knew the gap between Christ in them and their Christ likeness, then I would get a clear vision for how they could become more like Christ.

"But, when I looked for Christ in them, every single one of them opened up their heart of hearts to me so that I could fathom them each to the deepest and highest core of their very being. In every instance, their being became the Father. The Paradise Father. They were human Paradise Fathers, every one. Fully Father Fused.

"I could discern no way that they could become more like Christ. I looked into the brilliancy of the one who was holding my hand as if to say this, but I felt the urge to turn instead to the presence of God my Father within. And so, I looked Him in the face, into His heart of hearts, and I asked Him, 'Father, how can these ones become more like Christ when they are so much the Father?'

"At that, the Father gripped me and elevated me and we lifted up off the floor and came out of the roof of that Monastery's Sanctuary. Then we rose up above the monastery, then above the Wadi surrounding it, then above the land mass and above the whole Earth and then we traveled through galaxy after galaxy ever upward. We came to a region in the heavens where there was a veil. With a little pressure, my Father urged us through the veil and it released us to the other side, into the higher heavens. On and on we traveled, and I was fully conscious. At one point I looked back down the trail to the Sanctuary in the monastery on the Earth. They were still worshipping in the liturgy.

"As I turned my attention upward I found us coming into an area of brilliant light. It was so bright that I had no vision whatsoever. It was like a whiteout in the Winter snow.

"Then we came to rest. I felt myself being released from my Father's hold on me, as if he released himself from my very core.

"He prompted me to look around. And then I saw him. Christ the Son of God. In His own realm. I was flawed. I dropped to the ground and my whole being exploded in tears. I was so utterly small in the presence of His perfect magnificence. I suddenly found my heavenly Father, my Parent. It was so amazing for me. I can barely describe the experience."

There was a long pause. At the table in the refectory of Anaphora, Hsu sat with her eyes closed. Father Zakaria looked on as if looking at the face of an angel. Liam knew not to touch her, but he too was elevated in his whole being. Sister Elaria looked on and twinkled, as she always did when she and God were one heart and mind and soul, but as detached from the world as a whole other planet.

It was a God moment.

All around, the presence of the Paradise Father was palpable. People were looking at the four of them, and smiling, knowing God was doing something.

And God was generous. He wasn't being shy. He flooded the entire refectory, kitchen and all. God was showing up, as the saying went, and He was having a good time.

The love was so perfect that every heart and soul just melted with the love of God. The focus went off the four at their table and spontaneously turned exclusively to God. A couple of Pentecostals stood to their feet and shouted something about the Holy Spirit being in the house. Normally it would have alerted everyone to God doing a special thing, but in this instance it didn't. It came over simply as an acknowledgment about what everyone was experiencing, each in their own way.

As for Hsu, God had captured her mind and had reunited her to the realm of Christ in the heaven of heavens beyond the veil that separates time from eternity, and Nirvana from the endlessness of the divine and the personalness of Deity and deified beings.

When she opened her eyes and looked around, Hsu said, "You know, I don't think I have much to offer humanity by way of AI hoping them to become more like Christ. Artificial Intelligence will need soul, and soul will need the Spirit of Truth, and the Spirit of Truth will need the Father, and the Father will have to want to make something of it if AI is going to amount to anything more than just mathematics in an incestuous relationship with itself."

40

SAIHA MARY TURNS UP

PRIOR JAMES RETURNED TO THE TABLE in the midst of the glorious action of God. With him was Saieh Yousef and an older woman who looked rather simple, almost like a city beggar. Her robe was quite discoloured and barely covered her knees. She carried a shoulder bag and it hung from her left hand. There was something quite unusual about her, as if she was not your typical Egyptian grandmother.

As the glory of God became more down to earth, Saieh Yousef introduced her, saying, "Everybody, this is my friend, Mary. She serves the Lord with all her heart."

"Oh my goodness," thought Liam, "she's Saiha! That explains it." But he never said a word to the others. The thought crossed his mind that this was the Mary who visited Kyrillos, but in an instant it was gone. Still, he was curious why he couldn't focus on her. Or was it that she was a little out of focus. He settled in his mind that she was a bit blurry to look at because of the presence of God.

Father Zakaria stood up to greet her. He extended his hand with its cross in it and she stooped to kiss it as is the custom. "Bless me, my Father the saint."

Hsu stood up and stooped to kiss her hand, but Mary would have none of that. She stiffened, looked Hsu in the eye and patted her chest twice. It was sufficient a greeting. The rebuke didn't impact on Hsu at all, and she returned the heartfelt greeting with a smile.

Sister Elaria patted her chest twice while she looked into Mary's deep set eyes, and, smiling, Mary in turn patted her chest twice in reply.

Prior James just looked on, but no one noticed except Mary.

Saieh Yousef said, "Please, all sit down. I asked Mary to come here to give you all a word." Then he looked at Hsu, saying, "Hsu, I believe that you have seen Mary before. On the stairs to Saint Antony's Cave."

Hsu looked up at the old woman's smiling face. "No, Abouna. The lady I saw was Chinese. She spoke two Chinese languages, well, Mandarin and our local dialect. She wasn't an Egyptian woman."

Then, right before their eyes, Mary adjusted herself a little and said in English with a slight Italian accent that is common among many Egyptians who learned their English that way, "How about now? Xiànzài zěnme yàng?"

Hsu silently rose to her feet, drew her two hands together, one cupping the other, at the level of her chin, cast her eyes to the floor, bowed quite low and said, "I am honoured, blessed one."

Mary smiled. Her countenance was soft and fresh and lovely. Liam noticed that she was fully in focus now. She released an extraordinary sense of maternal love that engulfed Hsu. Then with the gentleness of a monarch butterfly, she lifted her cupped hands in reply. With a gentle nod of her head, she intimated that Hsu should sit down again. Abouna Zakaria looked on quietly and thought, "It's all God. This is all God. Everything is fine. I am so glad they are in my country."

41

SAIHA MARY'S WORD

THE LONGER MARY STOOD there beside Saieh Yousef, the more radiant she became. As the seconds turned into minutes, Prior James discerned that it was her staying in one place that allowed the fullness of the Father with her to materialise with her. The grace of God was all over her. The Father was generously spreading Himself out across the large refectory where others were chatting and waiting for the lunch bell.

Liam looked on her, saying to himself, "Saint Mary. Glory to God, Saint Mary." He could discern the fullness of her fusion in the Father. He melted into the exceptionally warm and welcoming feelings that emanated from her. In only a few moments, she had won him, heart and soul.

Hsu asked her, "Have you lived in Wudangshan, Blessed Mary?"

"My home is nowhere. I travel a lot," she replied. Then she smiled as she looked at Saieh Yousef, "Now, *HE* has a place to lay his head. Over there at the Descendants Monastery. He has a nice place. Sometimes I visit there and smell the flowers and the leaves of the trees.

"But Wudangshan? I can say that I have lived there but I have never had a place there. I have visited so many times. There are many monks and nuns and hermits there, Buddhist and Taoist, who call on the One True Source and I am asked to be a help to them. But not just there. At Shao Lin also, and the hermitages and temples of wu Tai and other great spiritual centres in that vast land."

"In what way do you help Taoists and Buddhists, dear Mary?" asked Liam.

"They need the Father. I bring Him."

"In what way do they need the Father, dear Mary?"

"In many ways, Liam. Some are following the path that is gilded with superstition and myths. When their hearts break, which is inevitable, they need energy and a word from a stranger who will bridge them to the actuality of spirituality. It is the actuality of spirituality that is often a person's first glimpse of the Father. It brings the actuality of sonship or daughtership with God, and it breaks apart the wonder of the mystery of faith.

"Others are meditators. They pursue mind and the nature of mind and the capacity of mind. Sooner or later they will want what lies beyond mind, and I am there for them with the actuality of the Father.

"And then there are the luminaries, those sages, men and women, old and young, who want the language of the Uncreate. I become their friend. I share time with them. I help the Father within each of them to actualise things of heaven in their consciousness that their previous explorations have bias against."

"Do you bring them to Christ?"

"No, not usually. I do the works of Christ. He did not strive to convert people away from their religious traditions, merely to link them to the Father."

"I thought that serving the Father would automatically preclude the notion that you would be bringing as many people to Christ as possible," said Liam.

"Your thinking will keep you out of the community of the Sowah, Liam," Mary replied. "I know that is a strong wish in your heart of hearts. Such notions of insisting that all people will belong to the Christian Church will keep you in bondage like the monkey who holds onto the handful of nuts and keeps himself trapped to the hole in the rock."

"How so, dear Mary?"

"It is not possible for a person to be Sowah and also be an Earth-bound Christian. Before you will ever become Sowah, you will find the Father will explode all your known boundaries and limitations until you have the love of the Father as it exists in heaven and in Paradise.

"To think that heaven is only occupied by Christians is far too small an idea. It cannot withstand the mighty love of Christ's perfect heart.

"To think that the people from this world, Earth, are the only people in heaven, is too small and idea for even the angels who minister across all of God's creation.

"To think that your own maximised spirituality is more than a single drop in the Atlantic Ocean is so poor a use of your mind that you should lay it down and take up the Father Fusion mind of Christ, as Saint Paul recommends in his letter.

"The Son of God, Christ, gives to us perfect divine love, and in utmost abundance. It never fails us. It never hungers or thirsts. Such universally divine love loves all people, for all the good and right and beautiful reasons. And loves them regardless of their intellectual view or ideation or decision power or actual pathway in life.

"Love, Liam, is greater than thought. The love-self in you is entirely bigger, better and more real than the thought-self in you. It is the guiding light for faith even.

"But love is not single and stationary. Love grows. Love experiences itself. Love knows perfection at different levels of life, over and over again, glory upon glory.

"Love that is locked is love that shuns others, and such a love has no place with God's highest servants. It is simply not real enough. It is powerless, impotent. It cannot carry your will into

THEOSIS AND ARTIFICIAL INTELLIGENCE

the places the Father would have you go and serve."

"Beloved Mary," said Hsu, "love is greater than thought. I agree. How then would we style artificial intelligence so that it transcends the very thought-type algorithms that enable AI to learn, communicate, and even become self-determined? How do we do that?"

"Dear child," Mary replied, "you have come this day from Abu Seifein and the convent of my Sowah sister, Tamav Erene. I want to share with you something from my own experience.

"When she was young and I visited her in the convent, I always felt an immense comfort and assurance. It came from her. It was not an assurance in the Church, nor in the monastic life, nor in being Christian. It was all of this, but so much more. It came from a higher point of focus, a higher source of assurance.

"Being near to Tamav Erene made me aware of the assurance God had for my eternal life in heaven and in Paradise.

"She confirmed for me the miraculous, the supernatural and the mystical. But more than that, she was a living testimony of the interaction with God at every level and in every place after my physical death.

"When I was with her, my God of Paradise opened up fully to me and I experienced Him in Paradise and in all the heavens between the Earth and Paradise, and in every place here on the Earth. My God was the God of Eternity, the Alpha and Omega, the ever present fullness of the living loving Source of all that is.

"That spoke to me a great deal in those days. It was a life changer for me. She was, and still is, a most beautiful creature of God. Tamav is refined, elegant, quick to smile and never jostled. I can trust her perfectly, and I do. And it is not because God had given her the gifts of miracles and teleportation and bilocation and the Motherhood to raise up generations of monastic Sisters in God's image. No. It is that she was for me a living universality of God's presence and destiny for all people. Not just Christians, but also Muslims, Jews, Druze, Bedouin, all people. Tamav Erene was and to this day is universal Cosmic God in His fullness and His everywhereness and His absolute I AM-ness. Past. Present. Future. Below. Above. Inside. Outside. Behind. In front. In the flesh life and in the Spirit life. And God is entirely personal.

"I took that away with me from Tamav Erene. I was already well esteemed and good at what I did to help people. But she elevated that even more for me. So much more.

"Her example shaped my questions to the Lord Jesus and to the Father when I was growing leaps and bounds in my own service for the Father. It was the Father who sent me to her. Not for a miracle of healing. Not for hearing a sound word of preaching. Not for association with the Sisters as a nun. Not to learn anything about bilocation or teleportation or intergalactic presence. No. He sent me to her to receive a silent and secret transmission by the Father through her. And I carry it to this day. She was the cup I drank, and the wine in the cup was the Father's ever present Face and eternal destiny for people.

"It is in this manner that I am used by the Father to minister to any human being on the Earth, in any generation, of any culture or religion, in any language, in any location at any time of the day or night. Because I am in the service of the Father, and I am in Christ when I serve, it is not for me to determine the worth of that soul whom I serve. It is enough for me to serve the Father's will. I have little or no speculation about the destiny of that soul in the hereafter that I can bring before the Courts of God. It is the work of those Heavenly Assessors so to administer that kind of determination as to how that soul continues in the hereafter. It is enough for me to know that I have loved that soul perfectly, according to the will of our heavenly Father.

"My place in the Father is the answer to my deepest prayer, Hsu. I am utterly unlimited in the Father through Christ Jesus.

"To the Christian, I am the Father. To the Taoist, I am an immortal in the Tao. To the Buddhist, I am an enlightened one in Nirvana, Nibbana: the Tathagata. To the Hindu, I am moksha. To the Celt, I am Culdee, a companion of God. To the lost person, I am a guiding light. To the helpless person, I am God the rescuer.

To the damaged goods I am the one who salvages and sets on solid ground.

"I am the Father's will for each people to receive, to hold onto, to stand on the rock when they were in the quicksand of circumstances. God is a God of provision. 'I am the God who heals you.' 'I am the Lord, your provider.' 'I am the Lord, your Shepherd.' 'I am the Lord, your righteousness.' 'I am the Lord who sanctifies you.' 'I am the Lord, your peace.' 'I am the Lord of Hosts.' 'I am the Lord who hears your prayer and it is I who sends to you the answer to your prayer, and my Word never returns to me empty and unfulfilled.' 'I am the Lord who can send to you the Christian who is in need, a Muslim with my Word for you, or a Jew with my Word for you, or a Buddhist, a Hindu, a Sikh, and Jain, a Taoist, a Confucianist, an Australian Aboriginal, a Maori or Islander, a Hawaiian Kahuna, with my Word for you. I can use anyone to be a help, and I do so because my energy and Spirit I have placed inside all human beings. They hear my voice. It is still and sweet and a joy to behold.

"All the while, the Father's only request of me, Hsu, is that I am simply myself. It cannot be easier, more simple or more effortless.

"There is a fusion of wills, Hsu, between the lover of God and the Lover of Humanity Himself, the Father. When that fusion is sealed, you and the Father are One. You still have yourself and the Father still has Himself, but the two wills can function as One Will, and do so at will.

"In this Father Fusion, there is no separation of personality or divinity. The Father has not become your essence and you have not become His essence. The union is between your wills: the desires of your heart of hearts. And they are yolked in the love that is unbreakable, and unshakeable, and impervious to ignorance and to error and sin.

"I believe that you have an experience of just this glory whilst you were at the convent of Abu Seifein. You saw the Fathers and Mothers of the Sowah and you saw their Father Fusion."

"Yes, I did," replied Hsu, non plussed that Mary should know such an intimate part of her own dream life. "And your explanation of your own Father Fusion clarifies so much of that encounter for me. I thank you with all my heart, Mary."

"Perhaps my prayer is also the prayer in your own heart, Hsu? I have ministered in all the leading centres of spiritual need around the world. Not only in your China but also in India, Tibet, Russia, South America, Australia, New Zealand, the Pacific Islands, Malaysia, Singapore, Sri Lanka, every African nation, the British Isles and Ireland, Canada and the American States, Central and South America and even in both Poles. I have attended to individuals who are totally off grid. I have saved lives, saved souls, ministered miracles of healing and brought material resources to people in dire need. Perhaps this is the desire of your heart also, Hsu, to do these works of Christ?"

"Yes, it is, dear Mary."

"Then understand this. Hsu. Liam. This day I am imparting to you the secret and personal transmission of the Father. The word I have brought to you both is the permission to release your project into the provision of the Father.

"In the Father's name and in the name of Christ Jesus the Son of God, I am giving you permission to release yourselves totally, with all your heart and mind and spirit. I am declaring in confidence that, in doing so, He will draw you further up into your own vocation in Him and He will enter into your project with artificial intelligence and your lives beyond your involvement with it.

"The quest to articulate how artificial intelligence can help us to become more like Christ places demands on the Father's provision. No human being can accomplish this on his or her own or with the imagination and creativity emerging from their own provision and skill. Artificial intelligence itself is wholly incapable of articulating it. It can point toward useful supports that human beings already know about, but it cannot yet engage God and stimulate spirituality by means of spiritual circuitry. Both you and

AI need to feed off the Father and thus be transformed by the Father so that you are both capable of becoming Christ.

"And this *is* Theosis. This *is* the teaching of Orthodox Christianity, our becoming God in Christ. This *is* the hope of the world, even if the scientific world is predominantly agnostic or atheist and unable to elucidate this hope of all ages. But not all, of course. In the field of quantum physics and quantum mechanics there do exist those who dare to dream of the shores of Paradise and its impact in their work.

"Without such a total investment of yourselves, the end result will be shallow and empty. It will leave people standing before the cross and shed blood of Jesus saying among themselves, 'He saved others but he cannot save himself.' They will not be given the spirituality to lift them off the ground and into the very heart of Christ. They will be fully entitled to be the heathen who rage against the religious and cause the religious to ask, 'Why do the heathen rage?'

"The hope of the world is to be shown God by those who know God. And to be shown with no ulterior motive, no hidden fine print, no curse of the wolf tucked away in the sheep's clothing of blessing.

"The hope of the world is to actually be lifted up to become like Christ in their religion of choice. And, once they are lifted up into the heart of Christ in their own culture and customs, to have the Father draw them deeper and higher out of time and space and into Himself Uncreate.

"The energy of God inside them knows this. He speaks into their souls saying, 'This is the way, walk therein and be blessed in Me.' And they may not hear the voice of Jesus. They hear the truth. And Jesus is the truth. They are not trying to hear a Jesus, they are listening for something that is beyond names. They are listening for the I AM that the Father told Moses to name Him to His people in Egypt.

"They want to engage life from the wholeness and all inclusiveness of the Father through Christ. By the time the saintly person of any religion or faith reaches the shores of the Divine, there is none of them who will shun Christ's invitation to take one step more and join the Father through Him the Son and the Way. Not one. They have it confirmed in their deepest truth, that their love will serve all creation and all created beings and all created things forever. They know that their own love will be God's love. They know that there will be a fusion of God's divine will and their own human will — eternal salvation. And they *adore* that!

"Hsu. Liam. Do you want this for yourselves and for the future of AI — salvation? You say that you have been seeking Christ. I believe that you have found Him. Will you now find more of Him? Truly find Him? Can you be that kind of a person? Can you die the second death into Christ so that the Father finds you in Him? This is who the world needs people to be. Are you willing to be all and do all that the Father wants for this world? Can you give so much of yourselves that the Father finds you within Christ in Paradise?"

"As you take this question away with you, I have something else to flavour it with. In answering the question, 'How Can AI Help Us To Be More Like Christ,' have you not found enough Christ-like men and women here in Egypt to prove to you that it is all sufficient to make an AI that is entirely Christ-centred?

"Could it be that you do not need to be inclusive of other religions? Could it be the Father's plan to exhibit Christ's power for generating Theosis in a human being and that if others from other religions want that then they will see the source of that Theosis and ask Christ for it? Could it be that Christ truly does draw all who believe Him to the Father?

"Your father, Hsu, once painted a lovely piece of art. He wrote in the right bottom corner, 'Just suppose its true,'"

Suddenly, that which was unclear became sparkling crystal clear. The focus was exclusively on Christ Jesus. He alone would work out how AI makes us become more like Christ in the religion of our choice. The seeking had reached its apex. Mary's Word had brought the project full circle back to its true Source.

The project creator. The project provider of resources. The project designer. The project implementer. The project upholder. The very evolution which was designed to act as a catalyst in any form of the divine gift of faith in the Earth. It was all in Him and no other Source. Christ alone. The relief and the joy was simply superb.

"In Christ alone," said Liam.

Saieh Yousef, Saiha Mary, Sister Elaria, Hsu, Liam, Abouna Zakaria and Prior James each placed their right hands on their chests and tapped twice and with one voice said, "In Christ alone. I believe."

The End of Mystic

FOLLOW THE ADVENTURE

Look at how far you have come by travelling with the team in Book One and Book Two. It's incredible! Well, now you can continue to follow the adventure of How AI Can Help Us To Become More Like Christ in our Religion of Choice in Book Three, **FINDING.**

What happens when RoboSaint arrives in Egypt?

How does the language of the ancient Hebrews suggest a way for AI to make direct contact with the Creator?

What extraordinary things in the desert does the Sowah, Saieh. Yousef, provide for his companions?

How does Christ the Son of God and the Lord of Lords begin to impress his heart's desire in the ambitions of AI?

And what is AI's unpredictable development?

Does the Ancient Chinese traditions of knowing God impact on the adventure through the long multi-religious history of Mount Tai and Wudang Shan?

And how do Prior James and Sister Elaria pour out possibilities that thrill and inspire Liam and Hsu?

All this and more awaits you in SEASEM Publications' everlasting adventure

THEOSIS AND ARTIFICIAL INTELLIGENCE
BOOK 3: FINDING

Keep on loving the adventure, all creation needs you to be the best that you can hope to be.
ADD A NEW BOOK THREE COVER PIC

www.ingramcontent.com/pod-product-compliance
Lightning Source LLC
LaVergne TN
LVHW051113080426
835510LV00018B/2009